The Midwestern Novel

The Midwestern Novel
Literary Populism from *Huckleberry Finn* to the Present

NANCY L. BUNGE

McFarland & Company, Inc., Publishers
Jefferson, North Carolina

LIBRARY OF CONGRESS CATALOGUING-IN-PUBLICATION DATA

Bunge, Nancy L.
　The midwestern novel : literary populism from Huckleberry Finn to the present / Nancy L. Bunge.
　　p.　　cm.
　Includes bibliographical references and index.

　ISBN 978-0-7864-9435-4 (softcover : acid free paper) ∞
　ISBN 978-1-4766-1785-5 (ebook)

　1. Populism in literature.　2. American fiction—Middle West—History and criticism.　3. American fiction—20th century—History and criticism　4. Middle West—In literature.　I. Title.
PS374.P633B86　2015
813'.009977—dc23　　　　　　　　　　　　　　　　2014039327

BRITISH LIBRARY CATALOGUING DATA ARE AVAILABLE

© 2015 Nancy L. Bunge. All rights reserved

No part of this book may be reproduced or transmitted in any form or by any means, electronic or mechanical, including photocopying or recording, or by any information storage and retrieval system, without permission in writing from the publisher.

On the cover: sunset in the heartland © 2014 iStock/Thinkstock

Printed in the United States of America

McFarland & Company, Inc., Publishers
　Box 611, Jefferson, North Carolina 28640
　　www.mcfarlandpub.com

For all the kind people
in La Crosse, Wisconsin,
who helped my parents raise me

Table of Contents

Preface **1**

Introduction **5**

One. Conformity's Consequences **19**

Two. The Redemptive Potential of Childhood **49**

Three. Valuing Women's Passion **77**

Four. The African American Dimension **104**

Five. Surrendering to Nature **130**

Six. Relaxing into Compassion **151**

Chapter Notes **175**

Bibliography **185**

Index **193**

Preface

I began the research for this book in 1971, when I had the chance to propose a new upper division English course at George Washington University. While exploring my options, I made a list of midwestern writers.[1] Although I loved many things about teaching in Washington, D.C., including my students there, listening to people brag about their ties to "the great" was not one of them. When others would boast of a friendship with a television news anchor or of a close bond with someone on the Brazilian supreme court, I felt bemused rather than impressed perhaps because I was apparently the only Washingtonian without distinction. And when I entered the classroom, the students' passivity stunned me. As a teaching assistant at the University of Wisconsin at Madison, I would often walk into a room filled with students animatedly debating the reading for that day. In one poetry section, my contribution consisted primarily of naming the poem we would discuss. Once, when the conversation stalled, I made a remark I hoped would move things forward and a student enthusiastically remarked, "Good comment!" When Harry Hayden Clark, the professor in that course, had me give a lecture on T.S. Eliot, one of the students confronted me afterwards with a reading of "The Love Song of J. Alfred Prufrock" that endangered the intellectual edifice I had just constructed with my talk. I enjoyed all of this immensely and found it tough to adjust to an environment where virtually all the responsibility for making the class work fell to me. I saw both the pointless boasting and my students' respectful silence as evidence of a faith in status that many of my students in Madison and I both lacked. So I welcomed the idea of exploring the literature of the Midwest in the hopes that it would help me come to grips with my cultural biases.

The length of my midwestern authors list astonished me. I realized that more American Nobel Prize winners came from the middle west than any other region and included Sinclair Lewis, Ernest Hemingway, and Saul Bellow. The poets that academics fixated on in those days, T. S. Eliot and Ezra Pound, had midwestern ties: For one thing, *Poetry Magazine* was published in Chicago. Moreover, the course would give my students and me a chance to consider authors like Theodore Roethke, whose enigmatic poetry fascinated us both and Richard Wright, whose novel *Native Son* raised the issue of racism, a new critical consideration in the early seventies. So I had no trouble filling a respectable English Department course with midwestern writers and, even more gratifying, so many George Washington students enrolled that I had to teach the course twice to facilitate the conversation that I insisted take place.

In 1972, the Modern Language Association program announced a discussion section on midwestern literature. To participate, one had to write David Anderson at Michigan State University asking for permission. That I received an extremely friendly reply to my letter would surprise no one who has ever met Dave Anderson. At that session, thrilled to meet people who might understand what I had just spent a semester teaching, I talked, I felt, way too much. But apparently no one minded, for I very happily accepted a job at Michigan State the following spring. My first papers and publications focused on midwestern writers and, eventually, many years later, after a wonderful year as a visiting scholar at Harvard Divinity School that also reawakened some of my regional biases, I worked on midwestern literature during my next sabbatical.

More than forty years after compiling my first list, I embarked on a new one and the number and quality of midwestern writers once again flabbergasted me. Many authors dominating contemporary literary discussions have midwestern roots, including Toni Morrison, Jonathan Franzen, Jane Smiley, Louise Erdrich, Charles Baxter, and Jim Harrison. I eventually limited myself to thirty authors and, to my delight, as I read, their work began clustering around themes some of which I had noted before. My first paper and subsequent publication, "Woman as Social Critics in *Sister Carrie, Winesburg, Ohio*, and *Main Street*," argued in 1974 that Sherwood Anderson, Theodore Dreiser, and Sinclair Lewis took women seriously long before it became fashionable. A 1977 article dealing with common themes in the novels of Saul Bellow, Ernest Hemingway, Anderson, and Lewis stressed these writers' emphasis on authenticity. As I picked up my research again, it pleased me to discover that midwestern writers not only persisted in developing these motifs, but also that they constantly questioned the social structure, standing at the forefront of those acknowledging the literary importance of children, women, African Americans, and nature.

Because I firmly believe that my midwestern dispositions rest in my bones, far beyond the reach of intellectual modification, I conclude that I acquired them as a child growing up in La Crosse, Wisconsin. Since I wanted to analyze writers with similar training in midwestern habits, I only considered authors who had spent a substantial portion of their childhoods in the middle west. That those I selected share many of my views, including the notion that one's childhood plays a huge role in one's values and interests, confirms the wisdom of this choice. The one exception is Richard Wright, who moved to Chicago at the age of nineteen; but after some debate, I made him an honorary midwesterner because the literary fathers he acknowledges in *Black Boy*, Theodore Dreiser and Sinclair Lewis, came from and wrote about the Midwest and because Wright's novel *Native Son* shares important traits with the work of midwesterners Nelson Algren, Chester Himes, James Farrell, and Willard Motley, as Wright implicitly acknowledges in both his essay "How Bigger Was Born" and in his introduction to the first edition of Algren's *Never Come Morning*. My only other standard was literary significance. I made no attempt to be comprehensive in part because collections of information and essays about midwestern literature have appeared in recent years, such as *The Dictionary of Midwestern Literature* (2001), produced by the Society for the Study of Midwestern Literature; *The American Midwest: An Interpretive Encyclopedia* (2007), edited by Richard Sisson, Christian Zacher, and Andrew Cayton; and *Midwestern Literature* (2013), edited by Ronald Primeau. Since midwestern literature as a significant subject came into existence in the early seventies, this broad exploration of new territory makes sense and certifies widespread interest in the subject. All this reconnaissance has also laid the groundwork for a comprehensive study.

Two recent focused studies of midwestern literature exist. William Barillas's *The Midwestern Pastoral: Place and Landscape in Literature of the American Heartland* (2006) discusses midwestern nature writing and includes some of the same authors I review in chapter five. But Barillas emphasizes the way in which this writing resembles that of Thoreau and Emerson; hence, the word "pastoral" in his title. I stress the striking ways midwestern nature writing differs from work produced by New Englanders in order to capture the essential midwestern character of this work. *The Midwestern Ascendency in American Writing* (1992), by Ronald Weber, considers only the period when he believes midwestern writing played a central role in American literature, a time which he defines as beginning after the Civil War and ending in the 1920s. He argues that this literature includes no masterpieces, a position he bolsters by declaring *Huckleberry Finn* an example of southern literature. My book covers a much broader range of work over a period of 130 years, makes much larger claims for midwestern literature, and locates Twain's novel firmly in the middle west, as do *The Dictionary of Midwestern Literature* and *The American Midwest*.

I owe an obvious debt to the late David D. Anderson and also to the late George McCandlish, who gave me the chance to teach midwestern literature at George Washington University so long ago, as well as to the enthusiastic students in that course. I also thank Anne Dubuisson Anderson for encouraging me to do this book and for giving me great advice as I worked on it. I thank David Izzo for his helpful counsel. I'm grateful to the Society for the Study of Midwestern Literature for allowing me to read papers at their conferences and for publishing a number of my articles on midwestern literature over the years. I confess I would not have had the insights into midwestern nature writing that constitute chapter five had I not audited Lawrence Buell's course on American environmental writing at Harvard, so I thank him for anything worthwhile in that section. I hasten to add that the responsibility for any errors in the book is mine alone.

Introduction

The shift that took place in American fiction between the publication of Nathaniel Hawthorne's *The Marble Faun* in 1860 and the appearance twenty-four years later of Mark Twain's *Huckleberry Finn* is massive. And yet the radical difference between the kind of fiction coming out of New England before the Civil War and that emanating from the Midwest after it has gone all but completely unacknowledged and unexamined for 130 years. The traditional histories of American fiction gloss over this change by declaring Melville and Hawthorne exemplars of the romantic tradition while calling Mark Twain and Henry James realists even though clustering Twain and James together makes very little sense. Henry James makes his debt to Hawthorne obvious by writing an admiring book about him. Moreover, Twain strives to render ordinary people as accurately as possible in *Huckleberry Finn,* even boasting of all the dialects he reproduces, while James writes almost exclusively about people so extraordinary that they rarely hold down jobs and never speak in dialect. Lawrence Buell's book *The Dream of the Great American Novel* may cast light on this odd pairing, for he argues that after the Civil War, when American critics "looked at what U.S. Fiction had thus far delivered, what they especially saw was a scene of disparate provincialisms, a failure at the level of imagined nationhood, that they then offered prescriptions to remedy."[1] And so they pretended that Twain and James produced the same kind of fiction because to acknowledge that James's affiliating himself with Hawthorne meant anything about his aesthetics or to admit that Twain's work concerned itself with entirely different issues than James's, would undermine the fantasy that America had a unified literature that clearly progressed. Wallace Stegner notes accurately that, in fact, when *Huckleberry Finn* appeared, it signaled a regional shift in American literature since Twain's "materials and his forms are an inheritance from the forming culture of the Mississippi Valley.... His achievement was to elevate these shapes of folklore and journalism, and along with them the vernacular in which they were expressed, into literature."[2] *The Dictionary of Midwestern Literature* (2001), produced by the Society for the Study of Midwestern Literature, and *The American Midwest: An Interpretive Encyclopedia* (2007), edited by Richard Sisson, Christian Zacher, and Andrew Cayton also see *Huckleberry Finn* as midwestern. But in the interest of constructing a coherent national literature, the obvious differences between, say, Twain and James got overlooked and their totally distinct work, strangely enough, became part of the same literary movement.

Another reason the movement of American literature's center to the west gets largely slighted is that the most obvious qualities distinguishing Twain's writing, his use of ordinary speech and characters, soon became national, as Ernest Hemingway famously acknowledged when he declared: "All modern American literature comes from one book by Mark Twain called *Huckleberry Finn*."[3] The impact of Twain's book on American literature as a whole may also reflect the reality that the literary center of the country had shifted to the middle, even though most literary critics have failed to notice.

The obvious question is: If so many writers have come out of the Midwest and if their work reflects this background, why has this gone unrecognized? In the one book addressing the subject, *The Midwestern Ascendency in American Writing*, Ronald Weber says midwesterners dominated American letters only from after the Civil War until the 1920s and reports that this writing "was given to mostly modest effects."[4] To arrive at this conclusion, he adopts the standards implicit in F. O. Matthiessen's phrase "imaginative vitality" from his book on the American Renaissance which took place in New England before the Civil War. Weber determines that if one uses the phrase "imaginative vitality" to appraise midwestern literature published after the Civil War, one must conclude that it "was surely important but only in a few instances of the very first importance" (4). Maybe so, but why would someone use a vague, impressionistic description of New England's literature to evaluate an entirely different kind of work? The primary concern of most midwestern fiction writers, unlike that of the writers from New England, is clearly not "imaginative vitality," but rendering and, hopefully, improving ordinary lives.

To strengthen his argument, Weber declares *Huckleberry Finn* a southern book, citing Kenneth Lynn's affiliation of the book with the South. True, Lynn declares that "Mark Twain was first and always a Southerner," but then he continues to explain that "Twain became the 'Lincoln of our literature,' in Howells's beautiful phrase, only by transcending the limitations of a sectional outlook without betraying its strengths." Lynn particularly focuses on Twain's attitude towards race, saying that Twain "shucked off forever the outlook of the slaveholding aristocrat."[5] And, indeed, since Lynn contends that "the South had always feared that the Negro was a volcano, ready to burst forth at any moment in violence and revolt" (111), Twain seems to have espoused an entirely contrary view in *Huckleberry Finn*: The character Jim in no way resembles a volcano and the entire novel issues a clear attack on racism.

According to Weber, midwestern literature ceased to matter after Sinclair Lewis won the Nobel Prize for Literature in 1930. This judgment not only dismisses the three midwestern writers who won the Nobel Prize for Literature after Lewis: Ernest Hemingway, Saul Bellow, and Toni Morrison, it also fails to acknowledge the many other important midwestern authors who followed Lewis, including Willa Cather, Langston Hughes, Jack Conroy, Gwendolyn Brooks, Nelson Algren, Tillie Olsen, and Richard Wright. Furthermore, in 2014, almost a century after Weber claims midwestern authors stopped playing important roles in American literature, the contemporary authors who garner attention and respect with each new book are often midwesterners: Jonathan Franzen, Toni Morrison, Charles Baxter, Jane Smiley, Jim Harrison, and Louise Erdrich. But Weber's claims go uncontested because very few people realize that all these authors come from the Midwest and the notion of the Midwest as culturally backward has become a comfortable cliché.

Still, attempting to prove that midwestern writers have produced a distinct body of literature over the last 130 years raises such large difficulties that meeting them requires a new kind of critical book. Earlier attempts to define what midwestern literature is often collapse into a collection of hints rather than into an overarching pattern. For instance, Marcia Noe's essay, "Midwestern Literature in Historical and Cultural Context," concludes by suggesting that attempts to generalize about the literature of the Midwest inevitably fail:

> Perhaps the multiplicity and diversity of the Midwest are most directly reflected in the number of different names we have for it. While the South is simply the South, and the same is true for New England and the West, we call the twelve-state region in the middle of the country by a variety of names, including the Midwest, the Middle West, Mid-America, Middle America, the Middle Kingdom, the Middle Border and, of course, the Heartland.[6]

In her essay "What Is 'Midwestishness'? The Evolution of Midwestern Literary Studies," Sara Kosiba declares the notion of a midwestern literature inherently amorphous: "Midwestern literature has never truly been at rest as a defined concept."[7] The lack of a clear definition for midwestern literature not only gives a comprehensive analysis of midwestern fiction little foundation to build upon, but raises the question of how one best attempts to convincingly demonstrate to those like Marcia Noe and Sara Kosiba that certain commonalities do, in fact, exist. It is clear that one cannot certify the consistency of the work produced by authors from an entire region by taking the normal scholarly route and looking closely at the work of a handful of writers. One must examine the work of a wide variety of authors over a broad time period. And in order to show general patterns in an intelligible way, one cannot hover over the critical controversies collecting around each author and each work in any detail for to do so would drag the analysis into one cul-de-sac after another. This means that such an argument must focus on primary work. Fortunately, the authors themselves help resolve this dilemma. Despite authors' general reluctance to associate their work with didacticism, a number of midwestern fiction writers declare that they have social goals for their work.

Even an author like Toni Morrison, who produces one aesthetically sophisticated novel after another, confesses that since her values must shape what she writes, she has no interest in producing work free of political content: "I'm not interested in indulging myself in some private, closed exercise of my imagination that fulfills only the obligation of my personal dreams—which is to say, yes, the work must be political. It must have that as its thrust. That's a pejorative term in critical circles now: If a work of art has any political influence in it, somehow it's tainted. My feeling is just the opposite: If it has none, it is tainted."[8] Morrison believes that the notion of individual freedom plays a central role in most literature: "Much of what we as writers do and how we do it is shaped by our belief in the sacredness of the individual artist and his freedom" (159). But she also values the community literature can establish, seeing the author's ability to help people enter into each other's lives as potentially revolutionary: The "real life" of the book, she explains, is "about creating and producing and distributing knowledge; about making it possible for the entitled as well as the dispossessed to experience one's own mind dancing with another's" (190).

Other midwestern authors who make their goals explicit articulate ideas perfectly consonant with Toni Morrison's declarations here. Nelson Algren argues that all literature is revolutionary: "Literature is made upon any occasion that a challenge is put to the legal apparatus by conscience in touch with humanity."[9] And Algren tries to make his own argument for decency by treating the lives of people who fall into the underclass in ways that generate compassion for them. He believes and attempts to show that these people feel frustrated with their lives, not because they have fallen under the influence of Communists, but "from the instruction of men everywhere where men wish to own their own lives" (106). Scott Turow praises the work of Tillie Olsen because it achieves the aim Algren refers to here: "The authorial persona in Tillie Olsen's work knows all, and like a God men have not dreamed of in centuries, she knows it with a compassion which requires articulation for those too tormented to speak for themselves, the transformation of all human feeling into the majestical, the poetical, the eternal."[10] James Farrell even associates authorship with a particular political stance: "It should become increasingly clear to the writer with a conscience that his long-run interests as a human being and as an artist fail to coincide with the interests of capitalism."[11] Saul Bellow hopes to help his readers discover their shared spiritual values: "Now, more than ever, it seems to me, it becomes the writer's job to remind people of their common humanity—of the fact, if you will, that they have souls."[12] And certainly critic after critic describes the work of these authors as offering a empathetic and honest discussion of social issues, often revealing the damage left by the competitive social structure that pursuing the American Dream leaves in its wake. This component of midwestern literature helped draw Richard Wright to Chicago. In *Black Boy*, he describes the impact of reading Theodore Dreiser's *Jennie Gerhardt* and *Sister Carrie*: "They revived in me a vivid sense of my mother' suffering; I was overwhelmed. I grew silent, wondering about the life around me. It would have been impossible for me to have told anyone what I derived from these novels, for it was nothing less than a sense of life itself."[13]

Since the social dimension of this work plays such an important role in the critical commentary surrounding it as well as in the author's explanations of their purposes, it seems logical to establish its consistency by focusing on its treatment of community norms. And these issues are overwhelmingly present in midwestern fiction. Authors from Twain to Theodore Dreiser to Sherwood Anderson to Willa Cather to Richard Wright to Nelson Algren to Toni Morrison to Louise Erdrich to Charles Baxter as well as the other twenty-four fiction writers discussed in the chapters that follow make rendering the American Dream's destructive consequences central to their work. That the analysis which follows considers these works primarily thematically does not violate them because these authors' political intentions often compel them to write prose easily understood intellectually. But, like *Huckleberry Finn*, they also challenge their readers to evaluate their own integrity and compassion. This helps explain why the New Critics paid little attention to this writing: It can but usually does not invite adjectives like "ambiguous" or "complex." But it does seem strange that aside from a few writers like Toni Morrison, Tillie Olsen, Richard Wright, and Meridel Le Sueur, the race/class/gender critics ignore this fiction which, from the beginning, has concerned itself with these issues. Mark Twain prides himself on his freshly accurate renditions of common people precisely because those who preceded him had so little interest in them. Sherwood Anderson's *Perhaps Women* articulated the largely overlooked strengths that women brought to American's cultural life, a stance complemented by the fiction of Dreiser, Twain, and Lewis until women authors appeared on the scene and spoke for themselves. William Dean Howells, Willa Cather, and Sinclair Lewis attempted to chip away at their contemporaries' prejudices by offering sympathetic portraits of African Americans before many African Americans could get published. Indeed, William Dean Howells helped Paul Lawrence Dunbar get into print by championing his poetry and writing an introduction for his first volume. Virtually every significant midwestern author writing fiction in the wake of *Huckleberry Finn* produced work empathetic to the middle and lower classes. But then it would probably disappoint those who thought that they revolutionized literary studies in the 1970s by introducing considerations of class, race, and gender to learn that midwestern authors had already focused on these concerns for almost a century. Similarly, in the past decade, critics seem to have discovered the importance of childhood, founding journals and writing books on the subject; midwestern authors began taking children seriously with *Huckleberry Finn* and have never stopped paying attention. Also, in the past couple of decades, the notion that nature writing should focus on nature itself rather than the people observing it has become prominent, but this view of nature has also played an important role in the literature of the Midwest since its beginnings.

The fundamental assumption undergirding midwestern literature is that people arrive on the planet with enormous decency which the American social structure with its emphasis on competitive triumph destroys, either by replacing the individual's inherent values with conventional ones or by harming the lives of those who either resist the dictates of the American Dream or cannot marshall the resources to follow them. This may, on its surface, sound like the same ideology that sits at the center of Ralph Waldo Emerson's and Henry David Thoreau's work, but Emerson and Thoreau consider most people permanently benighted and those who save themselves do so with a spiritual evolution only a few can achieve. As Huck's decency demonstrates, for midwestern fiction writers, kindness comes easily and naturally. And utterly nothing exists in midwestern literature that suggests its authors share Herman Melville's and Nathaniel Hawthorne's commitment to humanity's innate evil.

The first chapter of this book, "Conformity's Consequences," explores the damage these authors trace to the American Dream. Those who actively pursue success like, for instance, the King and the Duke from *Huckleberry Finn*, most major characters in the fiction of F. Scott Fitzgerald, and the characters in Jane Smiley's novels, *Good Faith* and *Ten Days in the Hills*, wind up with empty, desolate lives which they unsuccessfully strive to fill with sex, drugs, and/or alcohol. Those characters who most obsessively strive to fulfill their misguided ambitions usually come from outside the Midwest or flee it for one of the coasts or Europe as soon as possible. Thus, midwestern authors imply that the aggressive pursuit of success and prestige is fundamentally foreign to the region.

Middle-class Midwesterners, like George F. Babbitt, capitulate to conformity, passively attempting to fulfill the role they think society wants from them. They evade the agonies of the dramatically "successful" characters, but their fundamental alienation from themselves puts genuine happiness out of their reach. The most vital characters in this fiction come from the lower classes whose suffering makes it easy for them to understand the cruelty of the norms people from the upper classes attempt to realize at their expense. The people at the bottom of the social ladder include the men in Jack Conroy's *The Disinherited* or the women in Meridel Le Sueur's *The Girl* who retain enough of their emotional lives to care intensely about their friends and their family, but find themselves constantly fighting to collect enough money to survive. The lower classes in this fiction have greater emotional health than the elite, but they have little opportunity to enjoy it since finding jobs that provide them with enough money for food and housing necessarily consumes most of their energy and attention. But that they endure only through each other's kindness gives them an indelible lesson in the power of decency.

The second chapter, "The Redemptive Potential of Childhood," shows how these authors particularly value children. This makes logical sense since they believe that the emotional honesty that most human beings bring with them when they arrive on the planet makes them both vibrant and kind until convention begins its work on them. This focus on children contrasts sharply with the authors from New England that preceded them. None of these earlier writers describe children, aside from Nathaniel Hawthorne who tends to make the few children appearing in his fiction enforcers of social codes, like Pearl who torments her mother by calling attention to the scarlet letter in the novel of the same name. The children in midwestern literature, like Huck, may try to follow society's rules, but their innate ethical sense keeps them from succeeding. This rendition of children in midwestern literature persists to the present day. In 2013, Louise Erdrich's novel *The Round House*, which won the National Book Award, features a young native boy who kills his mother's rapist after it becomes clear that because of legal technicalities society would never punish him. These authors portray children as having such strength that, again, like Huck, they manage to heal the abuse they suffer at the hands of their caretakers. But they cannot overcome society's damage to them. A number of these writers consider the harm done when young men, seduced by society's claims about the rewards of patriotism, volunteer for the armed services. In Willa Cather's *One of Ours*, after falling in love with the adventure of traveling to France to fight, the protagonist, Claude Wheeler, gets killed almost instantly to his mother's relief: She celebrates that he died before his idealism. Ernest Hemingway's *In Our Time*, on the other hand, vividly portrays the damage done to young minds and souls by participating in war.

The third chapter, "Valuing Women's Passion," shows that these authors see women's emotional lives as potentially redemptive for society and believe that the devaluation of women's strengths hurts everyone. Only one of the writers from New England preceding these midwesterners wrote about women—Nathaniel Hawthorne—and he defined them entirely in terms of their relationships to men. Hester seem to achieve some stature since the townspeople in *The Scarlet Letter* decide that her *A* stands for angel, but Hester herself says her ignorance of sacred love means she has nothing to offer the women of her community who look to her for solace and insight. Sherwood Anderson's book *Perhaps Women* argues for a strikingly different view, suggesting that the machine age has rendered men impotent, but that women's vivid feeling lives keep them alive. The hope of Anderson's book is that if society would treat women with more reverence, their passion could help redeem it. A number of midwestern authors present male characters who could vastly improve their lives if they could own their softer sides, such as Studs Lonigan in the eponymously titled novel and Lefty in Nelson Algren's *Never Come Morning*.

Because the men generally refuse to cultivate their feelings, they tend to treat the women abusively, but some women come to understand that they collaborate with this mistreatment and become more independent so that they can resist male domination. So, finally, this literature comes down on the side of androgyny suggesting that women and men would improve their own lives, as well as their relationships with each other, if they cultivated traits associated primarily with the other gender.

The fourth chapter, "The African American Dimension," begins by pointing out that while the writers from New England failed to engage the African American experience, a number of white midwestern authors, including Mark Twain, Sherwood Anderson, Willa Cather, Sinclair Lewis, and Tillie Olsen, have written fiction portraying African Americans positively. Some critics have challenged the authenticity of these accounts, but no one can question their authors' good intentions. The chapter continues to point out that midwestern African American writers discuss the same topics as white midwestern authors, but the fact of racial discrimination causes them to sometimes offer a different perspective. For instance, because achieving wealth stood beyond their reach for so long and because of the clear link between greed and slavery, the American Dream does not tantalize the characters in the works by African American fiction writers. But like white midwestern writers, African American midwestern authors especially value their children. Because they know that racism means their children must learn to deal with particularly virulent and destructive social norms, African American authors worry about how to protect their children from this reality. Like white authors, they do not approve of their children going to war, but have additional concern about African Americans fighting to protect a nation that has never protected them. Because African American women and men see each other as collaborators in the attempt to evade racism's impact, the women tend to understand their mistreatment by the men as an offshoot of racism's power, so they try as best they can to regard it compassionately. The common enemy of African American men and women, the white power structure, unites them.

"Surrendering to Nature," the fifth chapter, talks about the distinctive way in which midwestern authors see nature as offering relief from the pressure to conform. While the transcendentalists also characterize nature as a refuge from social norms, they believed this happened through achieving the enriched awareness that gives one access to the spiritual dimension of reality. Midwestern authors have much lower standards for finding comfort in nature: They believe that anyone with a heart and eyes can discover freedom and happiness there, not by transcending it, but by observing and appreciating it. Nature has far too much significance and power for a mere human being to comprehend, let alone transcend. But those who find the humility to turn themselves over to it, discover enormous joy. Because midwestern fiction predominantly concerns itself with social dynamics, this view of nature stands primarily in the background of this work. But its consistency with the views implicit in the nature writing of the midwesterners John Muir and Aldo Leopold allow Muir's and Leopold's writings to sharply define midwestern fiction writers' views of nature and to clarify their conceptual backdrops. Like Leopold and Muir, all these authors associate nature not with solitude, as do the transcendentalists, but with connection. Not surprisingly, the most complete manifestation of this view appears in the work of native midwestern fiction writers like Louise Erdrich and Gerald Vizenor. As Vizenor writes in *Heirs of Columbus*, the human, the animal, the sacred, and the material dimensions of the natural world fuse:

> The Anishinnabe, the woodland tribe that founded his obscure tavern, the oldest in the New World, remember that Naanabozho, the compassionate tribal trickster who created the earth, had a brother who was a stone: A bear stone, a human stone, a shaman stone, a stone, a stone, a stone.[14]

The same pursuit of the American Dream that midwestern writers argue created destructive divisions between human beings also created a split between people and the other elements of the natural world, or as Vizenor puts it: "Once upon a time ... we dreamed humans into being, ... but humans lost their humor over land, gold, slaves, and time" (16).

Chapter Six, "Relaxing into Compassion," explores the ways these authors believe people can free themselves from the alienation generated by pursuing the American Dream, thus allowing them to know and pursue their own desires, enjoy honest and fulfilling connections with others, and savor the peace and happiness of resigning themselves to nature's power instead of striving fruitlessly to conquer it. Because achieving this freedom means overcoming well-established patterns, this is a fiction filled with benevolent breakdowns: Repeatedly, characters relinquish the struggle to triumph either voluntarily or because circumstances impede them. So multiple protagonists in Sherwood Anderson's fiction, Willa Cather's Alexandra Bergson in *O Pioneers!*, Saul Bellow's Herzog in the novel of the same name, Toni Morrison's Pilate in *Song of Solomon*, Fleur in Louise Erdrich's *Four Souls* and Nathaniel Mason in Charles Baxter's *The Soul Thief* all discover themselves and happiness when their attempts to secure success collapse. On the other hand, some characters in this fiction apparently enter the world wise, understanding from the start that what joy they will have depends on accepting and inhabiting the lives and feelings they were dealt: The archbishop in Cather's masterpiece *Death Comes for the*

Archbishop, and Donald in Jim Harrison's *Returning to Earth*. But whether they seem born with integrity or stumble into it, this self-awareness never leads to self-absorption. The characters either enter their fictional worlds possessing both integrity and kindness or discover that living honestly leads them into compassion. So this fiction argues that if the conventional enthusiasm for prestige and money melted away, the innate decency of ordinary people would reveal itself.

In 1894, Hamlin Garland predicted that the Midwest would produce significant literature of the type this book describes. In his *Crumbling Idols: Twelve Essays on Art, Dealing Chiefly with Literature, Painting and the Drama*, Garland anticipates that the artistic center of the country will soon move west from Boston. He identifies the distinguishing characteristics of this new art. First and foremost, it will focus on common people and common experiences: "If the past was the history of a few titled personalities riding high on obscure waves of nameless, suffering humanity, the future will be the day of high average personality."[15] The new writing undergirded by this attitude will use authentic speech: "We are to use actual speech as we hear it and to record its changes" (173). It will celebrate generosity, not domination: "If the past celebrated lust and greed and love of power, the future will celebrate continence and humility and altruism" (45). And it will include groups previously excluded from literature: "If the past ignored and trampled on women, the future will place them side by side with men. If the child of the past was ignored, the future will cherish him. And fiction will embody these facts" (45). Above all, it will rest on the honest perceptions of the individual: "This school will be one where most notably the individuality of each writer will be respected" (156). Garland identifies Chicago as the center of this new work, declaring that its large and diverse immigrant population makes it more American than the East. And Garland notes that "the great body of men and women who give strength and originality to Chicago are people who care very little what New York thinks of their work, and the doings of London and Paris are not more vital" (155). When Garland turns to the people of the Midwest who will produce this art, he exhorts them, above all, to honestly present their rendition of the world they see: "His first care must be to present his own concept. This is, I believe, the essence of veritism: 'Write of those things of which you know most, and for which you care most. By so doing you will be true to yourself, true to your locality, and true to your time'" (35).

Garland believed that fiction would most compellingly articulate these themes since it reflected everyday life better than poetry and the average reader could understand it more easily. But it would hardly surprise Garland that the same themes appear in midwestern poetry. A number of midwestern authors have produced both poetry and fiction, so, of course, their work in both genres includes similar themes. The writers whose fiction appears in the following chapters who also wrote poetry include Sherwood Anderson, Charles Baxter, Gwendolyn Brooks, Rita Dove, Jim Harrison, Langston Hughes, Clarence Major, and Gerald Vizenor. But themes that predominate in the fiction also appear in the work of midwestern authors considered exclusively poets.

The aversion to class divisions created by Americans striving for success and sympathy for the mistreatment of the working class play central roles in the poetry of Carl Sandburg and Philip Levine. The title of Sandburg's *The People, Yes!* indicates where his sympathies lie. And like the lower-class people in the fiction, those described by Sandburg and Levine, let everyone know that, despite difficult circumstances, they have retained their humanity by singing.

Children also function importantly in much of this poetry, most especially in that of Theodore Roethke, who writes: "Through the young, I shall recover my lost innocence."[16] He attempts to restore himself and the readers of his verse to childhood and does such a good job that his poems make little rational sense. Like a child, the reader must feel his or her way through the experiences the poems present and resist the temptation to analyze or understand them rationally. In poems like "Thinking for Berky" where he lies awake worrying about the fate of a promiscuous girl, and "Accountability," wherein he frets over what the school system does to its students, William Stafford establishes himself as poet concerned with society's treatment of children.

Rita Dove records the rich emotional lives of women in her poetry, while Gwendolyn Brooks ties women's passion to ethics in her poem suggesting that the white woman Emmett Till died for supposedly whistling at hates her husband for his brutality, but fears him too much to show it. Androgyny plays such an enormous and complicated role in Robert Bly's work that he has produced whole books considering the issue from multiple perspectives.

The views articulated by African American poets complement those presented in their fiction. Robert Hayden's poem "Middle Passage" and Clarence Major's poem "The Slave Trade: View from the Middle Passage" portray slavery's enormous damage. And, as in the fiction, African American poets recommend that blacks rely on their own considerable culture and abilities rather than on whites. In *Slave Moth*, a long poem about a slave named Varl who teaches herself to read and write despite her master's abuse, Thylias Moss affirms the faith that African Americans can save themselves. And African American poets, like African American fiction writers, weave music into their work. Langston Hughes sometimes includes musical notations along with his poems. In Rita Dove's *Thomas and Beulah*, music accompanies and consoles their difficult lives.

The views on nature that one uncovers primarily by looking very closely at the fiction through a lens provided by the work of John Muir and Aldo Leopold become much clearer in midwestern poetry. William Stafford, Jim Harrison, and Philip Levine all stress that nature far outpaces man in terms of size, duration, and power, so the notion of a human being attempting to transcend it becomes laughable. But people can profit enormously from turning themselves over to it. Theodore Roethke's poetry centers on the ecstasy of losing oneself in nature, as does James Wright's often-anthologized poem "A Blossom."

What poem could offer a clearer call to resist the social structure's emphasis on success and trust oneself than Theodore Roethke's "I Wake to Sleep and Take My Waking Slow"? William Stafford's poetry, along with his nonfictional comments, also focuses intensely on the value of accepting oneself. When asked to explain why he does not worry about success as a poet, Stafford replies that producing poetry "is the process of living centrally and paying attention to your own life. Surely that's worth doing. If you don't, who will? That's what living is about and you can be distracted from living by trying to create things that will last in the terminology and the mode of society."[17] and Stafford's integrity easily leads him to compassion, which saturates both his poetry and his teaching. Stafford's empathy explains why he believes that "even if there is such a thing as the lowest one in the class, they deserve the same level reception and cordiality as anyone else" (73).

But then it makes sense that midwestern poetry and fiction articulate similar themes: The same culture produces them. The populist stance implicit in midwestern fiction and poetry has moved into other media as well. Bob Dylan knew he shared roots with Carl Sandburg, so he sought him out and presented him with his album *The Times They Are a-Changin'*. Dylan closes his autobiography *Chronicles* by mentioning two other literary Minnesotans, F. Scott Fitzgerald and Sinclair Lewis and noting that because they "followed their own vision, didn't care what the pictures showed," they "would have understood what my inarticulate dreams were about. I felt like I was one of them."[18] Certainly Dylan's lyrics share the suspicion of the American Dream, greed, and conformity as well as reverence for common people that pervades midwestern literature. And what could be more populist than the films of Michael Moore? His *Roger and Me* (1989) articulates the notion pervading midwestern writing that too often decent, ordinary people pay for the elite's triumphs. What could be more consistent with the values of midwestern literature than the books Studs Terkel put together collecting the views of common folk on historical events, such as the Great Depression, but also on their daily work? And who spoke more articulately and passionately about the white social structure's oppression of African Americans than Malcolm X? And like other midwesterners, when Malcolm X moved away from Elijah Muhammad and found his way to integrity by relying on his own perceptions, he also discovered a compassion that allowed him to resign his hatred of whites.

A number of institutions that began in the Midwest reflect the region's focus on improving everyday life by helping people find ways to resist having their lives shaped by the powerful. The University of Chicago laboratory school, founded upon John Dewey's faith that children needed less instruction and more space to develop their possibilities, continues to function to this day. The University of Chicago itself, although an elite research university, spurned the lecture system in place on the East Coast at institutions like Harvard University and Yale University to adopt a participatory process wherein students and professors arrive at insights together through discussion. The belief that all people deserve access to higher education led to the establishment of land-grant universities in the Midwest. And the important centers of the labor unions that play such major roles in the fiction of Jack Conroy and Chester Himes are midwestern: The Pullman Strike, the Haymarket Bombing, and the founding of the International Workers of the World took place in Chicago, Detroit served as the epicenter of the powerful UAW, and Wisconsin first legalized collective bargaining by public employees.

So Garland's prophecy captures qualities that define and distinguish the literature and culture in the middle of the country to this day. But because many of its writers have succeeded spectacularly on the international stage without any acknowledgment of their origins and because the easy dismissal of the Midwest as "flyover country" has become routine, the importance and unity of midwestern fiction has gone unexplored. The chapters that follow correct this oversight.

One

Conformity's Consequences

Twain's *Huckleberry Finn* differs sharply from literature produced in New England earlier in the century even though the major authors directly preceding Twain, Ralph Waldo Emerson, Henry David Thoreau, Nathaniel Hawthorne, and Herman Melville, all agree with him about conformity's dangers. But their literature suggests that only a few enlightened people can resist capitulating to social norms while the ordinary language, characters, and events of *Huckleberry Finn*, as well as the community's collective joy at Jim's freedom from slavery, underline the book's commitment to the view that people have an innate sense of decency which the social structure undermines. To behave well, one merely needs the courage to follow one's natural inclination to act kindly.

For the writers from New England, conformity poses dangers because it obstructs higher awareness. Thoreau wants his readers to develop their "nobler faculties," so he condemns the passive way they read: "Most men have learned to read to serve a paltry convenience, as they have learned to cipher in order to keep accounts and not be cheated in trade; but of reading as a noble intellectual exercise they know little or nothing; yet this only is reading…[:] what we have to stand on tiptoe to read and devote our most alert and wakeful hours to."[1] Both Thoreau and Emerson believe that only by engaging texts in this wholehearted way can one experience the transcendental illumination the best writers offer. Emerson explains the nature of this insight in "The Divinity School Address": One learns that "this homely game of life we play, covers, under what seem to be foolish details, principles that astonish…[:] the perfection of the laws of the soul."[2] Thoreau adds that this kind of spiritual awareness comes only from engaging the written word, not listening to speech: "The noblest written words are commonly as far behind or above the fleeting spoken language as the firmament with its stars is behind the clouds. *There* are the stars, and they who can may read them.... They are not exhalations like our daily colloquies and vaporous breath" (98).

Thirty years after *Walden*'s publication, Mark Twain produced *Huckleberry Finn*, a novel that children can and do read, yet over time, it has achieved the same classic status as Thoreau's *Walden* and Emerson's essays. Twain values colloquial speech as passionately as Thoreau dismisses it, prefacing his book by assuring the audience of its various dialogues' accuracy: "The shadings have not been done in a hap-hazard fashion, or by guess-work; but pain-stakingly, and with the trustworthy guidance and support of personal familiarity with these several forms of speech."[3] Twain also shows little reverence for the spiritual transcendence Thoreau and Emerson hoped their readers would achieve. In his essay, "James Fenimore Cooper's Literary Offenses," he insists that "the personages of a tale shall confine themselves to possibilities and let miracles alone; or, if they venture a miracle, the author must so plausibly set it forth as to make it look possible and reasonable."[4] Twain does not want his readers to rise above commonplace reality; he wants them to face it.

While Emerson and Thoreau consider human beings fundamentally good but profoundly benighted, Herman Melville and Nathaniel Hawthorne argue for the corruption of the world and its inhabitants, often using allegorical characters to convey their general sense of people's sinfulness. Hawthorne's "Earth's Holocaust," a tale that describes the burning of symbols from destructive institutions like monarchy in a bonfire, culminates with the declaration that destroying these emblems serves no purpose as long as the human heart remains because "unless they hit upon some method of purifying that foul cavern, forth from it will re-issue all the shapes of wrong and misery."[5] Since Melville and Hawthorne characterize ordinary people as corrupt, it makes sense that they fill their fiction with allegorical characters like Captain Ahab and Hester Prynne. Nor would loyalty to colloquial speech interest them; so even when Hawthorne's Ethan Brand announces that he regrets losing his sense of community, he uses elevated speech: "'Oh, Mother Earth,' cried he, 'who art no more my Mother, and into whose bosom this frame shall never be resolved! Oh, mankind, whose brotherhood I have cast off, and trampled thy great heart beneath my feet!'"

Huckleberry Finn places at its center not transcendental truth like Emerson and Thoreau or universal depravity like Hawthorne and Melville, but the ways in which pursuit of social status seduce people away from their natural inclination to treat others well. Although it has gone unrecognized, many other writers who, like Twain, spent their childhoods in the Midwest, share his fascination with the destructive impact of conformity on people's behavior. Twain's interest in and evaluation of the power of social norms has not achieved the same general recognition as the impact of his use of common speech and ordinary characters, even though it resurfaces in midwestern fiction for over a century.

The social reality these authors focus on most persistently is the destructive consequences of embracing a definition of "success" that prizes proving oneself superior to others. According to one midwestern writer after another, striving to fulfill competitive goals demands an alienation from one's authentic desires in order for one to adapt to the market's demands. And the expectation that one prove one's worth by defeating others also alienates one from the kindly feelings that these authors consider innate in all human beings. In other words, these writers warn again and again that by fervently pursuing the American Dream, Americans destroy any basis for leading decent lives.

Unlike Emerson and Thoreau, Twain identifies some specific characters as evil, but unlike Hawthorne and Melville, he does not claim universal depravity. He locates it exclusively in those who intentionally exploit others, like the King and the Duke in *Huckleberry Finn*. Although they falsely represent themselves as royalty, Huck sees no reason to tell Jim that they aren't because "you couldn't tell them from the real kind" (221), establishing a clear link between corruption and the social triumph. Indeed, their names recall the robber barons of the Gilded Age who made their fortunes by taking advantage of others. Precisely because they lie and rob with impunity and even turn in Jim for forty dollars, Twain associates these two crooks with the elite. They also come from outside the community: Otherwise, people would have heard about their schemes and not have fallen for them. Moreover, they actively represent themselves as foreign, although they speak in accents so bad even the unsophisticated Huck can recognize their fraudulence. Huck immediately understands that they share the same personality type as his alcoholic, abusive father: They have become so completely detached from themselves and others that appealing to their benevolence makes no sense: "'It didn't take me long to make up my mind that these liars warn't no kings nor dukes, at all, but just low-down humbugs and frauds.... If I never learnt nothing else out of pap, I learnt that the best way to get along with his kind of people is to let them have their own way'" (186). Even the King and the Duke seem to recognize the desolation of their lives: They spend their free time drinking themselves into oblivion. Through their characterization, Twain raises questions about the values central to the American Dream since achieving it requires only that one collect more money and power than others. The King and the Duke energetically fulfill its imperatives; their triumph delivers them to emptiness.

The striving for domination at the heart of the American Dream strikes later authors, as it had Twain, as potentially destructive to all Americans, including those who apparently thrive. The King and the Duke do not have good lives by any measure and neither do the hugely "successful" characters in the midwestern fiction that follows *Huckleberry Finn*.

F. Scott Fitzgerald's career as a novelist consists largely of describing the vacuous lives of the rich. The main character in his first novel, *This Side of Paradise*, comes to understand the importance of integrity to a good life, but most of Fitzgerald's characters lose track of this truth or, more frequently, never understand it in the first place. Those born to wealth, like Anthony Patch, the protagonist in *The Beautiful and Damned*, aspire to nothing except accumulating money and status. When the uncle whom Patch expects to become his benefactor happens upon Patch and his wife as they host yet another drunken party, his uncle cuts Patch out of his will and Patch faces the horrifying possibility of working for a living. While Patch consoles himself with drink, his lawyer successfully challenges the will. At the novel's conclusion, Patch congratulates himself on resisting "unkind" attempts to make him accept his ordinariness: "Only a few months before people had been urging him to give in, to submit to mediocrity, to go to work. But he had known that he was justified in his way of life—and he had stuck it out stanchly. Why, the very friends who had been most unkind had come to respect him, to know he had been right all along. Had not the Lacys and the Merediths and the Cartwright-Smiths called on Gloria and him at the Ritz-Carlton just a week before they sailed?" Patch congratulates himself as the thought of his triumph brings tears to his eyes: "It was a hard fight, but I didn't give up and I came through!"[6]

The Buchanans in *The Great Gatsby* also live on inherited wealth and feel no obligation to do anything meaningful with their lives unless Tom Buchanan's expression of white-supremacist views qualifies as an effort to protect civilization: "'It's up to us, who are the dominant race, to watch out or these other races will have control of things.'"[7] After Daisy hits and fatally injures Tom's lover, Myrtle Wilson, she just keeps driving. Nick Carraway, the novel's moral center, describes Tom and Daisy as "careless people.... They smashed up things and creatures and then retreated back into their money or their vast carelessness, or whatever it was that kept them together, and let other people clean up the mess they had made" (180–81).

Gatsby actually makes his own money, but apparently illegally: Rumors suggest that he once killed a man. Nick meets one of Gatsby's friends, Meyer Wolfsheim, who wears cufflinks made from human molars, who fixed the World Series and who offers Nick "'a business gonnegtion'" (71)—all characteristics that make him unsavory. Nick repeatedly portrays Gatsby in an admiring fashion, describing his smile, for instance, as "one of those rare smiles with a quality of eternal reassurance in it, that you may come across four or five times in life" (48). He also lauds Gatsby's "incorruptible dream" (155), even though Gatsby wants Daisy because she introduces him to the pleasure of having lots of money: "Gatsby was overwhelmingly aware of the youth and mystery that wealth imprisons and preserves, of the freshness of many clothes, and of Daisy, gleaming like silver, safe and proud above the hot struggles of the poor" (150). Gatsby's aspirations are essentially the same as Anthony Patch's; he simply must work harder to achieve them. The brilliance of Fitzgerald's novel rests in his successfully revealing both the superficial attraction and the fundamental hollowness of Gatsby's life through Nick's perspective.

The appeal of the wealthy life destroys Dick Diver of *Tender is the Night*, even though he had once established a career as a psychiatrist and researcher. He understands the importance of integrity and tries to protect it, but after marrying Nicole Warren, a wealthy client, he enters her glamorous world and focuses on partying with the beautiful people. Slowly, the identity that had allowed him to define his world weakens. He realizes only in retrospect that he has obliterated his center: His involvement in an empty affair with a young actress named Rosemary forces Diver to examine himself critically: "He had lost himself—he could not tell the hour when, or the day or the week, the month or the year. Once he had cut through things, solving the most complicated equations as the simplest problems of his simplest patients. Between the time he found Nicole flowering under a stone on the Zurichsee and the moment of his meeting with Rosemary his spear had been blunted."[8]

His father taught him the importance of decency: "His father had been sure of what he was, with a deep pride of the two proud widows who had raised him to believe that nothing could be superior to 'good instincts,' honor, courtesy and courage" (204). But his father also endured poverty; Diver suspects that this history made wealth attractive to him because it could provide security he and his father lacked. Unfortunately, the money winds up owning him: "He had never felt more sure of himself, more thoroughly his own man, than at the time of his marriage to Nicole. Yet he had been swallowed up like a gigolo, and somehow permitted his arsenal to be locked up in the Warren safety-deposit vaults." His consequent vacuity leaves him out of control: "He was in love with every pretty woman he saw now, their forms at a distance, their shadows on the wall" (201). Like most of the other opportunists in these books, Dick Diver tries to fill his hollowness with drink. Eventually, his career, his marriage, and his family fall apart. He returns to Buffalo, where his father lived and died, and tries to begin a practice and research once more, but seems unable to rebuild his life. Indeed, Fitzgerald's novels primarily offer case studies of the void wealth leaves in its wake.

In *Elmer Gantry*, Sinclair Lewis shows the same destructive tendencies at work in an ambitious preacher. Gantry's first vigorous "religious" experience comes from his intense enjoyment of the power mouthing platitudes gives him over others: "He had little to do with what he said. The willing was not his but the mob's; the phrases were not his but those of the emotional preachers and hysterical worshippers whom he had heard since babyhood.... They were sobbing with affection for him."[9] Gantry easily adapts to the discovery that he can dominate others; he uses everyone: His parishioners, his family, and his nominal friends. When an auditorium catches fire during a service, he tells Sharon Falconer, the woman he supposedly loves, to go to hell when she ignores his instructions to leave. He then climbs over others to safety, leaving everyone else behind in the flames: "The door opened inward—only it did not open, with the score of victims thrust against it. In howling panic, Elmer sprang among them, knocking them aside, struck down a girl who stood in his way, yanked open the door, and got through it ... the last, the only one to get through it" (221). As he continues his cynical climb to the top, his aspirations become hopelessly grandiose: "He would combine in one association all the moral organizations in America—perhaps, later, in the entire world. He would be the executive of that combination; he would be the super-president of the United States, and some day, the dictator of the world" (393). Meanwhile, he demonstrates his contempt for even those closest to him, especially his wife, Cleo, by having one affair after another. Unimpeded by conscience, he steadily rises in status and wealth; still, his mother knows who he is: "You were always so quick with excuses! When you stole pies or hung cats or licked the other boys! Son, Cleo is suffering. You never pay any attention to her, even when I'm here and you try to be nice to her to show off. Elmer, who is this secretary of yours that you keep calling up all the while?" (404). But the rest of the universe admires him.

Con men persist in midwestern fiction. Three decades later, in *Seize the Day*, Saul Bellow portrays a hustling psychiatrist, Dr. Tamkin, who talks a desperate Tommy Wilhelm into writing a check for his last dollar to Dr. Tamkin so that he can invest it; Tamkin then disappears with Tommy's money. Tommy trusts Tamkin because he intersperses his ludicrous claims with accurate insights, like the notion that business has become a pestilence. Tamkin's comments should warn Tommy against investing with him; take this remark, for instance: "Money-making is aggression. That's the whole thing. The functionalistic explanation is the only one. People come to the market to kill" (69).

As Tamkin well knows, Tommy finds himself surrounded by people who only want something from him when he himself desperately needs help. After Tamkin disappears and his own father refuses him money, Tommy confesses his despair to the wife he has left when she calls to demand money. She does not respond sympathetically. He asks her how she can treat someone who lived with her and loved her for so long so cruelly. She replies, "'How did you imagine it was going to be—big shot?'" (114). Julia Eichelberger points out that the novel critiques an entire society of narcissists pursuing the American Dream: "The narrative diagnoses individualism, the belief that individuals shape their own destiny by seeking a favorable position in a hierarchy, as a veneer for greed. Individualism produces not wealth, but alienation from nature and from other human beings."[10]

In *The Twenty-Seventh City*, Jonathan Franzen portrays the damage done by a power-hungry police chief. At the start of the novel, Martin Probst is an honorable man with a healthy family life: "He was viceless, honest, capable, and calm to the point of complacency."[11] Susan Jammu, who has arrived from India to take charge of the St. Louis Police Department, wants to control him so that he will facilitate her ambitions; in order to acquire the knowledge she needs to do this, she bugs his home. Her colleague Balwin Singh joins her in St. Louis, eager to help implement whatever plots she sets in motion. He enjoys abusing others, so he relishes his assignment of seducing Probst's daughter Luisa: "He wanted Luisa Probst, too, with sudden criminal force. Wanted to break her. He removed a shoe and winged it fiercely at the skylight" (36).

Singh winds up seducing Probt's wife, Barbara, instead of his daughter. When he no longer needs her, he stages her death. Meanwhile, Jammu works on getting Probst to cooperate with her political goals by having an affair with him. As Probst becomes more involved with Jammu, he comes to share her cynicism and detachment. He realizes when he catches a glimpse of his daughter's back that he now sees her only as a thing: "What was happening to the city? He saw Luisa's naked back and paid as little attention to it as if it were a bathroom door; the funny ripples and blades turned livid as his stare lengthened in time and the snow falling outside the window faintly scuffed the nighttime. She was an object. This was what was happening" (373). From the superior perspective his new skepticism grants him, he begins judging others as moronic: "Who would be fooled by these hollow eggs? Kids, that was who. Kids were fooled. The economy was fueled by the stupidity of kids" (428). So this novel argues that everyone, no matter how old, no matter how noble, can become ensnared in corruption. Although *The Twenty-Seventh City* appears more than a century after *Huckleberry Finn*, both novels, along with *The Beautiful and Damned*, *The Great Gatsby*, *Tender Is the Night*, *Elmer Gantry*, and *Seize the Day* all locate evil in people who stalk the American Dream at others' expense.

Jane Smiley's novel *Good Faith*, with its detailed description of the transformation of the ethical real estate agent Joe Stratford into a scam artist, gives a sense of what pushes people towards the full-throttled pursuit of success, detaching them from themselves, others, and constructive lives. Joe sells a home to Marcus Burns, a retired IRS agent who convinces first Joe's boss, Gordon Baldwin, and then Joe himself that they can build a huge, profitable development on land that formerly constituted an estate called Salt Key Farms. Joe has serious doubts about the possibilities Marcus enthuses over, but the notion of becoming rich and powerful excites him so much that his exhilaration overwhelms his uneasiness. When he worries about what to tell engineers, inspectors, secretaries, and the like about the project, Marcus urges him to "try and figure out what they needed to know, what they were looking for, and then tell them that. The overall plan, he said, was a kind of beautiful dream.... It was my job to educate them so they would take their natural places in the plan."[12]

Joe finds exercising all this power so thrilling that he easily convinces himself that he has finally begun to realize the American Dream: "I had lived, without understanding it, the proper American trajectory, rising and rising, dropping off the first-stage rocket, then the second stage, then shooting into space, destined to orbit the earth for some uncounted number of times before splashing into the ocean off Florida, retired in the far-off twenty-first century" (274–75). He congratulates himself on leaving behind his religious parents' cautious approach to life.

His professional ascent fills Joe with confidence. He begins dating Susan Webster, who has few sexual inhibitions and shares her cocaine with him. Like almost every other tycoon in these midwestern novels, as he becomes more successful, Joe relies more and more heavily on sex and artificial stimulants for pleasure. He also enjoys succeeding in competitions, no matter how meaningless; he notes with pride when they go to a swimming party "that Susan was the youngest woman there and was unconsciously and naturally beautiful in her bikini, whereas the other women were a little defiant in their rather more sedate swimwear. Here, as in every other facet of her personality, was just that touch of the exotic that thrilled me—her bikini was an old one but that meant she had bought it in Europe, and it was cut just a little more stylishly than everyone else's Cole of California bathing suits" (348).

Eventually, Marcus disappears and everything collapses. Since Joe has acquired problems, Susan Webster loses interest, explaining that "it's going to take a long time to sort this out, you said so yourself, and I don't want to go through it with you" (408). Their relationship had so little substance that he finds himself astonished to discover that he doesn't miss her and that he considered marrying someone he cared about so little.

The characters who populate Jane Smiley's *Ten Days in the Hills* have either already arrived, like the Oscar-winning director Max and his ex-wife, the famous actress Zoe Cunningham, or have achieved success vicariously through their ties to these two. Members of both groups suffer from terminal emptiness. To amuse themselves, they use the same shallow solutions as all the other "successful" people in these novels: Sex, drugs, and alcohol; they also add a new escape: Exquisite food. Elena, Max's lover, also talks obsessively about the war in Iraq. But she admits to herself that this useless speculation attracts her because she considers it yet another way to validate her superiority: "Though no theory worked, she couldn't help toiling at her theorizing. Her fellow citizens had become unaccountable. She had lost even the most rudimentary ability to understand their points of view, but she could not stop theorizing. Each new theory was accompanied by a momentary sense of uplift."[13]

All these novels—*Huckleberry Finn, Elmer Gantry, The Beautiful and Damned, The Great Gatsby, Tender is the Night, Seize the Day, the Twenty-Seventh City, Good Faith*, and *Ten Days in the Hills*, suggest that pursuing success at all costs creates an inner void which people attempt to fill with domination, food, sex, drink and/or drugs. Considering American and foreign enthusiasm for the American Dream, this seems a surprising development, but, on reflection, why would anyone find a life that involves exploiting others in order to enjoy a sense of superiority rich and meaningful? All these works validate Charles Citrine's conclusion in Bellow's *Humboldt's Gift*: "And this was the famous Romance of Business? Why it was nothing but pushiness, rapidity, effrontery. The sense it gave of getting your own way was shallow.

Compared with the satisfaction of contemplating flowers or of something really serious ... it was nothing, nothing at all."[14]

Just as the King and the Duke represent themselves as foreigners, in these novels, people looking for triumph over others tend to flee the Midwest or arrive there from elsewhere. As Nick Carraway points out at the end of *The Great Gatsby*, he, the Buchanans and Gatsby were all midwesterners who moved east. Tom Buchanan, the book's most loathsome character, proudly asserts that he would never go back to the Midwest; while Nick Carraway, the book's moral nucleus, returns to Minnesota. Near the end of the book, Nick presents comparative images of the middle west and the East. Nick visualizes the East as a place where four well-dressed men carry drunken women in a white formal dress from house to house on a stretcher: "Gravely the men turn in at a house—the wrong house. But no one knows the woman's name, and no one cares" (178). When he thinks of the Midwest, he recalls meeting old friends in Chicago's Union Station as they all head home from school: "That's my Middle West ... the thrilling returning trains of my youth, and the street lamps and sleigh bells in the frosty dark and the shadows of holly wreaths thrown by lighted windows on the snow. I am part of that, a little solemn with the feel of those long winters, a little complacent from growing up in the Carraway house in a city where dwellings are still called through decades by a family's name" (177).

Only the dysfunctional rich populate *The Beautiful and Damned* and *Tender is the Night*, both of which take place on the East Coast and in Europe. Elmer Gantry grows up in the Midwest, but attends theological seminary in Babylon "a town which suggests New England more than the Middle West" (85) and the final certification of his success comes in the form of a pastorate in New York City. The whole of *Seize the Day* takes place in New York City, which Bellow portrays as a maelstrom of individuals driven by insistent needs: "The great, great crowd, the inexhaustible current of millions of every race and kind pouring out, pressing round, of every age, of every genius, possessors of every human secret, antique and future, in every face the refinement of one particular motive or essence—I labor, I spend, I strive, I design, I love, I cling, I uphold, I give way, I envy, I long, I scorn, I die, I hide, I want. Faster, much faster than any man could make the tally" (115). Julia Eichelberger agrees that Bellow's novel makes New York City look especially problematic: "Wilhelm ponders the alienation of all his fellow New Yorkers from each other, in a city where 'every other man spoke a language entirely his own.'"[15] In Jonathan Franzen's *Strong Motion*, Rene Seichek, the novel's heroine and a native of

Lake Forest, Illinois, finds Boston's mean spiritedness disappointing: "There's ... a coldness, an ugliness. I mean every week there's some incredibly twisted crime here. And somehow all the people who think Boston's a center of culture and education manage to ignore it.... But I look and I see overt racism and a rotten climate and elevated cancer rates and bad drivers and a harbor full of sewage, and I see all these young mothers with their Saabs in Cambridge blissing out on being in Cambridge, and who wouldn't be revolted?"[16] Evil in *The Twenty-Seventh City* jets into St. Louis from India with Susan Jammu. Smiley's novel *Good Faith* discusses only people on the East Coast, while *Ten Days in the Hills* includes a few expatriates from the middle west among its Californian cast. So, although midwestern authors persistently decry people using others and sometimes describe this kind of behavior taking place in the Midwest, they imply the malicious exploitation of others is fundamentally alien to the region. Perpetrators either immigrate into it or long to escape it.

And in *Duplicate Keys*, Jane Smiley associates the Midwest with authenticity and leaving it to achieve greatness as a move away from oneself. Alice, Jane Smiley's protagonist, realizes that her friend, Susan, who, like her, left the Midwest for New York City, has shot to death mutual friends who had also headed east looking for success in the music business. Susan could no longer stand their endless conversation about two brief reviews of their work in *Rolling Stone*. The murderess explains: "'I thought I was doing them a favor. Even if I left them and my life went on, their lives ... would be like listening to a scratched record play the same three notes over and over forever.'"[17] While they waited for their big break, these young men, like their ambitious compatriots in midwestern fiction, get involved with using and selling drugs. After digesting her friend's guilt, Alice wants to return to Minnesota and honesty and passion: "Her relatives seemed actually to have learned something from their long existences, which was perhaps why Alice had always liked them. They had not been battered by random events into numbness, as Alice felt in danger of being. Each of her forebears had a peculiar and fully branched inner life. Maybe that was the great compensation for living in the Midwest" (303).

In *Song of the Lark*, Willa Cather draws a portrait of Thea Kronberg, a young woman who like Cather herself, entered the art world from Nebraska. The novel suggests that the authenticity of midwestern living nourishes art along with integrity. The novel's narrator claims that Thea has an advantage coming from Nebraska, a place where "the important thing was that one should not pretend to be what one was not."[18] As a result, Thea develops into an adult who hates dishonesty. She vehemently explains: "If you love the good thing vitally, enough to give up for it all that one must give up, then you must hate the cheap thing just as hard. I tell you, there is such a thing as creative hate! A contempt that drives you through fire, makes you risk everything and lose everything, makes you a long sight better than you ever knew you could be" (383). Art, the novel's narrator maintains, comes from authenticity: Becoming an artist is essentially a process of honest self-realization: "Artistic growth is, more than it is anything else, a refining of the sense of truthfulness. The stupid believe that to be truthful is easy; only the artist, the great artist, knows how difficult it is" (398). This is how she evaluates the region that produced her: "Thea was glad that this was her country, even if one did not learn to speak elegantly there. It was, somehow, an honest country, and there was a new song in that blue air that had never been sung in the world before" (192).

Jim Harrison's novella "The Land of Unlikeness," portrays a sixty-year-old art historian who has settled in New York City and returns to Michigan to mother-sit. The humility that comes naturally from inhabiting the Midwest returns to him, freeing him to do what he wants. He wakes up one day to discover that as a result of moving home, he has "lost his self-importance."[19] So he falls in love again with the painting he abandoned because he thought he wasn't good enough at it. He now feels entitled to do what he loves, no matter how unimpressive the results: "Part of the grace of losing self-importance was the simple question 'Who cares?' More importantly, he didn't want to be a painter, he only wanted to paint" (88). So midwestern authors not only characterize mindless and self-destructive ambition as an import, they suggest that the Midwest's lack of pretense not only encourages rectitude, in doing so, it can nourish art.

Greed and power do not drive most of the midwestern people in this literature. Instead, they resemble the placid, fundamentally kind folk populating *Huckleberry Finn*. Twain focuses specifically on the issue of slavery, making it clear that people go along with it not out of meanness, but out of passivity, and even modesty. People have an innate sense of morality that tells them slavery is wrong, but they violate it in order to fit into society. This explanation of racism receives the clearest exposition in Huck's debate about whether or not to turn in Jim. Huck's attachment to Jim will not allow him to treat Jim the way society recommends, but rather than congratulating himself on his superior morality, Huck declares that with this choice he condemns himself to eternal damnation. Since he is completely lost, he vows to "take up wickedness again.... And for a starter, I would go to work and steal Jim out of slavery again; and if I could think up anything worse, I would do that, too" (292).

Huck's decision here has received massive critical attention, with people debating issues such as which philosophic ethical system best explains it and whether or not Huck truly transcends racism. But no one argues that Huck makes the wrong decision. For instance, Bernard G. Prusak writes, "In the end, he freely chooses, taking full responsibility for his choice, a course of action contrary to the prejudices of slaveholding society.... It is by virtue of his crises of conscience that he sets himself against slaveholding society and begins to free himself from its fetters."[20] Lionel Trilling finds Huck's debate so powerful that he argues no one who reads this novel carefully "will ever again be wholly able to accept without some question and irony the assumptions of the respectable morality by which he lives."[21]

Most community members also have compassion which reveals itself when social pressure to behave otherwise disappears. As she faces death, Jim's owner, Miss Watson, frees him out of shame that she ever considered selling him. When they learn that Jim has been freed, other whites besides Huck have no difficulty recognizing and celebrating Jim's uprightness: "When Aunt Polly and Uncle Silas and Aunt Sally found out how good he helped the doctor nurse Tom, they made a heap of fuss over him, and fixed him up prime, and give him all he wanted to eat, and a good time, and nothing to do.... And Jim was pleased most to death" (384–85). So these are not racist people but individuals who follow society's rules—to everyone's detriment.

Inborn empathy helps explain why people repeatedly treat Huck kindly even though he has no status or power. Judge Thatcher winks at the law in order to protect Huck's money from Huck's father. The people Huck approaches for help as he travels down the Mississippi usually take him in and care for him, even when he clumsily disguises himself as a girl. Those Huck encounters during his trip behave badly only when social pressure leads them astray, as when the mob pursues Colonel Sherburn after he has shot Boggs in the middle of town and then collectively slinks away after he calls them cowards.

This conformity not only allows these people to collaborate with slavery, when tricked by the King and the Duke into paying to attend their pathetic show, the Royal Nonesuch, their unwillingness to appear more foolish than the other townspeople results in those who've been cheated by encouraging their fellow townspeople to attend; they obscure their mistake by persuading their supposed friends to duplicate it. And they do a great job: "Next day you couldn't hear nothing around that town but how splendid that show was" (217). The third night, all the townspeople show up at the show with rotten vegetables to throw at the King and Duke, who collect the proceeds and escape before anyone has a chance to shower them with produce. In other words, they only act against the King and the Duke as a group. Other people who have heard that the King and the Duke use the Royal Nonesuch to cheat people before the pair arrives in town, appear at the first show prepared to tar and feather the two. No one knows better than Huck that the King and the Duke deserve punishment, but it still saddens him when he sees the results: "Well, it made me sick to see it; and I was sorry for them poor pitiful rascals, it seemed like I couldn't ever feel any hardness against them any more in the world.... Human beings *can* be awful cruel to one another" (311).

The feud between the Grangerfords and the Shepherdsons suggests that conformity overwhelms all common sense. No one can remember how the feud started or why it persists, but the Grangerfords and the Sheperdsons kill each other with rare abandon all the same. Huck strikes up a strong friendship with Buck Grangerford, but cannot stop him from joining the battle. When Huck comes upon Buck's dead body, he covers his face and "got away as quick as I could. I cried a little when I was covering up Buck's face, for he was mighty good to me" (175). So most ordinary people in *Huckleberry Finn* have a natural kindness, which conformity obstructs. In Twain's universe becoming a good person does not require two years of reflecting in the woods or embracing the world's eternal corruption; it simply calls for turning away from mob influence and trusting the empathy that all human beings possess and that binds them all together. So although *Huckleberry Finn*, like the literature from New England that preceded it, shares the suspicion of conformity articulated in that work, it rests on and reflects a much more sanguine idea of ordinary people's capacity for understanding and moving beyond the limits of social codes and a humbler view of what transcending conventional norms involves. These writers have no interest in inspiring brilliance; kindness matters much more to them.

A number of midwestern novels end with optimism that the protagonist or someone he or she cares about will achieve the kind of full life that comes only when one learns to trust one's own perceptions and emotions, not those approved by society. But these novels conclude only with a vague gesture towards a solution, much like the ending of *Huckleberry Finn*, wherein Huck vows, "I reckon I got to light out for the Territory ahead of the rest, because Aunt Sally she's going to adopt me and sivilize me and I can't stand it" (366). Sinclair Lewis produces this kind of optimistic but fuzzy conclusion in *Babbitt*, his clinical examination of a man who has turned his life over to social norms so successfully that he has almost no idea what he wants. When faced with his own confusion, George Babbitt often comforts himself, temporarily, by doing or buying something that he imagines will win him external approval. George goes after the same accoutrements of status that aggressively bad characters seek, but since, unlike those people, he has not turned his life over to the pursuit of power and wealth, he has just enough integrity to make him ineffectual, but not enough for it to shape his life.

His constant concern with society ties George's reflections in knots. After a long contemplation of his wealth which produces a clear understanding that he has very little of it, George finds himself buying a new cigar lighter. He has just quit smoking. Rather than questioning this acquisition, George rationalizes that he did not buy it to bury his suspicion that he has failed, but because he feels so successful: "Then he remembered that he had given up smoking. 'Darn it!' he mourned. 'Oh well, I suppose I'll hit a cigar once in a while. And—Be a great convenience for other folks. Might make just the difference in getting chummy with some fellow that would put over a sale. And—Certainly looks nice there. Certainly is a mighty clever little jigger. Gives the last touch of refinement and class. I—by golly, I guess I can afford it if I want to! Not going to be the only member of this family that never had a single doggone luxury!'"[22]

Babbitt's staggered speech reflects his personality. He has no firm sense of what he wants, so his life consists of his lurching from one temporary palliative to another. He controls nothing because he invests in nothing: All his standards come from outside himself, so he consistently fulfills them in a half-hearted way. Although he admires and purchases all the latest models, he cannot be bothered with understanding how they work. He buys a khaki blanket for a camping trip that he never gets around to taking, so he sleeps under it on his porch—a testimony to his virility he likes to mention to his luncheon pals. He frets over his children, but worries whether others will consider them a credit to him, especially since he has projected onto them his own lack of commitment: "Simply can't understand how I ever came to have a pair of shilly-shallying children like Rone and Ted. I may not be any Rockefeller or James J. Shakespeare, but I certainly do know my own mind, and I do keep right on plugging along in the office" (14). Babbitt does keep plugging along, trying to quit smoking by using the same external mechanisms that shape his life and failing, trying to turn his real estate business into a treasure trove despite his superficial awareness of architecture and failing, and finally, trying to convince himself that he's happy and failing: "He was conscious of life, and a little sad. With no Vergil Gunches before whom to set his face in resolute optimism, he beheld, and half admitted that he beheld, his way of life as incredibly mechanical. Mechanical business—a brisk selling of badly built houses. Mechanical religion—a dry, hard church shut off from the real life of the streets, inhumanly respectable as a top-hat. Mechanical golf and dinner-parties and bridge and conversation. Save with Paul Riesling, mechanical friendship—back-slapping and jocular, never daring to essay the test of quietness" (190).

Babbitt eventually realizes that his uneasiness stems from his inability to discover and trust his own opinions and needs; he never realizes what to do about it. The book closes with George congratulating his son on eloping because he sees it as a hopeful sign that Ted, unlike his father, will not sacrifice his life to upholding social codes:

> I've never done a single thing I've wanted to in my whole life! I don't know's I've accomplished anything except just to get along. I figure out I've made about a quarter of an inch out of a possible hundred rods. Well, maybe you'll carry things on further. I don't know. But I do get a kind of sneaking pleasure out of the fact that you knew what you wanted to do and did it. Well, those folks in there will try to bully you, and tame you down. Tell 'em to go to the devil! I'll back you. Take your factory job, if you want to. Don't be scared of the family. No, nor all of Zenith. Nor of yourself, the way I've been. Go ahead, old man! the world is yours! [319].

Then the novel ends.

Similarly, in Lewis's *Arrowsmith*, Martin Arrowsmith has tried over and over to find some institution that will allow him to do pure scientific research. At the novel's conclusion, he enjoys freedom and peace in the woods with another dedicated scientist, Terry Wickett. The imagery suggests that they have taken a large chance: "That evening, Martin Arrowsmith and Terry Wickett lolled in a clumsy boat, an extraordinarily uncomfortable boat, far out on the water." Martin ends the book with the same kind of uncertainty Babbitt had about achieving an independent life, but his comfort with failure suggests that no matter how it turns out he will enjoy the process: "'I feel as if I were really beginning to work now,' said Martin. 'This new quinine stuff may prove pretty good. We'll plug along on it for two or three years, and maybe we'll get something permanent—and probably we'll fail.'"[23] Because Martin knows what he loves to do and has found a way to put it in the center of his life, his situation offers more hope than Babbitt's. But Martin has known what he loves doing for some time and this knowledge has not prevented him from repeatedly caving into society.

Main Street, Lewis's novel about the stultifying conformity of small-town life in Gopher Prairie, has an independent heroine, Carol Kennicott. She flees to Washington, D. C., and enjoys the freedom of her life there, but misses her husband and her friends. So she returns and accepts the rituals of Gopher Prairie instead of resisting them, vowing to inoculate her daughter against the town's pettiness. But she not only knows that she has given up, she knows why: "She looked across the silent fields to the west. She was conscious of an unbroken sweep of land to the Rockies, to Alaska; a dominion which will rise to unexampled greatness when other empires have grown senile. Before that time, she knew, a hundred generations of Carols will aspire and go down in tragedy devoid of palls and solemn chanting, the humdrum inevitable tragedy of struggle against inertia."[24] Despite her vows, Carol's capitulation to passivity almost certainly puts a good life out of her reach.

Tommy Wilhem, in Saul Bellow's *Seize the Day*, repeatedly knows that people deceive him, but he goes along with them anyway because he cannot trust his own perceptions enough to act in terms of them. When a talent scout named Maurice Venice offers him a screen test that will make him "a lover to the whole world," Tommy knows Venice has no idea what he's talking about but still follows Venice's advice to Hollywood, where he fails so completely that Venice wants nothing to do with him: "This was typical of Wilhelm. After much thought and hesitation and debate he invariably took the course he had rejected innumerable times" (23). Wilhelm finds it impossible to rely on himself instead of on a talent scout or a psychiatrist he barely knows, so he rambles from one self-destructive choice to another, never acquiring a solid sense of what he desires.

Jane Smiley's *MOO*, a novel set at a large state university, presents a plethora of groups capitulating to expectations that they behave in certain ways. The members of each fraternity must live up to its stereotype. The junior faculty must act in ways their senior colleagues would approve in order to get tenure. Administrators must conduct themselves in ways that allow them to get along with and/or outwit each other. And money silently shapes everything. Dr. Gift, who urges his students, whom he calls customers, to cultivate indifference rather than empathy so they can see the truth, sees money as an untamable life force: "Individuals and individual companies were but flickering pauses in the eternal exchange of fiscal energy."[25]

The circles within circles of proscribed behavior constituting university life make all of its participants miserable. Tim Monahan, who teaches creative writing, realizes he's unhappy and says so to Marly Hellmich, a woman who has accepted a marriage proposal from Nils Harstaad only after establishing that he makes $121,000 a year, far more than she takes home from her cafeteria job. When Tim asks her, "'What do you do at a university party if you're tired of jostling for status and promoting your career? If you want to actually attain delight and selflessly celebrate the good fortune of others?" Marly responds by asking him if he'd like something to eat. After their conversation deteriorates even further, Tim heads home: "He was in the perfect mood for grading papers, because the one emotion his students could narrate without any coaching was sadness" (157–58).

Students are sad because the pressure to fit in so that one can enjoy security pervades all aspects of their lives, not just the university. For instance, when Tim discusses the *New York Times* in class, a student denounces it as the "'mouthpiece of Satan'" because those who read it "'are led to doubt the goodness of the Lord and are drawn away from their faith.'" Another student helpfully suggests that the class subscribe to both a Christian paper and the *New York Times* so they can compare the views presented by both papers (312). The students fear any activity that may undermine the certainties they have absorbed. No wonder Gary, a student in Tim's creative writing class, can produce only thinly disguised and largely meaningless reproductions of events from his life when asked to write a story. In the world he inhabits, using one's imagination to explore something one finds significant would interfere with adjustment to society's definition of normalcy.

Tim realizes that a yearning to fit in contaminates even his own writing. A colleague, Cecelia Sanchez, startles him by pointing this out: "'How cold your writings are, how cold you are, the way you talk about your career and the way you contain it all with some funny remarks. You're a nice person, but look at your life. There's nobody in it, you're not excited about anything'" (197). Tim resists facing this, but eventually he agrees. As he explains to his friend Margaret, "'You've read my work. Look at how relentlessly I've mined every romantic feeling and sexual desire for profit or career advancement. Look how carefully I've studied other authors for ideas about how to rework that material over and over for more profit and career advancement. Now everything I do reminds me of something I already wrote'" (240).

Cecilia can identify Tim's problem with such precision because she shares it. As a child of immigrants, she turned her whole life towards achievement; when she looks back, "all she could remember was an effort to establish her virtue, to transcend her circumstances, to be the daughter her doctor-father-turned-gardener and her accountant-mother-turned-bookkeeper relied on her to be. Elevating herself had been both her virtue and her reward" (263). After reflecting on this, she "felt a fourth presence enter the room. It was her own sadness" (266).

She "solves" this by having an affair with Chairman X, an unattractive man who has lived with a woman for decades as his wife, had children with her, and who "was so in the habit of mistrusting his desires that he never consulted them if he could possibly avoid it" (337). Cecilia fully understands that the relationship offers "her no social, emotional, or spiritual benefits" (308). But Chairman X's extreme anger draws her irresistibly towards him; she describes it as "the way he attached himself to things as easily and as wholeheartedly as a child" (308). Fortunately for Cecilia, Chairman X marries Beth, the woman who shares his home.

Jonathan Franzen's novel *The Corrections* shows how even though people who merely conform do not actively pursue evil, because the culture admires wealth, status, and power, they can easily find themselves implicated in the same kind of self-destructive behaviors as those devoted to dominating others. Gary, Denise, and Chip Lambert, the children of Enid and Alfred, all fulfill their parents' dreams of their rising in the world by moving east. As a result, it troubles Gary that so many other midwesterners have moved away because it diminishes his accomplishment: "Gary wished that all further migration to the coasts could be banned and all midwesterners encouraged to revert to eating pasty foods and wearing dowdy clothes and playing board games in order that a strategic national reserve of cluelessness might be maintained, a wilderness of taste which would enable people of privilege, like himself, to feel extremely civilized in perpetuity."[26] Gary lives in Philadelphia, where he eventually becomes the vice president of the CenTrust Bank and acquires the accoutrements of an impressive life, including an attractive wife and three children. But he struggles with depression, which he self-medicates with alcohol. He and his wife battle so constantly that their children desperately try to mediate.

Chip becomes a professor who rebels against his family's values by specializing in attacks on capitalism. When his sure track to tenure gives way, he tries to quiet his panic by having an affair with a student who shares her ecstasy supply. After losing his job, he moves to New York City, acquires leather clothes and an earring, and tries to write a film entitled "The Academy Purple" that he hopes will expose the problems with higher education. He fails at this. A Lithuanian politician then urges Chip to help him convince Americans to invest in his country. So after spending his academic career ranting about corporate greed, Chip moves to Vilnius and discovers the joy of cheating people: "He felt as if, finally, here in the realm of pure fabrication, he'd found his métier" (436).

Denise works as a chef in Philadelphia after dropping out of college, then marries and divorces an older chef. As her parents and Gary proudly note, she has done well enough as a restaurateur for the *New York Times* to feature her in an article. But by the time the central action of the book takes place, she has indulged in a series of random affairs with both men and women and repeatedly treated her most consistent partner, a woman named Robin, cruelly, again and again.

As a result of achieving the success their parents wanted for them, the Lambert children engage in the same self-destructive activities as other characters who confuse status and power with happiness: Drugs, alcohol, food, sex, and abusing others.

Their mother, Enid, convinces them all to return home for a last Christmas after their father, Alfred, has a health crisis. Gary tries to impose order on the chaos of his parents' lives as his father loses control of his mind and his bowels. In this desperate attempt to organize the unmanageable, Gary shows himself to be his father's son. Gary's competitiveness makes spending time in the Midwest painful for him. Even the way midwesterners conduct themselves in a museum irritates him: "They didn't jostle Gary or cut in front of him but waited until he'd drifted to the next exhibit. Then they gathered round and read and learned. God, he hated the Midwest!" (176). In this egalitarian world, he loses his cachet: "What Gary hated most about the Midwest was how unpampered and unprivileged he felt in it" (175). To escape realities he cannot conquer, Gary becomes absorbed in reconstructing the train set he had as a child. When forced to recognize the intractable nature of his family's problems, he goes home to Philadelphia.

Unlike Gary, Denise establishes bonds with her parents. During his ramblings, her father happens to tell Denise that he has known since her teenage years that she had a sexual relationship with one of his employees. The man tried to use the affair against her father, so her father quit his job to protect her. He never raised this issue with Denise, but instead boasted of her high grades and her successful restaurant. She knows for certain that her father has always loved her and responds to this awareness with the same compassion for him that he has shown her. She has never identified with her mother; now she condemns herself for lacking the imagination to grasp the difficulties of her mother's life: "She felt sorriest about her mother, because no matter how often and how bitterly Enid had complained to her, she'd never got it through her head that life in St. Jude had turned into such a nightmare; and how could you permit yourself to breathe, let alone laugh or sleep or eat well, if you were unable to imagine how hard another person's life was?" (521). As the novel ends, the narrator reports that Denise has started a restaurant in Brooklyn and looks happier to her mother, encouraging the reader to conclude that accepting and connecting with her parents has helped Denise find some peace and happiness at long last.

Chip has no intention of showing up for Christmas until violence breaks out in Vilnius; he then eagerly heads home. The man who could not bear to have lunch with his parents in New York a few months before now feels pain when he sees the ravages of his father's face. It amazes him that his father and sister willingly trust him, but he gratefully accepts the reliable identity they assign him. As Alfred's health deteriorates and all three children help out Enid, she becomes more accepting of the ways her children have failed to measure up to her standards. She finds it especially challenging to enjoy Chip's marriage to a Jewish woman who is seven months pregnant, but she does and knows that had she attended the wedding with Albert, she would not have. As Albert slips away from reality, Enid tries to straighten him out, telling him he should have been more loving to his family, but "the one thing he never forgot was how to refuse. All of her correction had been for naught" (566). After his death, she vows to change her own attitude towards life.

Franzen has produced a book about midwesterners who sought money and stature in the East and found the same kind of emptiness as the other status seekers in midwestern novels. But two of the Lambert children find a kind of peace in empathizing with the parents who encouraged them to aim high. When they learn to love their parents, they apparently begin to love themselves and to build lives based on genuine pleasure. When commenting on all the work Franzen has produced until this point, Ty Hawkins focuses on the change in Chip, the one child who returns to the Midwest: "The fact that Chip can take this step—... affirming love over liberation, and engagement over retreat—means he has come a long way" (82). Hawkins thinks that with this novel, Franzen has made progress, too, placing "him squarely on the brink of a metavision of community that could anchor the twenty-first-century social novel which effectively challenges the hegemony of self-interest."[27] Actually, with this validation of kindness, Franzen establishes himself as part of a long midwestern tradition.

All of these novels suggest that when conformity holds people in its grip, although they lack a genuine sense of themselves and, as a result, have no substantial connections to others, redemption remains possible. Whether or not they achieve it influences far more than their personal happiness. Sinclair Lewis in *It Can't Happen Here* and Jane Smiley in *Greenlanders* point out that conformity can destroy whole cultures.

In *Greenlanders*, Jane Smiley tells the story of a country pushed into oblivion by mindless loyalty to social codes. The Greenlanders fight ruthlessly with each other, often over land, creating separations between people who need each other's support to survive. The Thing, a legislative meeting that gives them a common bond, takes place less frequently as the years pass. People struggle alone with the inhospitable environment and, as a result, more and more of them starve to death. The Eskimos know how to work with the harsh habitat and prosper, but the Greenlanders would rather wither away than admit that these people whom they consider alien creatures have knowledge they could use. At the very end of the book Gunnar Stead regrets his choices:

> He cursed his own heart, for he, too, had turned his mind and his strength to such killing as this. Eight men had fallen by his hand, and through his enmity.... He fell upon his face in the grass, and he wept for these eight men, all of them his enemies, all of them who had done him injury, but all of them men. And then he saw what he was, an old man, ready to die, pressed against the Greenland earth, as small as an ash berry on the face of a mountain, and he did the only thing that men can do when they know themselves, which was to weep and weep and weep.[28]

As Neil Nakadate explains, the Greenlanders perish as a result of having "stubbornly embraced cultural reflexes and habits of mind—shared convictions, behavior and fate."[29]

In *It Can't Happen Here*, Lewis takes a look into the future, warning that conformity and greed may culminate in fascism. Doremus Jessup, a newspaper editor with integrity who serves as the novel's hero, notes with surprise and disappointment that when considering their options in the upcoming election, his countrymen prefer "the theoretically Democratic Buzz Windrip. And that preference, Doremus perceived, wasn't even a pathetic trust in Windrip's promises of Utopian bliss for everyone in general. It was a trust in increased cash for the voter himself, and for his family, very much in particular."[30] When Windrip establishes a fascist state, Doremus blames himself and everyone else who failed to fight Windrip as passionately as possible: "'The tyranny of this dictatorship isn't primarily the fault of Big Business, nor of the demagogues who do their dirty work. It's the fault of Doremus Jessup! Of all the conscientious, respectable, lazy-minded Doremus Jessups who have let the demagogues wriggle in, without fierce enough protest'" (169). He sees that going along with someone like Windrip follows easily from other common dishonesties like writing "advertisements for fraudulent mouth washes or tasteless cigarettes, or writing for supposedly reputable magazines mechanical stories about young love" (181). In order to reduce the number of people capable of protest in the future, Windrip and his followers reform universities, shutting down independent small colleges altogether and establishing a practical, modern curriculum for those institutions that remain. There, "students ... were not to waste their time on the so-called 'literature'; reprints from recent newspapers were used instead of antiquated fiction and sentimental poetry. As regards English, some study of literature was permitted, to supply quotations for political speeches, but the chief courses were in advertising, party journalism, and business correspondence, and no authors before 1800 might be mentioned, except Shakespeare and Milton" (188). In other words, higher education would focus on material transparently useful in climbing the socio-economic ladder. Meanwhile, Doremus uses his press to help reformers and "whoever they were, of whatever faith or station, Doremus found in all of them the religious passion he has missed in the churches" (230). Doremus happily works with them, even though he realizes that they probably fight a futile battle because too many have already given up.

Twain locates hope in Huck and Jim because they try to follow social norms, but cannot accept them and because they care deeply for each other. Their intuitive sense of rectitude guides them, interfering with their ability to resign their will to the mob. Other midwestern novelists like Nelson Algren, Jack Conroy, and Tillie Olsen also characterize outsiders, usually alienated by their poverty, as strikingly kind, particularly considering the harshness of their lives. They want the security pursuing what the American Dream supposedly offers to all, but find themselves thwarted at every turn. In a competitive society, someone must rest at the bottom of the heap and as Algren, Conroy, and Olsen show; those with more powerful positions have a deep determination to keep the lower classes on the bottom, scrambling to survive. Ironically, their social and economic frustrations seem to help these people achieve a personal richness which the wealthy people in their work lack. Conroy, Algren, and Olsen portray these workers as deeply loving, even while reduced to desperate measures by the brutality of their situations. Jack Conroy's *The Disinherited* and Tillie Olsen's *Yonnondio* focus on workers simply attempting to build lives for themselves and fulfill the American Dream, but perpetually frustrated by their employers' ruthless insistence at making sure their attempts at unionization fail. The perspective of eight-year-old Mazie Holbrook dominates *Yonnandio*, facilitating a particularly emotional and touching view of working-class existence. Mazie's parents want her to get an education so that she can escape the brutal life they all share, but circumstances keep the family constantly on the move, looking for a place to simply rest. Although their situation briefly improves, the long-term trajectory of their lives heads downward, no matter how hard they work. This makes Mazie's home life rough, especially since her father takes out his frustrations on his family. The people struggling through this life die easily. The novel opens with the sound of whistles waking Mazie into a world of dread: "The whistles always wake Mazie. They pierced into her sleep like some guttural-voiced metal beast, tearing at her; breathing a terror. During the day if the whistle blew, she knew it meant death—somebody's poppa or brother, perhaps her own—in that fearsome place below the ground, the mine."[31]

This life of constant striving also drives some people mad. One mine worker, Sheen McEvoy, tries to throw Mazie into the mind pit to stop the mine from taking men. Still, despite the endless suffering and sickness, these people never abandon hope that they will find their ways to peaceful, comfortable lives. They cling to joy and to life and both assert and cheer themselves with music. No matter how tough things get for the Holbrooks, Mazie's mother, Anna, reveals and nourishes her resilient spirit with song. Sometimes friends and family join in, freeing them all of their environment's desolation, if only momentarily: "They sang and sang, and a longing, a want undefined, for something lost, for something never known, troubled them all. The separate voices chorded into one great full one, their faces into beauty (75–76).

In *The Disinherited*, another miner loses his job and tries desperately and futilely to build a new life for his family. Like Mr. Holbrook, he works hard to get nowhere. Larry Donovan's father, like Mazie's, wants Larry to get the education he believes will liberate his son from a life of constant struggle and grief. Even while Larry has to work extremely hard for minimal pay, he finds the time and energy to study for a degree, but the same exploitive forces that run the rest of his life also dominate the educational system and his learning does nothing to rescue him from his desperation. Indeed, at school, workers hear insulting and ignorant platitudes about themselves. Bonny, the wife of a man who finances her education despite sharing Larry's difficult circumstances, announces to Larry Donovan that her professor "'said the trouble with the half-educated is that they cannot weigh things impartially.'" The same authority explains to her that "'most workers *are* perfectly content.'"[32] When she begins to quote her sociology professor on another occasion, after proclaiming, "'Heifer dust!'" her husband, Ben, snarls, "'Every time I hear of that danged college I feel like a man that has throwed good money in a deep well with no chancet of gittin' it back" (217). The empty promises of education become another way to exploit what hope the workers manage to keep alive.

Another institution, war, makes its appearance in this book and robs lives. But out of misplaced patriotism, the workers viciously attack those who oppose it. Some of them never return from battle and some who do bring with them damaged bodies and minds, the aftermath of wounds and post-traumatic stress disorder. When a little boy proclaims to the veteran Ed Warden that he looks forward to serving his country, Ed warns him that patriotism is a trap: "'Don't talk like that, you little fool,' hollered Ed. 'That's the way I was when I got into it'" (118).

Their brutalization has heightened these people's awareness of the power of destructive social forces so that they understand even prostitution results from an attempt to survive in the face of hostile circumstances, not innate evil or moral looseness. Larry hunts down and tries to save Helen Baker, a young woman who has fallen into that life, but he confesses to himself that "'I couldn't see any way back for us. I felt her fingers in my hair and with the touch the sense of irrevocable loss stabbed me more deeply" (200). He does not rescue her, but he does not blame her either.

Through all of this abuse, these people, like those in *Yonnondio*, keep their spirits and their hopes alive with music. One day, Larry Donovan awakens to hear children singing of the beauty of the green grass. Longing for sleep, he thinks of chasing them away, but his sympathy for their desperate hopefulness stops him: "They were forlorn tatterdemalions with stringy hair and spindly legs.... Solemnly, as though performing a religious duty, they joined hands and hopped about grotesquely in a circle. Their feet seemed several sizes too big for their legs" (169).

Finally, large numbers of these people begin to put away their dreams that if they work harder and submit more fervently to those who appear to have succeeded, they will enjoy decent lives. Unable to evade facing that they have been used all their lives, they unite to obstruct the auction of a farmer's property. And Larry Donovan and his friend Ed experience genuine exhilaration and hope for the first time in decades. As the book ends, Ed proclaims, "'Another hard Winter comin' on, Larry,' he said. 'But I won't mind it like the others. I'm beginnin' t' get some kick out of livin'. You and me both got a different spirit'" (284). Unity, or more specifically, union activity, seems the only genuine path out of lives of persistent exploitation. Whether or not Larry and Ed succeed, simply putting this essential work at the center of their lives allows them, at long last, to taste joy.

While Conroy and Olsen write about the Depression in *Never Come Morning*, Nelson Algren shows that conditions fail to improve for the lower classes after the Depression ends. His novel focuses on a young couple, Steffi Rostenkowski and Bruno "Lefty" Bicek, who grew up together fatherless in a Chicago Polish neighborhood. Lefty aspires to make it as a boxer, but while he waits for his big break, he makes money any way he can, including theft. His family consists primarily of other lost young men who roam the streets with him. His compatriots demand to know if he has had sex with Steffi and shortly after their inquiries, he succeeds at this test. He then takes her to the Riverview Amusement Park, a miraculous place for both of them although Lefty hides his pleasure at their outing as well as the genuine feelings he has developed for Steffi in accordance with his gang's determination to regard women as nothing but creatures for them to use. So when his friends corner him and Steffi and insist on having sex with her, Lefty resists until they ask if he loves her. He admits this would make him a weakling in their eyes: "What would Casey think of a president and treasurer who was lovesick? What kind of contender was it, who still scribbled with chalk on billboards, 'I love Steffi R.?'"[33] So men line up to have sex with Steffi while Lefty vomits. He recovers, hits, and kills one of the men standing in line, a Greek who is not part of his gang. Steffi later becomes a prostitute.

Algren hovers in Steffi's consciousness to show her rich awareness of her situation and her conflict between escaping through death and embracing life as fervently as she can. She sees that everyone in her world rests in lonely despair: "All men, all women, passed in darkness, like the shadows on the parlor wall, each on a separate journey. Each hurried, anxiously or eagerly, through narrowing streets to his own small and final place beside the city dump" (194). She even pities the kind of men who have destroyed her life with their greedy lust because "they went about as though their real selves were the mad selves, as though to be obsessed by drink and depravity was—between themselves—the normal way to be. She heard them speaking innocently of innocent things; yet heard always, behind their voices the tone of men locked in for life" (216–17). And she understands that access to more money could liberate them all: "Everything was so wrong.... What she needed most was money. That was what made everything so wrong" (244).

Despite Steffi's insight into the circumstances that trap her, she considers her life to be God's punishment for having sex with Lefty. So when she goes to church, seeking solace, she finds only shame. Then Lefty promises to make enough money with his fists for them to marry and Steffi knows "everything was going to be all right after all" (259). But after his successful fight, Lefty gets arrested for the murder of the Greek and the novel ends, leaving Steffi and the reader in despair. Algren's exploration of the lives of prostitutes, pimps, and hoodlums makes it clear that they have the same feelings and insights as everyone else, but considerably less control over their circumstances than those enjoying more prosperous lives. And the blame for that falls to the greed and complacency of those with more options. As Algren puts it, "The source of the criminal act ... is not in the criminal but in the righteous man: The man too complacent ever to feel that he—even *he*—belongs to those convicts and prostitutes himself" (xv). Algren's goal is obviously to make the rest of us face our ties to the Leftys and Steffis of the world. So, despite its improbability, Algren cannot resist presenting a policeman who understands the inappropriateness of his sense of superiority to those he arrests in *The Man with the Golden Arm*. Algren's fantasy detective comprehends that his unearned arrogance has cost him his life and his heart: "All errors must ultimately be punished. Yet for his own, that of saving himself at the cost of others less cunning than himself, the punishment must be simply this: More lost, more fallen, and more alone than any man at all." He has damaged the one capacity that could save him: "Only his heart might redeem him: Through tears or laughter. His heart that felt stopped by dust."[34]

Sherwood Anderson explains the vitality of the lower classes that Olsen, Algren, and Conroy portray. He argues that to compensate for the emptiness conformity produces, rich people buy things. This makes the wealthy boring and conservative: "The rich and the successful are inevitably tied to the possessions they have acquired. They are afraid of change." Anderson finds poor people more interesting; he sees their greater complexity as a product of their humility and believes that this finally gives them hope of changing their situations:

> Life will have beaten down upon such a man more. He will be less sure of himself.
> That would make him more open to new impressions, new impulses.
> New forces will have to begin moving, operating on men here.
> You successful men are so walled-in by your possession. You cannot receive any new impressions.[35]

This openness would also explain the greater capacity for love portrayed by one midwestern fiction writer after another.

Their singing suggests, even asserts, that no matter what society does to them, the lower classes remain healthy and whole just as in Louise Erdrich's *The Plague of Doves*, two Ojibwe men, lynched for something they did not do, sing a song that asserts their independence of their killers as they strangle to death.[36] In Saul Bellow's *Humboldt's Gift*, Charles Citrine explains that music allows one to transcend apparently impossible circumstances: "By means of music a man affirmed that the logically unanswerable was, in a different form, answerable."[37]

Theodore Dreiser's *Sister Carrie* encapsulates what these midwestern writers have to say about an American society dominated by greed. Those who, like Carrie, try to rise in the world through manual labor, find their hard work simply used to make others rich. But despite the comfort of their lives, wealthy people, like George Hurstwood, feel so desolate that a vibrant young woman like Carrie proves irresistible. So Hurstwood sacrifices his family, his reputation, and his professional accomplishments to elope with her. His past achievements can sustain him only briefly in a new environment: He falls rapidly. Carrie's success relies, always, on intuitions and impulses which serve her well, making her a famous actress, for her emotional integrity allows her to embody and express the hunger for substance, passion, and meaning everyone feels in a world driven by economic forces. That music strikes Carrie with particular power, certifies her emotional integrity. Robert Ames, whom Carrie recognizes as the wisest person she has met, explains her popularity: "'Most people are not capable of voicing their feelings. They depend upon others. That is what genius is for. One man expresses their desires for them in music; another one in poetry; another one in a play. Sometimes nature does it in a face—it makes the face representative of all desire. That's what happened in your case.'" And the desire her face embodies for the world is "a natural expression of its longing."[38]

Seventy-five years later, *Song of Solomon*, by Toni Morrison, does an even more complete job of rendering the interactions between the upper, middle, and lower classes.

Macon Dead is the aggressively successful man. After seeing whites kill his father to steal his land, Macon heads north and begins acquiring real estate with almost religious zeal. Determined to duplicate and even exceed his father's accomplishment, he acts ruthlessly, evicting tenants who can't pay, even if that means throwing a whole family onto the street. He demands that his wife and children behave in ways that will reflect well on his status. "The way he mangled their grace, wit, and self-esteem was the single excitement of their days. Without the tension and drama he ignited, they might not have known what to do with themselves."[39] To emphasize his preeminence, he takes his family for rides on Sunday in a huge car his neighbors call "Macon Dead's hearse" because his fellow citizens know that, despite all of his frantic activity, Macon Dead's life is empty. His wife, Ruth, cares too much about status herself to notice: She cherishes the watermark at the center of the dining room table left by the vase of flowers her family kept there because it helps her recall her elegant childhood as the daughter of a doctor whom she reveres.

Macon Dead's sister, Pilate, plays the role of the lower-class outsider in *Song of Solomon*: Her brother has nothing to do with her and considers her a disgrace, in part because she makes money bootlegging. To make matters worse, from Macon's point of view, she lives in a shack with her illegitimate daughter and her daughter's illegitimate child. These three women follow their impulses; if they feel like eating peaches, they do, for days, or until they feel like eating something else. And they sing. Macon's decision to take a route home that allows him to stand in the dark, listening to their music seems a silent confession that he knows his sister's life has a richness missing from his own.

While Macon makes his whole life an act of protest against what happened to their father and lets his rage choke all the pleasure out of it, Pilate lives as joyfully as she can. When young, she recognized and embraced her role as an outsider, realizing that it gave her the freedom to do whatever brought her the most satisfaction: "She tackled the problem of trying to decide how she wanted to live and what was valuable to her. When am I happy and when am I sad and what is the difference? What do I need to know to stay alive? What is true in the world.... Throughout this fresh, if common, pursuit of knowledge, one conviction crowned her efforts: Since death held no terrors for her ... she knew there was nothing to fear. That plus her alien's compassion for troubled people ripened her" (149). Pilate's empathy and integrity make her, despite all appearances, the novel's wisest character. Brenda Marshall agrees: "Pilate is outside society, often outside the laws of man, and seemingly outside the laws of nature, and yet she is the most reliable commentator on society, man, and nature."[40]

Macon's son Milkman spends the novel trying to decide whether he wants to be like his father or his aunt. First, he goes into the real estate business with his father and treats his girlfriend, Hagar, who is also his cousin, like an inferior while he dates more impressive girls. But this life soon bores him. He contemplates enlivening it by marrying and making even more money, but he immediately realizes that this will not solve his problem: "He ought to get married, Milkman thought. Maybe I should too. Who? There were lots of women around and he was very much the eligible bachelor to the Honore crowd. Maybe he'd pick one—the red head. Get a nice house. His father would help him find one. Go into a real partnership with his father and.... And what? There had to be something better to look forward to" (107).

He goes on a journey to find his aunt's gold for his father, but it becomes a quest to discover his family history which culminates in Milkman's understanding that he has behaved arrogantly, to everyone. This humility lays the groundwork for Milkman's first reciprocal relationship, with a prostitute named Sweet, and for his first experience of being fully, honestly himself, like his aunt. He enjoys it: "He was grinning. His eyes were shining. He was as eager and happy as he had ever been in his life" (304).

At the book's conclusion, as Pilate dies, she asks Milkman to sing. While doing so, he realizes that he loves her because "without leaving the ground she could fly" (336), meaning that living so intensely and truthfully frees Pilate from the traps that weigh down most people. Just before her death, Pilate declares, "'I wish I'd a knowed more people. I would of loved 'em all. If I'd a knowed more, I would a loved more'" (336). So Pilate becomes an embodiment of the passionate independence and kindness all of these midwestern authors hold as an unstated and unrealized ideal. Emotional honesty serves as an antidote to the destructive behavior encouraged by social norms. But most people embrace wealth, power, and status too virulently to enjoy it.

These authors, starting with Twain, suggest that people's desire for conformity runs so deep that they willingly sacrifice their emotional integrity to achieve it. This dishonesty harms everyone, but, ironically, is most damaging to those committed to cynically manipulating the system and other people, for succeeding in this process means violating and eventually undermining their capacity for probity and empathy. They try to reinvigorate their damaged lives with money and prestige, but their repeated and consistent reliance on temporary sources of elation like liquor, drugs, and meaningless sex underlines their desolation. Although these books repeatedly suggest that one can build the most fulfilling life by basing it on one's passions, as Pilate does, they give little specific sense of how one achieves that. Fortunately, other midwestern fiction authors suggest a broad array of solutions, the germs of which can also be found in *Huckleberry Finn*.

Two

The Redemptive Potential of Childhood

If a group of authors produces work that suggests all human beings enter the world with a natural integrity and kindness that a competitive social structure undermines, it would make sense for those writers to positively characterize children. And from *Huckleberry Finn* on, children not only play a large role in the work of midwestern fiction writers, like Huck, they could and sometimes do serve as models of authenticity and decency for the many adults who have lost their way. On the other hand, only one of the New England writers preceding Mark Twain even wrote about children: Nathaniel Hawthorne—and he did so infrequently. Moreover, while the children in midwestern fiction serve as antidotes to a corrupt social structure, Hawthorne's children reinforce community opinion. In *The Scarlet Letter*, Pearl so perfectly reflects communal codes that her inquiries about the scarlet letter make Hester suspect "providence had a design of justice and retribution, in endowing the child with this marked propensity."[1] Similarly, Joey in Hawthorne's tale "Ethan Brand" immediately recognizes Brand's evil; indeed, identifying Brand as problematic constitutes Joey's entire role in the tale and the corrupt citizenry in the story, who share Brand's coldness but refuse to acknowledge it, agrees with Joey's judgment.

By making Huckleberry Finn an exemplar of compassion in a society dominated by racism, greed, and cruelty, Twain suggests that people enter the world with an emotional purity that their social experiences immediately begin to challenge. The novel makes clear how quickly the pollution begins, by making another boy, Tom Sawyer, already so bound by conventional mores simply from reading romantic books that Huck finds it shocking when Tom enthusiastically helps him free Jim from slavery. The triumph of Huck's aspirations for Jim in the novel suggests that despite his cynicism about a range of matters at the time he wrote *Huckleberry Finn*, Twain embraces the view that people not only arrive on the planet with an intuitive ability to empathize with others, but also that the preservation of this naïveté could transform society. Huck's powerful sympathy inspires him to act: he does as much as one could expect from a small boy to protect Jim's freedom. When the King and the Duke try to cheat descendants of the recently deceased Peter Wilks by posing as relatives, Huck's disgust with their behavior compels him to thwart their plan. As George Monteiro argues, "For Mark Twain the child is the only bearer of those values espoused (if not practiced) by his society: honesty of perception and expression, and loyalty to one's friends."[2]

Sometimes the children in the fiction by midwesterners seem to have an almost preternatural ability to sense and attack adult misbehavior. As Gary and his wife, Caroline, shred their marriage with endless fighting in Jonathan Franzen's novel *The Corrections*, their child, Aaron, tries to stop them. At the end of Franzen's novel *The Twenty-Seventh City*, a book peopled entirely by corrupt adults, as arguably the book's most evil character, Balwan Singh, flies back to India to disappear, the infant sitting next to him on the plane delivers his only punishment. The child puts a mucous-covered fist in his eye, spits milk on him, dribbles juice on his glasses, vomits on his trousers, and spits egg down his Pierre Cardin dress shirt. In Louise Erdrich's *The Round House*, when a legal technicality prevents the punishment of the man who raped Joe Coutts's mother, Joe shoots the man himself with the help of his friend Cappy. A childlike woman from the reservation protects Joe by disposing of the murder weapon when she happens upon the spot where Joe hid it. So the notion of children as ethical enforcers in a corrupt world persists in contemporary midwestern fiction.

The quality that most distinguishes and undergirds the decency of these youngsters is compassion. In *Winesburg, Ohio*, Sherwood Anderson presents a clear exemplar of this quality. George Willard's empathy renders him almost heroic. The book presents the stories of sad people who struggle to hide the passions that place them outside the mainstream of their small town. They all trust one person: the young George Willard, who not only tolerates their tales but welcomes them. Ironically, many of these people have learned to hide their own enthusiasms, but since they believe George has the potential to resist convention's repression, they try to help him find the courage to function with integrity, for they well know the despair that results from spending one's life playing a socially acceptable role. For instance, the major character in "Hands," Wing Biddlebaum, was a devoted teacher who sometimes touched the shoulders and hair of his students, a physical manifestation of "the school-master's effort to carry a dream into young minds."[3] A disturbed young man imagined "unspeakable things and in the morning went forth to tell his dreams as facts" (120), setting off a series of hysterical imaginings which drive Wing from Pennsylvania to a lonely life in Ohio. Despite this history, Wing cannot resist urging George Willard to trust his own aspirations, no matter how eccentric: "'You must try to forget all you have learned,' said the old man. 'You must begin to dream. From this time on you must shut your ears to the roaring of the voices'"(11). George's English teacher, Kate Swift, appears stern, but she, too, opens up to George, because she considers him talented. She urges him to "'stop fooling with words'" (89) and instead cultivate rather than deny his instinctive connection with others: "'know what people are thinking about, not what they say'" (90).

One after another, the characters of Winesburg share their secrets with the tolerant and curious George Willard. His mother, however, has so thoroughly squelched her yearnings that she can only mumble platitudes to her son. When he tells her he wants to escape the town and the life that have suffocated her, Elizabeth Willard cannot express how ecstatic his choice makes her: "'She wanted to cry out with joy because of the words that had come from the lips of her son, but the expression of joy had become impossible to her. 'I think you had better go out among the boys. You are too much indoors,' she said" (22). As George leaves town, his father, a man who "had always thought of himself as a successful man, although nothing he had ever done had turned out successfully"(19), urges his son to understand and embrace competition: "'Be a sharp one,' Tom Willard had said. 'Keep your eyes on your money. Be awake. That's the ticket. Don't let any one think you're a greenhorn.'" But, instead, as he waits for the train to pull out, George's "mind was carried away by his growing passion for dreams" (138), a development that would please his mother. It makes sense that idealism undergirds George's deep and generous connections with others: if he lacked hope, how could he find the courage to open himself to so many external influences?

In his story "Gryphon," Charles Baxter describes a child who, like George, cultivates fantasy and trust with the encouragement of a substitute teacher, Miss Ferenzi. This unconventional woman ignores suggestions that she follow the normal classroom rituals: she skips the pledge of allegiance and eats her strange lunch with the children rather than in the teacher's lounge. And she offers unusual lessons, refusing to correct a student who claims that 11 × 6 is 68 and telling a student struggling to spell a word correctly that he can forget it and only use words he likes. She talks somewhat randomly about a variety of subjects: angels, Tarot cards, and a gryphon she claims to have seen in Egypt. When a student comes up with a Tarot card representing death, she urges him not to worry because "'it is not really death. Just change. Out of your earthly shape.'" The student reports her to the principal and she disappears at noon, leaving the students to spend the afternoon learning facts from a more traditional teacher. But the child who narrates the story regrets her departure, adamantly maintaining, "'She was always right! She told the truth!'"[4] He finds her imaginative musings more interesting and alive than data. Like George Willard, dreams interest him more than reality and probably help keep alive his passion and his vulnerability.

In the tale "Indian Camp," from the book *In Our Time*, Ernest Hemingway's Nick Adams uses fantasy to restore his hope and trust after his empathy prevents him from dismissing a woman's cries as his father performs a caesarian on her. After his father explains why the woman screams, Nick politely replies, "'I see,'" but he cannot sustain this cool perspective. He begs his father to relieve the woman's pain: "'Oh, Daddy, can't you give her something to make her stop screaming?'" His father explains that he has no anesthetic, adding, "'But her screams are not important.'"[5] The woman's husband finds the experience so troubling that he kills himself. But Nick quickly cheers himself up after encountering all of this sadness by deciding he will never die. Later, when he feels sad about breaking up with his girlfriend Margy, he consoles himself with the false but comforting knowledge that "nothing was finished. Nothing was ever lost" (48). The phrasing used to describe the moment when Nick decides he will never die suggests that same sense of connection that made the events he witnessed so painful for him, restores him: his bonds with nature and with his father convince him that death cannot touch him:

> They were seated in the boat, Nick in the stern, his father rowing. The sun was coming up over the hills. A bass jumped, making a circle in the water. Nick trailed his hand in the water. It felt warm in the sharp chill of the morning.
>
> In the early morning on the lake sitting in the stern of the boat with his father rowing, he felt quite sure that he would never die [19].

Similarly, Manolin, the boy who takes care of Santiago in *The Old Man and the Sea*, would dismiss Santiago's fishing failures and go out with him if his parents didn't insist that he join a more profitable boat. The boy apologizes to Santiago for this, explaining that his father "'hasn't much faith.'"[6] As the old man battles with the huge fish he has caught, he hopes no one will worry about his absence and then realizes that the boy "would have confidence. Many of the older fishermen will worry" (115). That the other fishermen laugh at Santiago does not discourage the boy, who helps Santiago pack up his gear every evening when he returns from the sea. Then the two go through the ritual of discussing the old man's plans to eat rice and fish for dinner, food they both know he does not have. After the boy offers to take care of the old man's nonexistent cast net to spare the old man's pride, he brings Santiago food, reprimanding himself for his thoughtlessness in failing to provide the old man the water, soap, and towel he needs to wash. When the old man returns home after three days at sea with an eighteen-foot fish skeleton, Manolin vows to fish with him, gets him food and papers, and then watches over him as the old man sleeps, dreaming of the lions on the beach he loved as a boy. Just as the boy's youthfulness explains his idealism and kindness, the old man's courage may well rest on his ability to lose himself in his childhood every night. He also maintains a childlike bond with nature: "His hope and confidence had never gone. But now they were freshening as the breeze rises" (13).

Thus, children in these books have enormous sensitivity to nature and to other people. Although these ties can cause them pain, children find ways to reestablish their sense of the world's goodness, even if they must build this faith on fantasy. As a result, generous behavior comes naturally to them. Just as Huck goes to enormous effort, however misguided, to save Jim, in Louise Erdrich's *The Plague of Doves*, the young boy Holy Track comes out from his hiding place when he hears his uncle, Asiginak, say that he doesn't want to die alone after whites seize him for murders he did not commit. The whites decide to lynch Holy Track, his uncle, and two other Ojibwe, Cuthbert, and Mooshum—all of them innocent. Johann Vogeli, the young son of one of the whites, weeps during the journey to the execution; his father responds by hitting his son. The boy fights against his father so passionately that Cuthbert declares, "'The boy's heart was good anyway.'" Because of his light weight, Holy Track dies a slower death than his companions, but he seeks and finds comfort in nature: "Behind his shut eyes, he was seized by black fear, until he heard his mother say, Open your eyes, and he stared off into the dusty blue. Then it was better. The little wisps of clouds, way up high, had resolved into wings and they swept across the sky now, faster and faster."[7] Children's union with people and nature both grows from and validates their hopefulness, thus supporting the accuracy of Charles Citrine's description of children in *Humboldt's Gift*: "That feverish beautiful state of childhood when we are beating all over with pulses—nothing but a craving defenseless greedy heart."[8] As a result, Citrine identifies childhood as "that early and sweet dream-time of goodness" (396).

Their optimism gives children courage. Huck does not hesitate to set off down the Mississippi by himself, and at the end of the book, he looks forward to taking off again because he doesn't want society shaping him. This bravery allows children to be enthusiastically themselves. Louise Erdrich agrees that children possess a wholeheartedness adults lose; this makes even children's temperamental outbursts amazing to her: "How I admire their tantrums, what awe! How do we lose the ability to pitch such magnificent fits?"[9] Erdrich points out that children love with the same intensity: "Her love is wholly of the child, pure in its essence as children are in their direct passions. Children do not love wisely, but perhaps they love the best of all" (117). In a letter to Marianne Hartley, Sherwood Anderson wonders why when the smallest events of childhood have so much richness, he and others have so many difficulties living vitally as adults.

> Again I begin the endless game of reconstructing my own life, jerking it out of the shell that dies, striving to breathe into it beauty and meaning. A thought comes to me. When I was a boy I lived in a town in Ohio and often I wandered away to lie upon my back thinking, as I am doing now. I reconstruct and begin to color and illuminate incidents of my life there. Words said, shouts of children, the barking of dogs at night, occasional flashes of beauty in the eyes of women and old men are remembered. I wonder why my life, why all lives, are not more beautiful.[10]

One answer to Anderson's query is that children's responsiveness to the life around them means that they feel intense pain as well as joy. By making the most sensitive and vulnerable of creatures, a little girl named Mazie, the point of view through which she presents the frustrating lives of the lower classes in *Yonnondio*, Tillie Olsen introduces the reader to the most sympathetic perspective possible on the Holbrook family's plight. As the family seems to escape the depressing world of the mining camp for their own farm, Mazie feels a happy bond with nature and finds solace there for the persistent difficulties in her household. When her parents fight, she runs outside, towards the sun: "There was a great star glowing in the heart of the sunset, like a still candle in the vast unmoving flame. She could feel its glow on her face. As it sank, she began to run across the fields, to follow it."[11] One night when Mazie is out studying the stars, she comments to an elderly neighbor, Elias Caldwell, that she thinks they are "splinters of the moon" or "flowers of the night." As he dies, Caldwell tells her, "'Live. don't exist,'" and adds that she need only trust the vulnerability she brings to her present in order for that to happen: "'Whatever happens, remember, everything, the nourishment, the roots you need, are where you are now'" (53). He has seen in Mazie's receptiveness to her environment qualities that could save her, if she nourishes them. When the Holbrooks must abandon their farm, the mother, Anna, comments: "'You'd think children wouldn't care'" (65). But their openness gives all the events of their short lives huge impact.

The enormous influence of one's youth on one's adult life serves as the central theme of Charles Baxter's novel *First Light*, which traces the relationship between an astrophysicist named Dorsey and her older brother Hugh by reversing normal chronology: the novel begins with the present and ends with Dorsey's birth.

Near the beginning of the novel, Dorsey needs to leave the West Coast quickly, so she calls her brother in Michigan, asking him to come pick her up. He hesitates only briefly before doing what she asks. As the novel traces their history, it becomes clear that Hugh's job since Dorsey's birth has been to take care of her, not himself. When he's still a small child, his mother forces him to raise his hand and promise that he will take care of Dorsey, always. Hugh concludes: "It's so clear: there's nothing he can do except what she wants."[12] He keeps this pledge, no matter how inconvenient it becomes. When he talks Dorsey into a winter expedition to a closed amusement park which leaves her too exhausted to walk, he carries her home on his back: "Trying to keep himself upright, he removes by mental force all the tiredness from his legs and chest as he totters and tips his way up the hill" (254). Indifferent to his own discomfort, he feels so guilty about putting his sister through this ordeal that when he reaches his room, he "does not snap the light on or stop whispering the foulest words against himself that he knows until he hears his sister pad into the bathroom and turn on the hot water" (255). Having broken his vow and put his sister in danger, he can relax only when she knows she is once more warm and safe.

Before Hugh marries, he has a series of affairs with attractive, lively girls and plans to enjoy this life for a while, but then he meets Laurie. He cannot understand her allure: "He puzzles himself sometimes, coming back to this woman who seems to offer him nothing but a long haul over bad roads in high, unforgiving country" (207). But the reader understands: Laura looks like

Dorsey and helping her solve her many problems allows Hugh to continue fulfilling his promise to take care of his younger sister.

At the very end of this book, when Hugh witnesses all the attention his baby sister gets during her baptism, it confuses him: "It's as though his sister is a magnet pulling at these people, so that they bend down over her and then straighten up again, bowing towards her, this baby. They're kissing her into the world. Why do they love her? Hugh wants to know. They don't even know her" (280). He asks his grandmother if this ever happened to him and she assures him it did, but he remembers only that everyone deferred to his sister, giving him a sense that his sister matters more than he does. That he feels and understands this love himself binds him to his sister even more tightly. The final scene of the book shows his intense attraction to Dorsey when first introduced to her in the hospital: "Hugh feels himself moving toward her, and as he says her name, 'Dorsey,' he holds his right hand out, his index finger pointing down. His sister's skin is the quietest human thing he's ever seen: it hardly seems part of the world at all.... The index finger still pointing out and down, he reaches forward and, with unpracticed tenderness, touches his sister's hand for the first time" (286).

Baxter's novel shows that the same openness to the world that makes childhood so moving allows witnessing even a pedestrian ritual like baptism to have overwhelming power. Hugh's deep love for his sister from the instant he sees her locks him into a lifetime of trying to meet her needs.

And as Elias Caldwell tries to tell Mazie, this undefended child constitutes one's emotional core. As a result, character after character in Sherwood Anderson's novels having achieved successful but desolate adulthoods, struggle to recover their youthful passion. In *Windy McPherson's Son*, Sam McPherson grows up in a town full of people who laugh at his "war touched" father while his "stoop-shouldered, silent mother with the deep lines in her long face"[13] eternally washes clothes in a desperate attempt to keep the family afloat financially. Sam vows to leave this life behind by becoming rich. But John Telfer, a resident of Caxton who loves art, gives Sam a sense of the imagination's importance. As a result, the "boy, who had quit school to devote himself to money making, read Walt Whitman and ... looked at the stars and listened to the night noises, so filled with longing that the tears spring to his eyes" (29). But Sam puts these feelings aside in order to succeed in Chicago. Eventually, he comes to recognize the meaninglessness of his new life and hopes to recover the emotional richness of his childhood. The book ends as he vows to return to his wife and make their marriage work by recapturing his younger self: "The boy of Caxton was still alive within him. With a boyish lift of the head he went boldly to her" (328).

Hugh McVey, the central character in Anderson's novel *Poor White*, enjoys spending his time dreaming on the riverbank, in a state not unlike that which Anderson portrays positively in this letter to Marianne Hartley: "His life, lying on the river bank through long summer afternoons or sitting perfectly still for endless hours in a boat, had bred in him a dreamy detached outlook on life."[14] Hugh lives with his employers, Henry and Sarah Shepard, and Sarah, a flinty New Englander pushes him to achieve so relentlessly that he becomes driven and ambitious. Eventually he invents a successful corn-planting machine, but like Sam McPherson, his life feels meaningless. He meets a woman named Clara Butterworth who has a fantasy that suggests conforming will deaden her to life:

> An obsession, that the whole world was aboard the moving train and that, as it ran swiftly along, it was carrying the people of the world into some strange maze of misunderstanding, took possession of her. So strong was it that it affected her deeply buried unconscious self and made her terribly afraid.
> It seemed to her that the walls of the sleeping-car berth were like the walls of a prison that had shut her away from the beauty of life. The walls seemed to close in upon her. The walls, like life itself, were shutting in upon her youth and her youthful desire to reach a hand out of the beauty in herself to the buried beauty in others [177].

Not surprisingly, she most values Hugh's imagination, not his success. Indeed, his fantasy life produced his invention: "The dreams he tried so hard to put away from him and that the New England woman Sarah Shepard had told him would lead to his destruction had come to something" (225). When she meets him, Clara finds herself most moved by the hunger and integrity she sees in his eyes: "He was, she decided, very like a horse; an honest, powerful horse, a horse that was humanized by the mysterious hungering thing that expressed itself through his eyes" (248). They marry, and after initial difficulties, they connect with each other after Hugh recovers a dimension of himself he had buried: "The new thing he had found, the thing inside himself that responded to the thing inside the shell that was Clara his wife, did not stumble. It flew like a bird out of darkness into the light" (318–19). But he returns to work and their struggles continue. Near the book's end, Hugh finds himself playing with colored stones while on a business trip and condemns his childish behavior: "'What a silly fellow I have become, playing with colored stones like a child,' he thought, but at the same time put the stones carefully into his pockets" (356). Later, his thinking becomes playful: "The same light that had played over the stones in his hand began to play over his mind and for a moment he became not an inventor, but a poet" (358). He comes to understand that their hostility to play has deadened the towns of the manufacturing age: "He looked at the towns and wanted light and color to play over them as they played over the stones" (361). Hugh arrives home and rejoins the pregnant Clara; the novel concludes with their going into their home together and with the optimistic hope that Clara will help Hugh fully recover his capacity for dreaming. As Walter Rideout notes, "Most of Hugh's life in Bidwell shows the warping of his personality by his own willed repression of the desire to dream."[15] He can achieve peace and wholeness only if he can reignite the imagination that shaped his childhood.

In Jonathan Franzen's *Freedom*, Patsy and Walter Bergland must both recover their pasts to move forward with their relationship. Their apparently successful marriage depends upon Patsy ignoring her attraction to Walter's promiscuous best friend. When she capitulates to this temptation, their marriage falls apart and they head in different directions, but the paths both take lead them to a more genuine sense of themselves. Childhood plays a role in their evolution. Patsy has always gotten along well with children, so she works with them. And Walter embraces an isolated life at a cabin in the Minnesota woods, not unlike the family cottage he yearned to stay at alone in high school. Both emerge from this regression healthier and more complete and, as the novel closes, they reunite; only this time, their relationship has a firmer basis since both of them have lived out and accepted multiple dimensions of themselves instead of trying to construct a marriage while playing beautifully executed roles.

If a relatively benign and innocent childhood can have this impact, what about one like Huck's, pervaded by abuse? Despite his naïveté, Huck knows better than to expect anything good from his alcoholic father. Rather than protecting him, his father beats him and demands Huck's money. Huck fights back: "He catched me a couple of times and thrashed me, but I went to school just the same, and dodged him or out-run him most of the time." When his father runs off with Huck, holding him captive, Huck finds a way to enjoy his imprisonment, finding it "kind of lazy and jolly, laying off comfortable all day, smoking and fishing, and no books nor study." But when his father beats him, leaving him "all over welts," then takes off for days at a time, leaving Huck locked up and goes after Huck with a knife when drunk, Huck executes his escape.[16] Some critics, including Toni Morrison, explain Huck's evasion of the mistrust and cruelty that might be expected in a child with this history, to Jim's influence. Morrison writes: "The consolation, the healing properties Huck longs for, is made possible by Jim's active, highly vocal affection."[17] The other midwestern writers who address the issue of child abuse seem to generally share the optimistic view articulated through *Huckleberry Finn* that someone else often steps forward to help children in an abusive situation, providing enough nurturing for them to rest in a positive attitude towards life. And if no savior appears, the children often have the resources needed to heal themselves.

Because he understands the damage child abuse leaves in its wake, Detective Sunderson, the protagonist of Jim Harrison's novel *The Great Leader*, becomes so obsessed with catching a religious leader who abuses children that he continues to investigate him after his retirement and finances his own efforts. This persistence reflects the power of his own childhood, for at the age of seven, he decided to make the world a better place and has never abandoned this goal: "Of course he had to destroy the Great Leader to save the innocent, both children and adults. The worst criminals were those who took advantage of weakness through greed, lust, and religion."[18]

These abusers sometimes have failed to overcome negative experiences they had as children. Billy Peace in Erdrich's *The Plague of Doves*, like the Great Leader in Harrison's novel, uses religion as a cover for hurting others. He learned this behavior through his own mistreatment. His wife has a talent for imagining and describing situations. At his request, she draws a verbal picture of Milwaukee, where he spent his childhood, but he can't bear it, even though she avoids the objects most closely related to his childhood suffering: "I steered away from the burning welts, the scissors, the pinched nerves, the dead eye, the strap, the belt, the spike-heeled shoe, the razor, the boiling hot spilled tapioca, the shards of glass, the knives, the chinked armor, the sister, the basement, anything underground."[19]

Louise Erdrich's *The Beet Queen* makes clear the contrasting fates of children raised with or without loving caretakers. The mother of Mary and Karl Adare literally takes off with a pilot in an airplane, leaving them waiting for her to return. Mary winds up being raised by their aunt Fritzie in Argus; with time, she takes over Fritzie's butcher store. Despite her apparent success, she remains detached all her life. Similarly, her brother Karl becomes a salesman who constantly manipulates people. They contrast with Dot and her mother, Celestine, who love each other intensely. Dot writes of her mother: "In her eyes I see the force of her love.... I walk to her, drawn by her, unable to help myself." As the novel ends, Dot has the impassioned response to the world and others that these authors again and again identify as characteristic of a person with their childish side awake and functioning: "Low at first, ticking faintly against the leaves, then steadier, stronger on the roof, rattling in the gutters, the wind comes. It flows through the screens, slams doors, fills the curtains like sails, floods the dark house with the smell of dirt and water, the smell of rain. I breathe it in, and I think of her lying in the next room, her covers thrown back too, eyes wide open, waiting."[20]

Most of the abused children in these novels, like Huck, find ways to mitigate the damage done to them and retain their sense of connection to others and to nature. As *A Thousand Acres* opens, Ginny and her husband, Ty, seem to have a good life. She and her sister Rose and their husbands live on land her father earned and gave to them. Then Ginny recalls her father's sexual and physical abuse, which Rose confirms. Achieving this terrible knowledge brings Ginny a fresh sense of herself: "I felt intensely, newly, more myself than ever before."[21] Her comfortable life suddenly becomes unacceptable to her: "Our cautious lives had grown intolerable in retrospect and every possibility of returning to them equally intolerable" (322). A lawsuit their younger sister, Caroline, a lawyer, helps her father bring against her sisters underlines the division between them, making it impossible to go back to the way things were, even if she wanted that. Ginny leaves her husband, moves into the St. Paul YMCA, and gets a job as a waitress. When her sister Rose dies, she takes care of Rose's daughters, Pammy and Linda. When her husband asks that she return to the farm, she turns him down because she sees a link between her father's abuse of his daughters and the way he exploited the land; she's determined to leave that way of life behind: "'He had lessons, and those lessons were part of the package, along with the land and the lust to run things exactly the way he wanted to no matter what, poisoning the water and destroying the topsoil and buying bigger and bigger machinery, and then feeling certain all of it was "right"'" (343). The novel ends with muted hope: at least she now knows herself and thus has a basis for building a new life and helping her nieces do the same. The protagonist of Sue Miller's *Lost in the Forest* not only overcomes the damage of her childhood sexual abuse, she achieves a positive attitude towards life. She has become an actress who understands from the inside the optimism Miranda, the character she plays, expressed in Shakespeare's *The Tempest*: "She thinks of being Miranda, enchanted by her father into a capacity for love, astonished at what life has brought her—an innocent, open to everything."[22]

In Toni Morrison's *Sula*, two young girls named Sula and Nel ostensibly have kind, responsible families, but they receive little encouragement to honor their own insights and desires. They nurture each other because their mothers cannot. Sula overhears her mother admit that she has never loved her and watches her grandmother burn her own son to death. Nel's mother sacrifices her daughter to her own need for control: "Under Helene's hand the girl became obedient and polite. Any enthusiasms that little Nel showed were calmed by the mother until she drove her daughter's imagination underground."[23] Together, Sula and Nel give each other the courage to be themselves: "In the safe harbor of each other's company they could afford to abandon the ways of other people and concentrate on their own perceptions of things" (55). They stick together even after Sula throws a smaller child in the water, expecting him to surface. When he drowns, this shared secret further binds them to each other.

Nel's parents have worn her down enough for her to obey convention and marry: "Her parents had succeeded in rubbing down to a dull glow any sparkle or sputter she had. Only with Sula did that quality have free reign" (83). Also, Nel enjoys getting attention from her fiancé, Jude: "And greater than her friendship was this new feeling of being needed by someone who saw her singly" (84). Sula leaves town; when she returns ten years later, Nel laughs wholeheartedly for the first time in years, but she then discovers Sula and her husband in the midst of incriminating sexual activity, so she separates herself from both of them. Sula finds Nel's reaction bewildering because she has never cared enough about a man to feel possessive until Nel turned her back on her. She understands Nel's rage, but still feels so close to Nel that as she dies, she thinks, "'It didn't even hurt. Wait'll I tell Nel'" (149). After Sula dies, Nel realizes that when she caught Sula with Jade, she was jealous of Jade, not Sula, and begins to cry: "It was a fine cry—loud and long—but it had no bottom and it had no top, just circles and circles of sorrow" (174). Thus, two girls who failed to get support and love from their families give it to each other; it remains the strongest human bond they have for the rest of their lives. Karen F. Stein argues that Sula continues to nurture Nel's growth even after her death: "When she weeps for Sula, she is freed from the old constraints and misconceptions, stripped of her false moral pride and smugness. Through this mourning for her dead friend/self at Sula's graveside, Nel is symbolically reborn as the surviving self, continuing the process of growth and self-awareness that Sula began."[24] The intensity of this link between Nel and Sula shows the essential role validation by other children plays in one's life; not even marriage and death can disrupt the relationship built on it.

Toni Morrison's novel *Love* portrays another close relationship between two young girls. The book's narrator describes Heed's and Christine's attachment to each other: "It's like that when children fall for one another. On the spot, without introduction. Grown-ups don't pay it much attention because they can't imagine anything more majestic to a child than their own selves.... Whatever kind they are, their place is secondary to a child's first chosen love." Then Christine's grandfather fondles Heed and they separate, but their attachment endures: "Heed and Christine were the kind of children who can't take back love, or park it. When that's the case, separation cuts to the bone."[25]

Louise Erdrich's books present multiple children who find constructive ways to soften the destructive impact of their abuse. In *The Bingo Palace*, Albertine knows that because her rigid, isolated mother could give her no warmth, there "would be no end to what she needed from a husband, a lover." So she concludes that "the only answer to her need would be realized in healing others the exact way she herself needed to be helped."[26] She uses her history positively and becomes a doctor. June Morrisey's rape during childhood helps explain how she could abandon her own child, Lipsha, in a slough. This hurt gets passed onto her son, which explains why Lipsha feels envious when he sees Shawnee Ray being kind to her son Redford: "There is no way I can imagine June Morrisey doing that to me, and my thoughts veer away in longing. The subject makes my throat choke up in envy" (165). Lipsha summarizes the cycle of harm that establishes itself: "Pain comes to us from deep back, from where it grew in the human body. Pain sucks more pain into it, we don't know why it lives, and we harbor its weight. When the worse comes, we will not act the opposite. We will do what we were taught, we who learnt our lessons in the dead light. We pass them on. We hurt, and hurt others, in a circular motion" (217).

But in *Love Medicine*, the reader learns that Lipsha turns out just fine, thanks partly to his grandparents, but mostly to his innate generosity. Lipsha says he can never forgive what his mother did to him and considers his grandmother Kashpaw his mother, even though she "'just took me in like any old stray'" and constantly reminds him that she saved him.[27] In fact, later events suggest that his grandmother invented the story about his mother leaving him in a slough to enhance her stature with Lipsha: June simply left him with his grandmother. Although the recipient of little kindness from others, Lipsha has an ability to comfort people with his massages and he's especially gentle with his grandmother, massaging her cramped legs. When he learns of his grandfather's unfaithfulness to his grandmother, he tries to kill geese so that he'll have the hearts to use in an Ojibwe love medicine ritual. When he fails to kill the geese, he concludes that faith supplies the important part of the ritual, so he gets some frozen turkey hearts, blesses them himself with holy water, and gives them to his grandparents to eat, so that their relationship will be healed. Unfortunately, after eating a heart, his grandfather dies, but his grandmother thinks she sees his ghost and attributes this to the love medicine. Lipsha tells her the truth about the flawed ritual he performed and explains that Grandpa's love for her must be bringing him back. His grandmother gets "the look of mothers drinking sweetness from their children's eyes. It was tenderness" (257). Despite his rough start in life, Lipsha radiates thoughtfulness and eventually gets rewarded with his grandmother's love. Similarly, LuLu LaMartine sees a kindness in her children that astonishes her because she did so little to nourish it. Her eight sons ignore her missteps and remain loyal to her: "They kept me company through loneliness. And they would look aside and never notice what my wildness made me do" (278). And so, in *Love Medicine*, Louise Erdrich portrays children who shape themselves into decent human beings even when their caretakers have little to give them. This theme comes through so clearly in all of Erdrich's work that Jill Deans argues her writings reveal "a remarkable, if complicated, sensitivity to adoptees and individuals who have fallen between the cracks of conventional family structures."[28]

In *Tale of a Sky Blue Dress*, Thylias Moss shows that these optimistic fictional accounts of child abuse reflect reality more truly than versions that claim that the child can never recover from the damage. Moss courageously tells her own story, which shows how kindness and understanding can mitigate the damage of abuse. Moss had parents for whom she expresses nothing but love and admiration. Her betrayal came at the hands of a teenager supposedly taking care of her. Too young to fully understand the inappropriateness of the girl's behavior or object to it, let alone report it, Moss brushed off Lytta's pinching her, knocking cigarette ashes into her hair, finishing off her ice cream, and then wiping her hands in Thylias's hair and even pushing the heel of her pump into Thylias's palm, ostensibly to help her become like Christ. In retrospect, Moss offers a number of explanations for her silence, but at the center of them rests her apprehension of the world as good. As Moss puts it: "*At night, braids undone, I slept, my hair a circle of dark daisy on the pillow. When I woke, sunbeams surrounded my bed like a tent.*"[29] When Lytta orders her brother Trevor to sexually assault Thylias, who is nine, she cannot evade the reality that something terrible has happened to her. Still, the positive elements of her life sustain her: "A dark cloud moved into a position just above my shoulder, but there was enough sun to stave it off, burn away its vapor. This impresses me now. I was nine in my last encounter with Lytta; just nine, yet I managed to salvage my pride in my other life. I cracked but didn't break because at the root was something unbreakable" (80–81).

In high school, Thylias feels betrayed by her voluptuous body, which brings her unwanted attention from "*nasty boys*" (182). She loses her balance and becomes involved with Hector, four years her senior. The first time she has sex with him, she "cried silently through the whole act" and afterwards, "I smoothed my skirt again and again, while I learned to hate myself" (189). She later discovers that he also has sex with five other girlfriends regularly. His brother Hollis pretends to rescue her, but then simply abuses her himself. She becomes pregnant at sixteen. When she calls his home to tell Hollis, she discovers he is married. She has an abortion and six weeks later meets her husband, Wesley.

She expects him to treat her the way Hollis did, but Wesley treats her with respect and patiently helps her gain control of her body, which facilitates her control of all her life: "Intimacy became the sacrament it can be. Intimacy remade me; from this point I started over; my vision slowly improved. A return of reverence. I began to emerge; my faith was re-outfitted with both wings and crown" (211). Wesley continues to support her after their marriage; as Moss puts it: "I was a wife before I was my own person, but I was able to become that person in my marriage because of my marriage" (238). Although her memoir makes clear that the support and love of many people contributed to her life, her husband's love played a crucial role because of his sensitivity to the vulnerabilities her childhood abuse left in its wake and his determination to heal them.

These authors suggest children's openness makes compassion come naturally to them, but the events they encounter as they move through the world will encourage them to abandon this sympathetic stance to protect themselves. But hopefulness is essential to constructing a good life. Thus, living well means hanging onto one's optimism and one's particular perceptions and feelings no matter how difficult this becomes. A number of midwestern writers, including Toni Morrison and her son, Slade; Louise Erdrich, Thylias Moss; Jane Smiley; Langston Hughes; and Jim Harrison all encourage children to cultivate their own insights and emotions in spite of external pressures by writing children's books that articulate this message. These books present children (or, in the case of the Morrisons, a cloud), who triumph by remaining true to their inclinations even in the face of hostile events. Jane Smiley's book presents girls whose love of horses leads them to satisfactory developments. Louise Erdrich's Birchbark series follows the adventures of an Ojibwe child named Omakayas whose bravery and compassion allow her to help in a small pox epidemic and survive removal with her family. Roni Natov comments that "in her portrayal of Omakayas, Erdrich offers a vision of power that encourages children to listen with their senses, with their bodies, to experience a deep listening."[30] In Jim Harrison's *The Boy Who Ran to the Woods*, a young man blinded in one eye by a playmate overcomes his feelings of isolation and alienation through his connection with nature. In Thylias Moss's *I Want to Be*, a young girl reviews all the things she wants to experience, concluding, "I want to be life doing, doing everything."[31] In Toni and Slade Morrison's *Little Cloud and Lady Wind*, even the cloud finds success, declaring, "I am me and all the things I dreamed of."[32] As George P. Cunningham explains in the Afterword of Langston Hughes's *Sweet and Sour Animal Book*, "He is introducing young readers to a complex life, and most importantly, he offers the gift of humor as a means of transcendence. In the face of adversity, Hughes encourages us to just be ourselves."[33] So these authors not only characterize children positively, they write children's books urging their young readers to remain loyal to their distinctive feelings and thoughts no matter what problems they encounter in the world.

Thus, a fundamental incompatibility exists between the kind, passionate, courageous, and resilient stance of most children and the cynical, greedy adult universe shaped by the standards of the American Dream. Sherwood Anderson's story "I Want to Know Why" presents a young boy's initial awareness of adult corruption. The tale's narrator loves horses so much that he eats a cigar to stunt his growth so that he can ride them all his life. He sees race horses as beautiful and pure: "There isn't anything so lovely and clean and full of spunk and honest and everything as some race horses."[34] He especially loves a horse named Sunstreak, which he describes as "a girl you think about sometimes but never see" (10). His enthusiasm for Sunstreak makes him feel close to Jerry Tillford, the horse's jockey, because he thinks Jerry understands the horse the same way he does. After Sunstreak breaks the world's record for the mile, the boy wants to share his elation with Tillford, so he hunts him down at a farmhouse, where he sees Jerry with a prostitute. When the narrator sees how Jerry "looked at the woman in there, the one that was lean and hard-mouthed and looked a little like the gelding Middlestride, but not clean like him, and his eyes began to shine just as they did when he looked at me and at Sunstreak in the paddocks at the track in the afternoon," he recognizes that Jerry does not share his love for racing's purity. The boy regrets learning this lesson: "I stood there by the window—gee!—but I wished I hadn't gone away from the tracks, but had stayed with the boys and the niggers and the horses" (12). The boy wants to understand why seeing Jerry Tillford with this woman has ruined the track for him. The reader could explain: he sees a decadence in the jockey incompatible with his own unalloyed adoration for beautiful horses and begins to understand that aging inevitably brings corruption with it.

Hemingway's *In Our Time* includes "My Old Man," a similar story about a boy who shares his father's love for racing and for horses. His father, a jockey, was supposed to throw a race in Italy, but didn't. So the two move to France, but the boy never understands why. Eventually, the father buys a horse to race himself, even though his age makes it difficult for him to stay in shape. The boy loves the horse and the fact that that his father rides: "Now it was so I couldn't hardly sleep the night before a race and I knew my old man was excited, too, even if he didn't show it. Riding for yourself makes an awful difference." Like the boy in "I Want to Know Why," he intuitively values integrity. Then the father has a fatal accident and after the ambulance leaves, the boy hears a man say, "'He had it coming to him on the stuff he's pulled,'" presumably because his father could not throw the race as he promised. Another jockey, George Gardner, assures the boy, "'Your old man was one swell guy.'" But the young boy remains confused and discouraged as the story ends: "But I don't know. Seems like when they get started they don't leave a guy nothing."[35] Like the narrator of "I Want to Know Why," he has discovered that the joy he and his father found in racing and in horses cannot escape society's corruption. So Hemingway believes society itself offers a greater threat to the richness of childhood than particular abusers, perhaps because the wide and deep impact of social norms makes them inescapable.

Similarly, in *Saul and Patsy*, Charles Baxter presents Gordy Himmelman, a boy so badly hurt by life that he shoots himself on the lawn of Saul and Patsy's house while they watch from their bedroom window. Afterwards, Saul sees the picture he gave his students of his own adored child on prominent display in Gordy's room. Saul, who became a teacher to save young people, worries that the photo helped Gordy understand the desperation of his own situation. Saul stops teaching school. Instead, he writes muckraking columns for the local paper. The book never gives explicit reasons for this choice, but, presumably, Saul has come to think that trying to save individual children is hopeless; after all, what could he have done to rescue Gordy? But mending society may improve the lives of everyone it shapes. His columns attack a new chemical plant that will burden the area with toxins and perhaps contaminate the ground water. And, indeed, how can a community that elevates economics over its own health produce children who value themselves? More specifically, Gordy lived with his exhausted, impoverished aunt. Since no one seems to care about either her or Gordy, his aunt's hitting Gordy with a hammer when she thinks he misbehaves makes depressing sense: where would she have learned compassion and how would she find the patience and the energy to exercise it? Thus, Baxter links society's obsession with wealth and personal success to the destruction of children. Similarly, in Gerald Vizenor's *The Heirs of Columbus*, the tribal reconfiguration of American culture will heal all the children damaged by the toxins a society driven by greed has produced. Yvette Koepke and Christopher Nelson explain that "the novel implies that 'chemical civilization' views children in general as 'cancers.'"[36]

Society's responsibility for damaged children also seems a secondary theme in Jane Smiley's *Good Will*. Certainly the controlling father in that story helps explain his rebellious child, but the boy singles out a black girl for his abuse, calling her "a Nigger." This shocks the father, who never uses such language himself. Although his parents have little interest in collecting wealth, the boy has obviously learned somewhere to envy the rich and the girl's beautiful home, doll, and coat, all of which he ruins, make it clear that her family has more money than his. Although his father needed to give him more freedom, society, not his parents, has made the boy angry at those who own more than he and has encouraged him to express his anger by attacking someone of another race.

So although the children in this fiction have the emotional resources to overcome childhood abuse, the social structure operates much more relentlessly and destructively on them than individual perpetrators. The contrast sits at the center of Gerald Vizenor's *Father Meme*. Father Meme sexually abuses native altar boys, who take revenge on him through an elaborate series of acts. As the narrator notes, "The altar boys refused to be priestly victims. We were never native victims, although the priest pursued us as sexual prey. Yes, we were casualties of his perversions and bear that by memory, but we sacrificed that depraved priest."[37]

But Dane White, who is arrested for truancy and jailed by the authorities, sees no escape for himself, so he hangs himself with his belt: "Dane White was a native renounced by the church and the court…. He had no voice, no tease, no friends, no play, no humor, no clothes, no home, no parents, no protection, no love, no sense of presence, no ordinary nights and rights, and no one heard his stories. Dane was forever alone and could not endure the turn of a blind eye, that passive pity" (34).

The issue of society's impact on children struck James Farrell as so profoundly central that he wrote two novel series, each about one young man growing up in Chicago. Farrell reports on *Reflections at Fifty* that reading Sherwood Anderson's *Tar* gave him hope that his own childhood could provide the basis for a book: "My ambition to write was solidified and strengthened. I thought of writing a novel about my own boyhood, about the neighborhood in which I had grown up. Here was one of the seeds that led to *Studs Lonigan*."[38] The fates of these two men, Studs Lonigan and Danny O'Neill, contrast even though they spend their youths dealing with essentially the same general environment as members of lower- to middle-class families with large ambitions on Chicago's South Side. Although both families struggle with poverty and O'Neill's also deals with alcoholism, Studs's family never takes him seriously. His parents see him as a way to fulfill their ideals: his mother wants him to become a priest, and his father wants his son to work with him. Neither pays the slightest attention to what Studs wants. He understands at a young age that his parents and his school have empty values, but he sees no other options for himself except cynical and destructive gang activity. As Carla Cappetti notes, "The gang, it turns out, is but a prosaic bohemia whose only message of liberation is self-destruction."[39] He has powerful feelings of attachment to a girl named Lucy Scanlan and even to a nun affectionately nicknamed Battleaxe Bertha. But because Studs prides himself on his toughness and because he feels closest to the young men with whom he roams the streets, he learns to value, above all, the ability to defeat others in fights. So he struggles against all soft feelings and prides himself on his ability to shut them off: "Whenever Studs had queer thoughts he had a good trick of getting rid of them. He imagined that his head was a compartment with many shutters in it, like a locker room. He just watched the shutters close on the queer, fruity thoughts, and they were gone, and he'd have a hell of a time bringing them back; even if he wanted to."[40] The only problem is that Studs shuts downs the feelings that could allow him to build a life truly his own. Instead of this, he roams around with various gangs, ignores Lucy and focuses on Iris, who will have sex with anyone. Studs dies in his twenties.

Although his parents' determined refusal to take his needs or claims seriously certainly played a large role in his tragic life, they simply reiterated the values of their culture. When his father congratulates himself on the way he has raised his children, he reviews how well he has fulfilled conventional standards: "They had given the kids a good home, fed and clothed them, set the right example for them, sent them to Catholic schools to be educated, seen that they performed their religious duties, hustled them off to confession regularly, given them money for the collection, never allowed them to miss Mass, even in winter, let them play properly so they'd be healthy, given them money for good clean amusements like the movies because they were also educational, done everything a parent can do for a child" (21–22). Donald Pizer comments, "One of Farrell's principal themes in *Studs Lonigan* is that the social institutions which should play a role in encouraging Studs to grow beyond his childish street roles and to accept the prompting of his 'soft' inner nature fail to do so."[41] Because he understands the importance of behaving properly, instead of valuing his unique feelings, Studs represses them. Instead of building a life around doing what he truly loves, he moves from one false conquest to another. Instead of cultivating compassion, he nourishes the contempt behind the ethnic and racial slurs he hears all around him. As Daniel Shiffman points out, "Such assertions of entitlement may be self-deluding, but they make failure seem righteous; they take blame away from one's self and place it onto others."[42] These choices not only leave him empty and depressed, they eventually kill him.

Studs repeatedly identifies Danny O'Neill as odd, or as "goofy young Danny O'Neill" (7). The opening of Farrell's first book about Danny O'Neill, *A World I Never Made*, contrasts sharply with the opening of *Young Lonigan*, perhaps to some extent because Studs graduates from high school at the start of his book and Danny is just a small child when his begins. But the opening of *A World I Never Made* makes clear that Danny has a richer inner life than Studs. He wonders at great length about whether or not his not attending church would offend God because he'd prefer to play in the green space he sees across the street from his home: "The lot across the street now, that was a place to play in! He would like to be in it right now, climbing signboards, where his aunt and grandmother couldn't see him and tell him not to climb, playing he was Buffalo Bill that Uncle Al had told him about, shooting Indians and saving a beautiful white girl, as beautiful as his Aunt Louise who had gone to heaven only a little while ago, saving her from the savage Indians who wanted to tomahawk her. But, gee, he did have to be getting himself dressed and go to church."[43] Danny would probably want to play baseball there because he has an especially deep passion for the game, although he admires just about everything he notices. Studs, on the other hand, has fallen into all but complete skepticism. About the only activity that brings him pleasure is beating up people: "It was a better day than he imagined. A sun was bursting the sky open, like Studs Lonigan busted guys in the puss. It was a good day" (117).

Danny, unlike Studs, lives in a home where he enjoys not only attention, but an aunt and a grandmother who adore him and rush to his aid when his uncle treats him a bit harshly. His aunt finds even Danny's declaration that he can dress himself remarkable: "'Aren't you the big man, though?'" his aunt lovingly said" (8). The uncle soon regrets his unkindness to Danny, although his guess that Danny uses his supposed illness to manipulate his way out of attending Mass is more accurate than anything Danny's adoring aunt and grandmother believe. And his uncle's punishment consists of a mild reprimand, followed by his allowing Danny to attend a White Sox game with his brother, Bill. When his uncle Al thinks about the future he hopes to give Danny, he relishes the soft feelings that assault him, the same kinds of emotions Studs has learned to shove away: "Carried away on his hopes and on soft sentimental feelings, he stood by the window playing his mouth organ" (16).

In contrast, Studs's parents seem all but incapable of seeing him. Until his death and beyond, his mother thinks he would make a fine priest. When Studs proposes working after graduating from grade school, his mother worries what the neighbors will think of that choice: "It would look like they were too cheap, or else couldn't afford to send their boy to high school" (56). And as Mr. Lonigan contemplates the success of his children, he fails to even mention Studs: "Frances was going to be a beautiful girl who'd attract some rich and sensible young fellow.... Martin would be a lawyer or a professional man of some kind.... And Loretta, he just didn't know what she'd be, but there was plenty of time for that. Anyway, there was going to be no hitches in the future of his kids" (19).

In Jack Conroy's *The Disinherited* and Nelson Algren's *Never Come Morning*, their protagonists' strengths result from their preserving values they acquired in childhood and somehow, despite the fierce environments they must contend with, never lost. *The Disinherited*'s Larry Donovan carries forward the values he learned from the father who died during his childhood when he happily commits himself to union activity at the novel's end. His mother reminds him: "'Your father would want you to do something like that. Don't you worry about me.'"[44] And to the end of *Never Come Morning*, Lefty retains the deep attachment to Steffi that he has held since childhood. While Studs represses his soft feelings for Lucy Scanlan, Lefty hopes to build a life with Steffi. But when Steffi recalls their childhood together, the contrast between the dreariness of her present life as a prostitute and the joy she took in small events as a child causes her such pain that she retreats from reality into memory: "Each time she permitted herself some recollection of childhood her fevered mind tricked her into some monstrous confusion with the present, till she feared the past as fully as the present."[45] And, indeed, Lefty's attachment to Steffi leads to his winding up in jail, certifying Maxwell Geismar's judgment that Algren's novel conveys a "sense of stunted (and potentially vicious) children."[46]

The narrator of Tillie Olsen's "I Stand Here Ironing" concludes her musings about her daughter's life with the realization that her child has not and never will realize her potential: "She kept too much in herself, her life was such she had to keep too much in herself.... She has much to her and probably little will come of it." The mother blames this on the child's society: "She is a child of her age, of depression, of war, of fear."[47] The mother comforts herself with the reality that this fate waits for virtually everyone.

Catholicism strongly and negatively impacts both James Farrell's Studs and Nelson Algren's Steffi, making it difficult for them to trust their own reactions, or even forgive their mistakes. Neither suffers from an excess of self-trust and this institutional encouragement to judge themselves enhances the difficulties of their situation. Algren makes his view of the church clear in an interview with Robert A. Perlongo: "I'd say the church does gently what the police do roughly."[48] Danny O'Neill opens his book and Farrell's rendition of his life by resisting the demands of Catholicism, trying to figure a way to evade church, also noting that although his aunt skips church, nothing terrible seems to happen to her. This independent thought probably helps explain the relative vitality and happiness of Danny's life: he eventually becomes an author, writing books that articulate his perspective for others to consider.

Several authors characterize war as a particularly virulent social force on the lives of young men. The good qualities these writers associate with youth invite adolescents to idealize defending their country in battle. Frederick Henry, the main character in Hemingway's *A Farewell to Arms*, reports that after seeing what actually happens in war, he finds "abstract words such as glory, honor, courage or hallow ... obscene" (185) because they so often get invoked to encourage idealistic young people to fight.[49] Participating in battle also fulfills the desire of many young people to test and expand themselves by taking risks. Donald, in Jim Harrison's novel *Returning to Earth*, offers a summary of war's impact: "Men are always quick to go to war and if it doesn't kill them it kicks the shit out of them."[50] The work of Willa Cather, Nelson Algren, and Louise Erdrich suggests that they agree with Harrison and Hemingway.

Willa Cather's novel *One of Ours* shows war's seductive adventure and idealism at work on Claude Wheeler, a young man from Nebraska, who participates in the First World War. He finds the experience so thrilling that he can't believe his luck: "Two years ago he had seemed a fellow for whom life was over.... All his comrades had been tucked away in prairie towns, with their little jobs and their little plans. Yet here they were, attended by unknown ships called in from the four quarters of the earth. How had they come to be worth the watchfulness and devotion of so many men and machines, this extravagant consumption of fuel and energy?"[51] He sees serving in the military as a way of becoming a larger and fuller person, even though young men perish all around him: "He awoke every morning with that sense of freedom and going forward, as if the world were growing bigger each day and he were growing with it. Other fellows were sick and dying, and that was terrible,—but he and the boat went on, and always on" (265). When a Frenchwoman seeing the Marines arrive proclaims them "a new man!" (332), Claude embraces the notion that he and his comrades help bring about a fresh way of life: "Ruin and new birth; the shudder of ugly things in the past, the trembling image of beautiful ones on the horizon" (333). Claude proclaims that the war gives his life deeper meaning by giving him a chance to fight for principles, not money: "'I never knew there was anything worth living for, till this war came on. Before that, the world seemed like a business proposition" (356). Now, he understands that "ideals were not archaic things, beautiful and impotent; they were the real sources of power among men" (357). He anticipates that those who survive will enjoy beautiful memories which they will yearn to bring to life again. The beauty of France moves him so that he entertains fantasies of settling there after the war.

Claude gets killed almost as soon as he enters combat. His mother takes solace in his early death because it spared him the disillusionment that extended participation in the war would necessarily bring: "He died believing his own country better than it is, and France better than any country can ever be. And these were beautiful beliefs to die with. Perhaps it was as well to see that vision, and then to see no more" (390).

Ernest Hemingway's book *In Our Time* explains with great specificity how war undermines the spirits of the young people who become involved in them. The first half of Hemingway's book includes stories about Nick Adams growing through the normal experiences of childhood and adolescence: sorting through his feelings about his parents, his first girlfriend, and his first breakup. These tales of normalcy and innocence alternate with descriptions of war that reflect what it inevitably does to the idealistic young men sent off to fight it.

The disjunction between Nick's ordinariness and the horrors he encounters in battle stresses the trauma that young warriors must learn to handle and validates Jeffrey Walsh's claim that, for Hemingway, war involves "a youthful culture betrayed by a paternalistic hegemonic one."[52] The opening chapter, "On the Quai," makes it clear that far from serving idealistic principles, the war makes no sense whatsoever. Even normal patterns of cause and effect do not hold: "They screamed every night at midnight. I do not know why they screamed at that time. We were in the harbor and they were all on the pier and at midnight they started screaming. We used to turn the searchlight on them to quiet them. That always did the trick" (11). James Barloon points out that even Hemingway's pronouns reflect the devastating consequences of participating in a war: "With only a few exceptions..., the men are unnamed, referred to only by pronouns, having no more individuality than the words 'we,' 'they' and 'he' can convey. This strategy ... emphasizes implicitly that war effaces individuality."[53]

Getting thrown into this chaos terrifies the soldiers who try to calm themselves with drink: "The whole battery was drunk going along the road in the dark" (13). But rather than calming them, it heightens their paranoia. The adjutant keeps insisting that they must extinguish the kitchen fire so that no one will see it from the front—fifty kilometers, or about thirty miles—away. The soldiers endure their situation by throwing themselves into the work of killing people. They come to take pleasure in performing this role as well as they can:

> *We'd jammed an absolutely perfect barricade across the bridge. It was simply priceless. A big old wrought-iron grating from the front of a house. Too heavy to lift and you could shoot through it and they would have to climb over it. It was absolutely topping. They tried to get over it, and we potted them from forty yards. They rushed it, and officers came out along and worked on it. It was an absolutely perfect obstacle. Their officers were very fine. We were frightfully put out when we heard the flank had gone, and we had to fall back* [37].

Enjoying slaughtering other people requires a detachment completely incompatible with the compassion characteristic of Huck Finn and other children. Nick even becomes distant from himself. As he leans against a wall with a spinal injury, his friend Rinaldi *"lay face downward against the wall"* and dead bodies line the street. Rinaldi struggles to breathe and Nick's *"legs stuck out awkwardly,"* suggesting a serious injury. Nick responds to this terrifying situation by making a joke and then feeling disheartened that Rinaldi does not laugh: *"Rinaldi was a disappointing audience"* (63).

The vulnerable young people sent off to war by their society return radically changed: they've had to cultivate a toughness that makes it difficult for them to feel empathy for anyone, including themselves. That's why in "Soldier's Home," Harold Krebs has no ambition and does not love anyone: he abandoned these qualities to survive the war. And he can't discuss the moments when he enjoyed the war because it would appall people. So he lies, even when talking to other soldiers: "He fell into the easy pose of the old solider among other soldiers: that he had been sickeningly frightened all the time. In this way he lost everything" (70).

In other stories about soldiers dealing with the aftermath of war, like "A Way You'll Never Be" and "Now I Lay Me," Hemingway offers a literary rendition of post-traumatic stress disorder. Intrusive mages of what they endured and saw during the war haunt them, making sleep difficult. Seeing so much death and destruction makes closeness to others challenging, not only because they have cultivated detachment but also because they fear losing those they love. In "In Another Country," an Italian major declares marriage impossible because "he should not place himself in a position to lose that. He should find things he cannot lose."[54] Back in the States, Nick Adams thinks in much the same way. In "Summer People," Nick knows that a woman named Kate finds him attractive, but he's afraid to get involved with her: "*He, Nicholas Adams, could have what he wanted because of something in him. Maybe it did not last. Maybe he would lose it*" (218). He winds up having a sexual experience with her, then calling her a slut and leaving her outside while he goes back to his room where he feels "good in bed, comfortable, happy, fishing tomorrow" (228), presumably because they are all situations he can control more easily than Kate, or any other woman.[55] It seems clear that Nick's coldness towards Kate derives from a terror of getting emotionally involved with others, a legacy of watching comrades die that he brought home with him from the war.

The concluding story of *In Our Time*, "The Big Two-Hearted River" describes Nick's attempt to heal himself by returning to a place he camped and fished when young. He finds the trout still there "keeping themselves steady in the current with wavering fins.... It was a long time since Nick had looked into a stream and seen trout. They were very satisfactory" (133–34). When the trout move, he "felt all the old feeling" *(*134). So, his return to this place promises to restore at least some of the emotions buried while at war. A fire has burned the area since he last saw it, but "it could not all be burned. He knew that" (135). And sure enough, as he continues to hike, he finds "the country alive again" (136), suggesting that Nick, too, will recover his emotional vitality.

Alex Vernon argues that Nick's using isolation to heal himself underlines the essential tie between war and society. He cites Michael Reynolds's comment in *Hemingway's First War: The Making of* A Farewell to Arms, *The Novel*, that in *A Farewell to Arms* Frederick Henry progresses "'from group participation to total isolation.'" Vernon notes that Nick follows the same pattern: "Nick Adams' solo journey in 'The Big Two-Hearted River' portrays another veteran seeking escape from social allegiance. For an American male to escape war, he must escape social ties."[56]

Louise Erdrich's *The Master Butchers Singing Club*, which appeared seventy-eight years after Hemingway's *In Our Time*, offers many of the same criticisms of war. Young people who go to war find horror there rather than glory and so they deaden themselves in order to bear it. This is true of Fidelis in the First World War: "In order to endure all that the war necessitated, including his own filth, Fidelis had shut down his senses."[57] His son Erich stands the Second World War the same way: "He'd made his heart numb" (351). When his son Franz returns from World War II, he has lost the emotional center that gave his life direction: "Returning from the war, he felt tremendously strange, dislocated, even menacing, like a ghost that comes to spy on the living" (355). In Erdrich's *Love Medicine*, Henry Lamartine Junior's tour of duty in Vietnam leaves him shattered. His brother, Lyman, tries to resurrect the brother he knew by trashing the red convertible they bought and worked on it together in order to give Henry a constructive, absorbing project. This seems to work, but after a night of fighting and drinking with his brother, Henry drowns after leaping into the river

Nelson Algren's *The Man with the Golden Arm* describes the struggle of a fundamentally good man to free himself of the drug addiction he acquired when wounded in the service. When Molly, the woman he loves, tells him he needs to leave his mentally ill wife in order to recover from his drug addiction, Frankie tells her that the cause is not his wife, but that his war wound still bothers him sometimes. But even Molly accuses him of making romantic excuses. And the longer his addiction goes on, as he tells his friend Sparrow, the further Frankie gets away from his emotional center. As he flees the police, Frankie enjoys a false confidence, like the one he felt when he left the service and believed that the rest of his life would go well because of the discharge papers he received from the authorities. He thought that he would leave the war's pain behind and resume his life, but as Cather, Hemingway, Harrison, and Erdrich point out, the negative impact of participating in a war often ceases only with death. And that is the escape Frankie eventually chooses for himself.

These writers express enormous faith in children, indicating that, like Huck, they can find ways to preserve their idealism and kindness even in the face of cruel treatment from inadequate caretakers. But they have far more difficulty arguing that a young person can evade damage at the hands of a thoughtless society. Like Huck, they consider civilization dangerous.

Three

Valuing Women's Passion

It makes complete sense that a group of writers committed to the view that social norms encouraging achievement and domination produce nothing but misery for all concerned would portray women positively. Although women recently have acquired professional aspirations, they rightfully retain their association with the nurturing tolerance these authors see as an antidote to ambition. These writers characterize women not as creatures appropriately controlled by successful men, but as, ideally, models of the kind of compassionate behavior that could go a long way towards redeeming society. This, again, sets their work in sharp contrast to that of their New England predecessors. Only one of these East Coast authors, Nathaniel Hawthorne, included significant female characters in his work. And Hawthorne's women usually found themselves victimized by men, like Beatrice Rappaccini in "Rappaccini's Daughter" or Georgiana in "The Birthmark." Beatrice spends her life as an unknowing participant in her father's scientific experiment; this experience leaves her poisonous. Georgiana collaborates with her own abuse, congratulating Alymer, her scientist husband, on the nobility of his aspirations as she dies from his obsessive attempt to remove a birthmark from her face. Other women redeem their men, as does Rosina in Hawthorne's "Egotism: The Bosom Serpent," wherein her love teaches Roderick to overcome his self-absorption. None of these women has any value independent of the men who rule them. Hawthorne's most vivid female character, Hester Prynne, appears to have constructed a productive life: after all, her townspeople come to believe that the "A" on her breast stands for "able." It makes sense that other women in the novel struggling with "the continually recurring trials of wounded, wasted, wronged, misplaced, or erring and sinful passion,—or with the dreary burden of a heart unyielded because unvalued and unsought" ask her "why they were so wretched, and what the remedy!" She assures them that in "heaven's own time, a new truth would be revealed, in order to establish the whole relation between man and woman on a surer ground of mutual happiness." She thought that perhaps she could help bring this about, but concluded that "the angel and apostle of the coming revelation must be a woman indeed, but lofty, pure, and beautiful; and wise, moreover, not through dusky grief but the ethereal medium of joy; and showing how sacred love should make us happy by the truest test of a life successful to such an end!"[1] In other words, even though Hester has become respected, she believes that women can build decent lives only after some utterly pure female shows the others how to achieve "sacred love," presumably through marriage. Once again, Hawthorne locates a woman's value in the strength of her bond with a man.

When Toni Morrison comments that she found some of the women characters in *Huckleberry Finn* "interesting," she does not refer to anyone who has achieved "sacred love." Instead, she cites "the clever woman undeceived by Huck's disguise" and "the young girl whose sorrow at the sale of slaves is grief for a family split rather than conveniences lost."[2] In other words, she lauds women whose actions and decisions rest on their own perceptions, judgments, intuitions. and emotions. When Mary Jane, Susan. and Joanna Wilks burst into tears after learning that their slave families will be separated, they show that empathy matters more to them than social norms. Miss Watson makes the same choice: faced with death, she trusts her own shame at participating in the convention of slavery and frees Jim. Jim and Huck both signal solidarity with these women by wearing dresses as they seek freedom. When Huck attempts to pass himself off as a girl, the woman Morrison appropriately describes as "clever," intuits his real gender and then finds ways to validate her guess with a series of questions and tasks, like asking him to throw a brick at a rat. So emotional integrity, intelligence, and independence distinguish the women in *Huckleberry Finn*. These same qualities frequently distinguish the female characters in the Midwestern fiction that follows. From the start, and long before women supposedly began liberating themselves in the 1970s, Midwestern authors populate their fiction with powerful women who resist conforming to social norms. Consider Carrie Meeber in Theodore Dreiser's *Sister Carrie*, Carol Kennicott in Sinclair Lewis's *Main Street*, and Kit Brandon in Sherwood Anderson's novel of the same name.

The emotional richness of these female characters makes it difficult for them to embrace a clear-cut ideology. A number of prominent female protagonists in this literature grope their way towards positions, sometimes not even realizing that they have formulated a point of view. Carrie in *Sister Carrie* follows her impulses from man to man and situation to situation, never really developing a plan or a position. Her affections direct her movement. The narrator divides mankind into two types: "Thus in life there is ever the intellectual and the emotional nature—the mind that reasons, and the mind that feels. Of one come the men of action—generals and statesmen; of the other, the poets and dreamers—artists all." Carrie clearly belongs to the second group: "She was an illustration of the devious ways by which one who feels, rather than reasons, may be led in the pursuit of beauty." And her emotional responsiveness to the world means that Carrie will never reach any clear conclusions or destinations: "Know, then, that for you is neither surfeit nor content."[3]

Similarly, Steffi, in Nelson Algren's *Never Come Morning*, should hate Lefty since his standing by while his friends rape her leaves her no option besides a life of prostitution. But she neither hates him nor her customers, even though she despises the life their behavior has shaped for her so completely that she considers suicide. But she also loves so intensely that she must continue to live: she would "again convince herself that her life was over, that there was no further meaning to it. Yet she felt so only out of a greed for life. She fought greedily for every moment of it."[4]

Carol Kennicott in Sinclair Lewis's *Main Street* attempts to make a clear decision and execute a clean break with the town that she believes reduces her life to empty routine. So she moves to Washington, D.C., and succeeds at building a life she enjoys. But her attachment to her husband and to the other people of Gopher Prairie pull her back there even though she understands intellectually that she commits herself and her daughter to comfortable emptiness.

In *The All-True Adventures of Lidie Newton*, Jane Smiley suggests that the empathy Lydia's gender brings with it even prevents her from espousing a definite intellectual position on slavery. After growing up in a family mostly inimical to abolitionism, she marries Thomas Newton, an abolitionist from New England. They move to Kansas, where abolitionists and people who advocate slavery clash frequently and violently. Her husband dies in one skirmish and Lydia vows to avenge his death, certain she knows his killer's identity. She disguises herself as a boy and goes on the hunt, only to discover that she has no idea who killed her husband. She survives after being taken in by a family of slave owners whose kindness to her complicates her hatred of such people. Nonetheless, she attempts to help one of their slaves, Lorna, escape; but she fails. Eventually she winds up back home with her family and discovers that abolitionist views no longer engage her. When she travels east to stay with her husband's family, his mother urges her to make an abolitionist speech. She resists because she no longer can sustain the clear notions of good and evil she once held: "She was very kind and loving to me, and she made up her mind that I must do this lecture for Thomas and his beliefs and what he died for. I couldn't explain that I found myself increasingly unable to speak about any of these issues—that the very certainty of everyone around me drove all certainty out of me." Although she thought she would find relief among Thomas's relatives in the East, instead, she feels extreme discomfort there because, to them, she serves as a symbol of a particular political stance: "The more they embraced me and drew me in, the less I felt like one of them, like a woman, even like a human being. I felt like a new thing, hardly formed, wearing a corset and a dress and a shawl and a bonnet and a pair of ladies' boots, carrying a parasol in my gloved hand, but inside that costume something else, which didn't fit, something I felt myself to be but couldn't name." She becomes convinced that conceptual analysis cannot accurately render the situation in Kansas or Missouri because reality has an emotional dimension that could only be conveyed through some kind of bond: "To say what was true, you had to look into the eyes of your interlocutor and see something there that you recognized."[5] This sense of connection that Lidie associates with truth-telling, makes all absolute judgments false. So rather than distorting reality for Lidie, feminine compassion becomes essential to it.

In Willa Cather's *O Pioneers!*, Alexandra's sympathy serves her well. It compels her to protect Ivar when others want to institutionalize him. She realizes that he understands animals better than anyone else around because she, too, has an emotional tie to nature. She buys up land while others flee the country because "she had felt as if her heart were hiding down there, somewhere, with the quail and the plover and all the little wild things that crooned or buzzed in the sun. Under the long shaggy ridges, she felt the future stirring."[6] Her brothers question her decision to mortgage what they have in order to invest in more land because so many of their neighbors want to abandon their property and move to the city. Alexandra's reliance on her emotional attachment to the land leads her and her brothers to prosperity. Nonetheless, when the same passionate responsiveness causes Alexandra to affiliate herself with Carl, who has not enjoyed success, her brothers accuse her of humiliating herself and them. Their conviction that Alexandra behaves disgracefully runs so deep that the siblings no longer speak with each other. Once again, Alexandra trusts her emotions and, as the novel ends, she declares herself certain she will enjoy happiness with Carl: "I think we shall be very happy. I haven't any fears" (122). Judy Jones Tisdale points out that although Alexandra, along with her pioneer sisters in *My Antonia* and *Song of the Lark*, "can be viewed as a version of the American self-made individual, their achievements (both financial and personal) are grounded in a sense of community. Cather celebrates working women who do very well in their chosen trades or professions and who do not succumb to the selfish and isolating influences generally considered the price of advancement in the traditionally male world of work."[7]

Annie Eliza, the African American woman in her seventies who narrates Clarence Major's novel, *Such Was the Season*, accepts herself and her world so completely that she first appears ignorant: she loves television, thinks she looks wonderful in her red wig, laughs when her teeth fall out, and fails to appreciate the accomplishments of her nephew, Juneboy, a professor at Yale who visits her in Atlanta while in town to report on his sickle cell anemia research. When he starts musing aloud about his search for identity, she "cut him off cause I thought he was talking crazy talk. I said, 'Juneboy, how was your flight down?'"[8] By the end of the novel Annie Eliza admires Juneboy, not because of his worldly accomplishments, but because of his kindness. She particularly appreciates that he asks her to dance: "For the first time in many a years, I felt young and happy" (124). But she also values his generous behavior with other family members and with his white girlfriend. Annie Eliza easily recognizes and understands Juneboy's sensitivity to others because she possesses so much of it herself. And, by the novel's end, the reader also grows to understand and appreciate Annie Eliza's wisdom.

Renee Seitcheck, in Jonathan Franzen's novel *Strong Motion*, has plenty of intelligence. A Harvard scientist, she uncovers the environmental damage perpetrated by a chemical company called Sweeting-Aldren. Her concern with minimizing the damage's impact shocks her boyfriend, Louis: "'You actually believe in this stuff? Service to Mankind and all that?'" His reaction makes Renee so furious that "in the calm upper stories of Renee's face a powerful furnace kicked on suddenly, a bank of white jets of anger."[9] Although Renee wants to do everything she can to impede Sweeting-Aldren's harming others, the compassion that directs her behavior makes it impossible for her to achieve the detachment necessary to hate them, or anyone else. Louis, on the other hand, indulges in global rants about corruption: "'I hate this country. I hate the piggishness. Everywhere I look I see pigs.'" Renee, like Lidie, rejects grand generalizations and points out the problems with them to Louis: "'Think about the people who make the subways run. Think about nurses. Mailmen. Lobbyists for good causes. They're not all pigs.'" Louis counters that trying to heal this corrupt world makes little sense: "'Things are so fucked up it seems pathetic to try to be a useful citizen.'" Renee's response certifies her refusal to buy into this false absolutism: "'We are going to have to do something about you'" (187). So, like other women characters in these books, grand declarations do not impress Renee. She relies on her own insights and her own empathy when she makes decisions. While she knows that Sweeting-Aldren does enormous damage and that this undoubtedly puts them in the same category with other corporations she doesn't know about, she refuses to fall into cynicism. She sees both good and bad, everywhere, and tries to do what she can to cultivate the positive component.

In *Perhaps Women*, Sherwood Anderson offers an explanation for these brave women who rely on their emotions as well as on their reason for their decisions. He argues that the machine age has destroyed everyone, but especially men, pointing out that in adapting to the mechanisms that allow them to work more efficiently, men lose control: they no longer shape their environment and their lives the way craftsmen did. To compensate for their powerlessness, men collect possessions and activities that give them a sense of vicarious strength. Making global assertions would also help someone towards a false sense of mastery and superiority. To give a sense of his meaning, Anderson talks at length about the thrill of stepping on the gas and roaring past other people on the road.

Anderson believes the industrial age further encourages meaningless competition by undermining awareness of the connections between people: "The workman in the furniture factory has no sense of the lumberman cutting trees in the hills.... One of the striking things about the modern labor world is the loss of a sense of a common interest."[10] He argues that the stronghold of the machine and its vicarious power over men has injured them beyond redemption. But he believes women remain relatively free of this damage because they have a more passionate inner life than men: "The women in the factories, in the offices, and the shops are still alive. They are not enervated spiritually by the machines. They have not accepted the vicarious feeling of power, got from machines, as their own power. The power of women is more personal. It is a matter of human relations. It operates directly on others. It is a power the machine cannot touch" (142). As Precious McKenzie Stearns points out,

Anderson considers women so strong that they can save men: "Because of their awesome life-giving power, they are capable of reuniting disillusioned and fatigued modern men with life and nature."[11]

Louise Erdrich's *Four Souls* suggests that the machine can undermine women temporarily, but their nature tends to restore them to their sympathetic selves. Fleur leaves her native community for the city where she hopes to take revenge on the man who took her land. At first, she feels uncomfortable there because "the movement of mechanical, random things sickened her."[12] Eventually, she marries the man she intended to kill, has a son with him, and becomes an alcoholic. When she returns to the reservation, Margaret Kashpaw tells her she can only heal herself through fulfilling her role as a woman and acting out of love, not anger; only in this way can she win her children's love: "How can they love a mother who forgot to guard their tenderness, and her own? ... Forget your power and your strength. Let the dress kill you. Let the dress save you" (206). The book concludes with Fleur abandoning her attempts at revenge and resettling in the woods where she enjoys a spiritual life: "The woman once called Fleur Pillager and now named Four Souls as well as another name nobody speaks, is now understood by the spirits. Like the spirits, she lives quiet in the woods" (209).

Anderson particularly credits the fact that women give birth with connecting them to the earth: "The machine can never bring children into the world" (140). The work of a number of midwestern women fiction writers suggests their agreement with Anderson. Louise Erdrich writes an entire book, *The Blue Jay's Dance*, describing pregnancy and childbirth. She asks, "Why is no woman's labor as famous as the death of Socrates?" Then she answers her own question: "In our western and westernized culture, women's labor is devalued beginning with Genesis. Eve's natural intelligence, curiosity, desire, and perhaps sense of justice causes her to taste the fruit of good and evil, the apple of knowledge. Thereafter, goes the story, all women are condemned to bring forth children in pain. Thus are women culturally stripped of any moral claim to strength or virtue in labor."[13] Erdrich contends that childbirth has also positively impacted her writing: "Without my children, I'd have written with less fervor. I wouldn't understand life in the same way.... I'd probably have become obsessively self-absorbed or slack off."[14] Jane Smiley agrees that having children enriched both her life and her work: "Motherhood is not a simply Madonna picture, or a simple witch picture, but a hugely profound, complex, and, most importantly for a writer, interesting mix of evolving forces that challenge and change the self and the world. Imagining motherhood opens the door to imagining every power relationship, every profound connection."[15] Sue Miller's *The Good Mother* presents a vivid account of how the intense bond between mother and child puts entirely independent actions and decisions out of reach for the mother who consistently considers her child's well-being. Tillie Olsen's "I Stand Here Ironing" enters into a mother's contemplation of and worry about her daughter's emotional vitality. In the end, the mother vows to help her daughter understand the value of and cultivate her inner life: "Only help her to know—help make it so there is cause for her to know—that she is more than this dress on the ironing board, helpless before the iron."[16]

A number of recent women fiction writers certify that mothers or not, women focus on their emotional lives, just as Sherwood Anderson claimed. Some of the stories Rita Dove collects in *Fifth Sunday* have no larger meaning beyond exploring the reality and power of young love. For instance, the title story concerns Valerie's attachment to a boy named Andrew. When she anticipates that she might run into him, she "felt a glow inside her chest—like a net with brilliant fish struggling to escape—and she felt strong."[17] In some stories, love proves more powerful than common sense. In "The Zulus," no one can believe that the exemplary Caroline Mosley could love the fast Leander Swope, but she does and after her marriage to him seems completely blissful. In "Second-Hand Man," Virginia threatens her husband, James, with a gun when she discovers that he neglected to tell her about his earlier marriage, which produced a child. But "she couldn't shoot him when he stood there looking at her with those sweet brown eyes, telling her how much he loved her" (28), and so they settle into a happy marriage, having a child named Belle: "That's French for beautiful. And she was, too" (29).

Meridel Le Sueur's *The Girl* also explores the power of relationships with men, concluding with the birth of a child facilitated by a group of women. The novel's unnamed protagonist develops from a shy, country girl into a bank robber anxious to help her boyfriend acquire the funds necessary for them to establish a life together. The bank robbery seems an almost reasonable way to collect money since the Depression has left them with few other options. And this shy, country girl proves an accomplished getaway driver. But her boyfriend gets wounded and dies as she drives them away from the scene of the holdup. After abandoning his body, she returns to St. Paul and reconnects with her female friends, all of them with little money available to meet their many needs. They settle together in a warehouse. One of them, Clara, dies and the rest cultivate a hatred of those who deny them what they need to live: "Who killed Clara? Why didn't she have milk and iron pills? Who didn't care if she died? Who doesn't care that we are hungry?"[18] The protagonist gives birth and the women celebrate that the child is one of them and will acquire their strength: "Her name is Clara, the women said, a kind of woman's humming was all around me. I saw mama in them all, the bearing the suffering in us all, their seized bodies, bent bellies hanging, and the ferocity of their guarding. I felt fierce" (181)

Ann Pancake points out that that unlike the traditional *Bildungsroman*, in *The Girl* "a girls's heterosexual maturation and pregnancy"[19] shape the novel's movement. Melody Graulich argues that, in *The Girl*, Le Sueur "creates a community of women whose united voices assert that women's devalued strengths—nurturance, vulnerability, interdependence—can and will prevail."[20] Some critics find this problematic, including Paula Rabinowitz, who acknowledges that "by constructing a narrative of female desire in which a mythic maternal power is put into process through heterosexuality, Meridal Le Sueur revises the proletarian novel to speak a language of women's memories and experiences." But Rabinowitz notes that "her evocation of femininity, however, verges on essentialism, because it invokes women's biological capacity to bear children without interrogating the cultural platitudes surrounding motherhood."[21] But most critics make positive judgments of the novel's ending. Erin V. Obermueller writes, "Le Sueur uses the labor and delivery to signify an emerging political consciousness.... Le Sueur thus invites the reader to see the female body as a site for political resistance, a response to the system that tortures and controls."[22] Laura Coltelli says in the novel, "The ultimate meaning of maternity, above and beyond its biological manifestation, resides in the construction of a community based on solidarity, which sustains, nourishes, transforms."[23] Douglas Wixson generalizes about the broad implications of this author's work: "Le Sueur's writing calls upon us to engage with her in seeking new habits of thought more compassionate and just than those that dominate Western societies wedded to capitalist economic systems."[24]

Anderson explains that men who have lost themselves and who attempt to compensate through order and control, rule society. As a result, women attempting to realize their feelings encounter frustrating social limits. The men and women in Anderson's *Winesburg, Ohio* embody this conflict in exemplary fashion. In the series of stories entitled "Godliness," Jesse Bentley, an intensely religious man wants, above all, to prove his superiority: "As he looked about at his fellow men and saw how like clods they lived it seemed to him that he could not bear to become also such a clod."[25] So, he makes his farm into the most productive one in the vicinity by enthusiastically embracing industrialism: "He began to buy machines that would permit him to do the work of the farms while employing fewer men and he sometimes thought that if he were a younger man he would give up farming altogether and start a factory in Winesburg for the making of machinery" (40). But since merely satisfying his greed does not bring Jesse peace, he also wants a sign from God.

As his wife gives birth to their child, Jesse asks God to send him a son whom he would name David. Instead, his wife passes away shortly after the birth of their only child, a daughter named Louise. Louise has a boy named David, whom Jesse eventually raises as his own. But during the second of two episodes when Jesse takes David into the woods and demands a sign from God, David flees and vanishes.

David would never run to his mother for comfort after his grandfather scares him because her father's irritation with her gender has left Louise angry at men. When he is lost on an earlier occasion and she treats him lovingly after he is found, it shocks David so that he "thought she had suddenly become another woman": "Her habitually dissatisfied face had become ... the most peaceful and lovely thing he had ever seen" (38). Louise hoped to escape her father's coldness when she went to live with the Hardys while attending school in town, but since the Hardy girls resent her academic achievements, she finds little warmth in their home. Desperate for connection, she sends an inviting note to their brother John Hardy, which he interprets as a sexual invitation; willing to settle for attention of any kind, Louise cooperates and soon false pregnancy fears bring about their marriage. Despite the comfort of her married life, Louise hates it. The impulses that made her yearn for contact with others become invested in anger, which she exorcizes with vigorous carriage rides.

Indeed, this lethal combination of controlling men and passionate women leaves the streets of Winesburg teeming with frustrated females at night. Kate Swift goes on energetic walks. Alice Hindman takes off her clothes and runs out into the rain: "Not for years had she felt so full of youth and courage. She wanted to leap and run, to cry out, to find some other lonely human and embrace him. On the brick sidewalk before the house a man stumbled homeward. Alice started to run. A wild desperate mood took possession of her. 'What do I care who it is. He is alone, and I will go to him'" (63–64). She calls out for him to wait, but his deafness brings her adventure to an abrupt halt. As he calls, "'What say?'" Alice collapses on the grass and waits for him to leave. George's mother married Tom Willard thinking that would provide the love she sought; when she concludes she has, in fact, entered a trap, she takes a carriage ride in a storm, beating the horse because "I wanted to get out of town, out of my clothes, out of my marriage, out of my body, out of everything" (127).

Lucy Gayheart in Willa Cather's novel of the same name also has a passionate nature and when she leaves Haverford, Nebraska, the town where she grew up, to study music in Chicago, she meets a distinguished musician named Sebastian who understands and comes to share her enthusiasm for life. She loves Chicago because living there allows her enormous freedom; for the first time in her life she can conduct herself with the abandon usually reserved for men. When Harry Gordon, an arrogant and determinedly sensible young man from Haverford, travels to Chicago and proposes, she confesses her attachment to Sebastian, inviting Harry to assume, falsely, that she has engaged in an affair. She fears a relationship with Harry because, although she cares about him, when with him she loses the magical sense of life's possibilities that allows her to take advantage of so many options in Chicago. She most wants to live out her longings: "If only one could lose one's life and one's body and be nothing but one's desire."[26] Although Harry has always loved Lucy, he marries someone else soon after his return from Chicago.

Lucy and Sebastian begin a relationship in spite of his strained marriage and she has good reason to believe it will continue. But he dies suddenly in a boating accident and she returns to Haverford, brokenhearted. Once home, Lucy tries to explain the true nature of her relationship with Sebastian to Harry, but Harry makes certain that they have only superficial interactions. One evening, she finds herself freezing on a country road when he comes by in his carriage. She asks him for a ride, but he continues on to an appointment. She tries to hasten her trip home by skating across the ice, but falls through and drowns. Harry knows her so intimately, he has no trouble imagining how this happened: "He understood well enough why she hadn't noticed the change in the river; he knew what pain and anger did to her. It was that very fire and blindness, that way of flashing with her whole self into one impulse, without foresight or sight at all, that had made her seem wonderful to him. When she caught fire, she went like an arrow toward whatever end" (186). It is precisely the fact that he lacks Lucy's passion that makes her so tantalizing to him: "It was a gift of nature, he supposed, to go wildly happy over trifling things—over nothing! It wasn't given to him—he wouldn't have chosen it; but he liked catching it from Lucy for a moment, feeling it flash by his ear" (188). Her commitment to an emotionally vibrant life along with his insistence that she satisfy these needs in a way that meets the requirements of his commonsensical view of life, leaves her dead and Harry Gordon desolate.

Some of the married women in Cather's novels fare little better. In *My Mortal Enemy*, Cather describes the disappointing life of Myra Henshawe, who married for love and found herself disinherited as a result. She throws herself into her social role, but as the years pass, she finds it fails to satisfy her deepest needs. Near the end of her life she explains that she continues to continue playing the part she adopted when young to avoid hurting her husband: "'I was always a grasping, worldly woman; I was never satisfied. All the same, in age, when flowers are so few, it's a great unkindness to destroy any that are left in a man's heart.'" Still, as she dies with her husband at her side, Myra declares that she hates him: "'I could bear to suffer … so many have suffered. But why must it be like this? I have not deserved it. I have been true in friendship; I have faithfully nursed others in sickness…. Why must I die like this, alone with my mortal enemy?'" The novel's narrator looks at Myra's husband, Oswald, sitting there listening, and comments, "I had never heard a human voice utter such a terrible judgment upon all one hopes for."[27]

In *A Lost Lady*, Cather presents Mrs. Forrester, a woman who lives in a mansion with her husband, Captain Daniel Forrester. At first Niel Herbert, whose perspective shapes the story, finds her hopelessly charming, but eventually he comes to see both that she behaves dishonestly and that her husband understands her completely. When Daniel Forrester dies, at first, she lacks the ability to shape her own life, but eventually, she rejects people who considered themselves her friends: "All those years he had thought it was Mrs. Forrester who made that house so different from any other. But ever since the Captain's death it was a house where old friends, like his uncle, were betrayed and cast off, where common fellows behaved after their kind and knew a common woman when they saw her."[28] Like *My Mortal Enemy*, *A Lost Lady* presents a grim view of marriage. Myra and Mrs. Forrester seem to play along with their husbands' demands because they have little choice: they need their husbands' support. But the novels give no sign that the women get much else from these unions.

Jane Smiley's *Greenlanders* presents a passionate woman in the midst of a male-dominated, competitive, self-destructive culture. The red dress Margaret wears signals her commitment to living fully: "In the red dress, she seemed to burst forth like a phoenix, burning up everything around her."[29] As a result, she finds herself incapable of resisting her attraction to a lover: "At the same time that she knew this as sin and vanity she fell into the terror of never seeing such a look on his face again" (106). Her husband kills her lover with an axe, but this death seems acceptable to her fellow citizens since "he was a Norwegian after all, and given to wearing peculiar bright clothing" (158). People blame Margaret for refusing to give up her independent, impulsive ways, but she cannot live any other way: "By the time of her late marriage she was much accustomed to having her own way, and so when Skuli Gudmundsson presented himself, she had her own way in that, and after his death, she ordered things so that she continued to have her own way, in spite of her sin" (235). Not surprisingly, when Margaret is asked near the end of the novel, "'How do men journey back from passion?'" she replies, "'It seems to me that most do not'" (560). Surely, she does not even though her culture constantly pressures her to conform.

When Jane Smiley writes about a twentieth-century marriage, women have more options; but she still stresses that marriage can stifle the women who enter into it. *Private Life* describes Margaret Mayfield's life from the late nineteenth century until World War II. Faced with a future as an old maid, she happily accepts the proposal of the brilliant Captain Andrew Jackson Jefferson Early and submits to all his wishes and demands. Indeed, given his extreme intelligence, she seems lucky to have married him. But decades into their union, she finds letters that make it clear he had a breakdown before he married her which made both her mother and his consider her a good match because of her passivity: "She thought of her mother and Mrs. Early. The one so busy, the other so elegant. They had known what marriage was like. They had known what *Andrew* was like. That they had colluded in bringing this very moment about made her tremble with something unspeakable."[30] When it becomes clear that her husband has gone completely mad, she does what she can to keep him from humiliating himself and her, but he figures out a way to evade her and goes to Washington, D.C., to let those in power know what his supposed surveillance has uncovered. When his accusations cause the death of her friend, Margaret finally confronts him, saying, "They did act on the one report, and they threw Mrs. Kimura in jail and interrogated her and now she's dying of pneumonia she contracted there. The whole thing makes me both angry and sick" (315). As the book ends, she announces to a group of women friends, "There are so many things that I should have dared before this" (318).

Anna Robison, a contemporary wife and the central character in Smiley's *At Paradise Gate*, waits for her husband, Ike Robison, to die. Although Ike brutalized her and her daughters, she stays both because she loves him and because she feels an obligation to take care of him. Unlike Margaret Mayfield, Anna has asserted herself with Ike; when she says, "'I don't want to fight with you, Daddy,'" he replies: "'Since when?'"[31] And, in fact, unlike Margaret, Anna does not know whether or not to label herself a casualty: "Which was true: victimized or victimizing? Would Ike know? She dared not ask" (217). When he does die, she worries about how she'll get through the nights. She begins to consider possibilities: maybe her granddaughter Christine will teach her to drive. And then she starts planning a trip to the West. But soon, fear of handling her new role sets in again and she recalls leaving her mother to go get married. Now, she'll begin being a widow. So, *Paradise Gate* contains far more ambiguity about marriage than *Private Life*, but the same kinds of problems with obeying dominant men persist.

The women apparently fear that if they assert themselves, the man will abandon them, a dread that *Never Come Morning* seems to validate. Although Lefty loves Steffi, merely imagining that others will recognize and publicize his attachment to her makes Lefty step aside and allow his friends to rape her. He tries to maintain his equipoise during this event, telling himself that she needs the experience, but he feels overwhelmingly sick. He attempts to regain control by singling out a Greek man standing in line with the others waiting to rape Steffi and beats him up, eventually killing him. Hearing Steffi call out "Next!" from the room where she is being raped, suggesting that she understands she has no choice but to accept her fate, spurs on his attack. One of Lefty's friends describes Steffi as incapable of implicating any of them in the Greek's murder: "This one wouldn't be up to putting a finger on a man for anything. Not yet. A woman had to go to the wars to get mean. They weren't born that way, any of them" (77). And Steffi's vulnerability explains why these men who have completely disowned their own find her so irresistible. The barber who becomes her pimp feels enormous desire for her because "weakness had always aroused him. It had been so long since he had seen anything so young, so helpless. So wonderfully lost" (78). Independent women fail to attract him: so, he "ignored women possessing strength and health, unless they appeared stupid enough to trick in some easy fashion; there was nothing in health or strength to excite him" (78). Tillie Olsen's "Tell Me a Riddle" suggests that such compliance extracts a high cost. After forty-seven years of marriage, a dying wife pleads only for enough solitude to explore her thoughts and emotions. She knocks away the pill her husband gives her, saying, "'No pills, let me feel what I feel.'"[32] (89). James R. Giles notes that the men also pay for these roles: Algren's men turn away from insight into how to redeem their lives when they dominate rather than empathize with women: "Throughout Algren, female characters are shown as more capable than male characters of a passionate indomitability, of confronting the essential challenge of existence through a full acceptance of life."[33]

In *Paradise*, Toni Morrison describes two different communities, one ruled by men, the other by women. In the town of Ruby, men dominate; seventeen miles away, damaged women find refuge in a place called the Convent. One of the women, Pallas, feels confident that she can achieve integrity while there because the absence of men generates an atmosphere of freedom: "The whole house felt permeated with a blessed malelessness, like a protected domain, free of hunters but exciting too. As though she might meet herself here—an unbridled authentic self."[34] Connie, the woman who runs the house, gives those women who arrive at her door the uncompromising love and acceptance they ideally would have received from their mothers, so eventually, the women feel so secure in that house that they begin articulating their deepest emotions and thoughts out loud, sometimes in the form of a cry. As a result of this process, the women achieve peace.

Because the men rule them, the women in the town of Ruby do not enjoy this kind of serenity and when their situations become intolerable, they come to the Convent for relief. The men must run things to compensate for their own insecurities. This solution does not really work: one wife notes that the more successful her husband becomes, the emptier he gets: "Dovey has watched her husband destroy something in himself for thirty years. The more he gained, the less he became" (287). When problems emerge in the town, the men have no capacity for taking responsibility for them and solving them since that would involve admitting their failings. After concluding that the women in the Convent have created their problems, a group of armed men attack. Connie gets shot through the head and the men fire their guns at other women who flee, but no bodies are found. So when some of the women who lived at the Convent appear at the novel's conclusion to heal old relationships, the book invites the notion that they have become spirits. J. Brooks Bouson reports that African American folklore supports this explanation: "The disappearance of a body is one indicator of the magical power of its inhabitant" (146).

Billie Delta, one of the women from Ruby who has found refuge at the Convent, knows the return of the women would be miraculous but nonetheless she expects it: "When will they return? When will they reappear, with blazing eyes, war paint and huge hands to rip up and stomp down this prison calling itself a town…. A backwards noplace ruled by men whose power to control was out of control and who had the nerve to say who could live and who not and where; who had seen in lively, free, unarmed females the mutiny of the mares and so got rid of them" (308). The book ends with the suggestion that the compassionate, loving stance of these women will survive simply because human beings need it so badly. Someone named Piedade sings "of reaching age in the company of the other, of speech shared and divided bread smoking from the fire; the unambivalent bliss of going home to be at home—the ease of coming back to love again" (318).

These books fail to offer real solutions. Instead, they seem to validate the vision of Sherwood Anderson's *Beyond Desire*, which traces a number of relationships between men and women, virtually all of them disastrous. The men and women in this book find themselves attracted to each other, but their impulses have become so distorted by social norms that they come together only to damage each other: "People were perpetually doing it to each other. It wasn't just this one thing ... two bodies clasp together trying that."[35] The only successful relationship in Anderson's novel takes place between Neil and a schoolteacher, both revolutionaries who believe that people need to concern themselves with reforming society.

The most constructive choice seems for the women to develop some of the same ability to shape their lives that the men have so they can free themselves when they feel trapped and ignored. This happens at the end of Jonathan Franzen's *The Corrections*. The father has an astonishing rigidity which his wife lectures him about on his deathbed, but he simply cannot give it up. She can. After his death, she decides to live more ardently: "He was as stubborn as the day she'd met him. And yet when he was dead, when she'd pressed her lips to his forehead and walked out with Denise and Gary into the warm spring night, she felt that nothing could kill her hope now, nothing. She was seventy-five and she was going to make some changes in her life."[36]

Charles Baxter's *Shadow Play* suggests that over the generations, this kind of assertion has become more possible for women; as a result, the relationships between men and women have improved. Wyatt, the main character, for instance, enjoys women: "He was one of those boys who was not only attracted to young women but who loved them as well."[37] His grandfather is precisely the opposite: he feels attracted to women but dislikes them: "[His] stony reciprocal contempt for women was visited upon his face when he looked at them, a look he also cast upon dogs. At the spectacle of womanly sociability he turned away, but he could not find a fortress safe from their terrible capacity to attract." A cold man whose "heart he had hidden away like a stone in a forest," his marriage survives, but their "hatred burns steadily like a pilot light. They did not converse. They muttered comments and corrections to each other." His wife "grew to loathe all men for their obdurate silence and rigidity. Their laws were bad enough—and they were always making the laws—but their willfulness was worse. They hammered and plowed and drilled" (170–71).

Their daughter Ellen marries, divorces, and raises nephews and a niece. Still, she prefers solitude, which she uses to think about God. She has concluded that the harshness of daily life argues for an at best indifferent God who amuses himself by watching people struggle. At her nephew's funeral she declares that people need to take care of each other because God is unreliable: "Love is to me looking better than almost anything else. It's the only weapon we've got against this God. We've got to love each other, because God won't" (300). Wyatt's mother, Jeanne, who has retreated so far from reality that she lapses repeatedly into her own language, stands to applaud Ellen's theology. This reaction gives the reader a possible explanation for Jeanne's extreme withdrawal from life. And, of course, a male attendee berates Ellen's blasphemy.

But Ellen guesses that relationships between the sexes are improving. Her nephew Wyatt, for instance, prefers women with self-esteem: "These young women Wyatt sought out were proud and strong-willed—what Ellen noticed about them first was the way they stood, as straight as soldiers, and a particular way of looking around a room without fear—as it seemed that perhaps there was, after all, cause for optimism in what had happened between the sexes, at least in this one respect, that perhaps the young men and women liked each other more than they had in her father's generation. No more angry stoicism, or prideful unexpressed resentment" (191).

As the book ends, Ellen feels herself swept up in light: "This voice is absorbed into the winter light, soaked and raptured directly into it, and the light moves around her and past her. It seems, this call, this voice, to be beginning its way on an endless circular journey. Holding herself still, Ellen feels herself being gathered up. She will be here for one moment longer, while gravity holds her" (399). So the women in Baxter's book not only value love, the novel suggests this connects them with larger forces; their stance has a universal validity and a power that male attempts at control and conquest lack. But Wyatt's enthusiasm for women gives hope that men, too, begin to move towards this more compassionate stance.

Toni Morrison's *Home* portrays a woman freeing herself from male domination by cultivating her own strength. The book's protagonist, Frank Money, has a sister named Cee whose dependence on him has been essential to his self-esteem. It seems especially important to him to rescue her after he failed at saving the two friends he saw die while fighting in the Korean War: "'*No more people I didn't save. No more watching people close to me die. No more.*"³⁸ Cee agrees that Frank can save her from anything: "She knew that if she could see him, tell him, he would not laugh at her, quarrel, or condemn. He would, as always, protect her from a bad situation" (51). Their relationship has nourished Frank's positive view of himself, unfortunately, at Cee's expense: "*She was the first person I ever took responsibility for. Deep down inside her lived my secret picture of myself—a strong good me*" (104). But when he returns with Cee to Lotus, the town where they grew up, after she has been badly injured, strong women take charge of Cee and tell Frank to stay away. As Cee proclaims her helplessness, these women demand that she take responsibility for her own life: "Two months surrounded by country women who loved mean had changed her.... They didn't waste their time or the patient's with sympathy and they met the tears of the suffering with resigned contempt" (121). As a result, the Cee that emerges from their caretaking has a new strength that makes the idea of turning her life over to Frank or anyone else repugnant: "She wanted to be the person who would never again need rescue.... If she did not respect herself, why should anyone else?" (129). She vows to figure out what she most loves and build her life around this. Cee plans to adopt and cultivate more of the power commonly found in men.

In *The Last Report on the Miracles at Little No Horse*, Louise Erdrich presents a woman who becomes very accomplished at seeing things from a male perspective because she lives as a man for decades. After her common-law husband dies violently, Agnes Dewitt comes upon the corpse of a priest named Father Damien Modeste; she had encountered him earlier and learned that he traveled to work as a missionary to the Ojibwe. She buries his body, appropriates his things, including his clothing, disguises herself as Father Damien and takes up his assignment. She gets along well with the Ojibwe, some of whom recognize that she is a woman. For one thing, she empathizes with women who suffer sexual abuse. For another, she/he has enormous warmth. Even after Father Damien has retired, people come to him/her: "Something in the quality of his forgiveness really made people feel better— his human sympathy, or his divinely chosen penances. He was in demand. Therefore, Father Damien studiously kept confessional hours."³⁹

When a young priest named Gregory Wekkle lives with Father Damien, he wonders about his sexuality as he finds himself attracted to him/her. Eventually, he comes to understand that she's a woman and that he "knew himself and knew his love for Agnes was a good love, filled with tenderness and light. He tortured himself to find evil in his actions, but knew only harmony and righteous peace." She has the same feeling: "Her desire was one with a kind regard that felt both sinless and irresistible" (204). He tries to get her to leave with him, but she says she cannot abandon herself. He points out that she is a woman and she retorts: "'I am a priest'" (206). When he tries to convince her that she commits sacrilege, she replies: "'No,' she said, looking at him with her heart tearing, helpless against the simplest truth, 'I am nothing but a priest'" (207).

And so these novelists and poets suggest that although men and women see the world in contrary ways, and since men generally dominate, women frequently endure enormous frustration, to the extent that each can understand the way the other apprehends reality, good relationships are possible. If women could cultivate strength along with their emotional responsiveness, they can find happiness. In other words, these authors recommend androgyny. This truth explains the presumably happy marriage of Alexandra and Carl in Willa Cather's *O Pioneers!* The opening description of Alexandra emphasizes a strength that Cather explicitly identifies as masculine: "His sister was a tall, strong girl, and she walked rapidly and resolutely, as if she knew exactly where she was going and what she was going to do next. She wore a man's long ulster (not as if it were an affliction, but as if it were very comfortable and belonged to her; carried it like a young soldier)" (2). Her father recognizes that she has more competence than her brothers in financial matters, so, as he dies, he leaves her in charge of the family's land. She does extremely well with it, over her brothers' protests. Cather initially describes Carl, whom Alexandra will eventually marry, as "a thin, frail boy, with brooding dark eyes, very quiet in all his movements. There was a delicate pallor in his thin face, and his mouth was too sensitive for a boy's" (4).

Alexandra's focus on making her farm prosper impedes her understanding of relationships, the domain of women. She fails to notice that her brother, Emil, loves her best friend, Marie. Carl, on the other hand, knows intuitively when he sees them together that they care about each other. As she wonders how their affair could have happened, he replies, "You remember that Sunday when I went with Emil up to the French Church fair? I thought that day there was some kind of feeling, something unusual, between them" (120). Eventually, Carl helps Alexandra understand the relationship between Marie and Emil. Alexandra tells Carl how lonely she has felt. Alexandra, it is revealed, has feelings; she simply has not made them central to her life. At the book's conclusion, Alexandra's emotions make themselves felt and she guesses that she and Carl will have a good marriage: "'I think we shall be very happy. I haven't any fears.

I think when friends marry, they are safe. We don't suffer like—those young ones" (122). Dana Kinnison points out when Cather presents "males and females who are not drawn according to rigid gender prescriptions," she "invokes new possibilities ... for men's and women's relationships."[40]

Toni Morrison says that in *Song of Solomon* she tried to show the importance of having role models from both genders in one's life. Pilate grew up with an influential father and brother. As a result, she learned from them how to consciously shape her existence as well as respond passionately to it. And so Pilate has much more self-control than her granddaughter or daughter, Hagar and Reba, whom she (and she alone) has raised. For instance, Pilate is able to manipulate the police into freeing Guitar and Milkman, but Hagar can neither stop trying to kill Milkman, nor do the job effectively. On the other hand, as Morrison explains, Milkman "is in a male, macho world and can't fly, isn't human, isn't complete until he realizes the impact that women have made on his life. It's really a balance between classical male and female forces that produces, perhaps, a kind of complete person."[41]

As Morrison points out, just as women need to cultivate their masculine side in order to become whole, the men in midwestern fiction tend to succeed or fail depending on their ability to own their more tender feelings. Studs Lonigan believes that "he couldn't let himself get soft about anything, because, well, just because he wasn't the kind of bird that got soft. He never let anyone know how he felt."[42] By the time he graduates from primary school, he has become adept at shutting these feelings out, but Studs's gentle side emerges repeatedly in the shape of longing for Lucy Scanlan. He believes as he sits next to her, swinging his legs and enjoying nature, that this moment will transform his life, making it wonderful. But he also worries about this change rendering him effeminate: "He usually thought it was sissified to listen or pay attention to such things as birds singing; it was crazy, like being a guy who studied music, or read too many books, or wrote poems, and painted pictures" (101). Then people report his affection for Lucy in chalk all over his neighborhood, fatally chilling their relationship. Studs swears off any public affection for girls: "He loved her, but after what had happened he was even ashamed to admit it to himself. He was a hard-boiled guy and he had learned his lesson. He'd keep himself roped in tight after this when it came to girls" (111). Mark O. Noe sees Studs's inability to own his vulnerability as the central cause of his tragic life: "He builds himself a paradise out of a few minor childhood incidents and plenty of dreams. But his paradise is all illusion: he fails to find any success in life because he never thinks of life beyond the macho construct in his mind."[43]

Just as women have difficulty owning their strength, the problems men have integrating their vulnerability into their lives helps explain why so many men in this literature have an obsessive, irrational faith that a woman can save them. Instead of owning their own capacity for tenderness, they look for salvation from women. Since they make no attempt to deal with the real issue, their inability to own their emotional lives, their "love" for women often fails to correlate in any meaningful way with the qualities the women they seek actually possess. For instance, for reasons best known to himself, Gatsby builds his existence around the fantasy that union with the mean-spirited, egotistical Daisy will redeem his life. Perhaps because he's a psychiatrist, Dick Diver in *Tender is the Night* knows that the actress he yearns for and eventually beds has no qualities that he needs or wants, especially since his relationship with her jeopardizes his marriage, but, still, he must have her at any cost. In *The Beautiful and Damned*, Anthony's self-destructive debauches also involve his wife, Gloria; Anthony knew when he met her that "she was the end of all restlessness, all malcontent."[44] In Charles Baxter's story "Flood Show," Conor, who is "the sort of man who believes that love and caresses are probably the answer for everything," married Merilyn because her beauty overwhelmed him.[45] She finally leaves him because she can't take his adulation any longer. He remarries and Merilyn comes back to town to see their son. Conor just happens to show up across the river from where Merilyn and their son Jeremy meet. At first, Conor notes that Merilyn's weight gain has changed her appearance. But then he looks more closely: "Through the binoculars a trace of a smile, Conor believes, has appeared on Merilyn's face.... In the middle of her pudginess, this smile is the same one that he saw sixteen years ago. It's the smile he lost his heart to. A little crow's-foot of delight in Conor's presence. A merriment" (249). So he wades through the freezing river water to go to her, almost perishing on the way. When he arrives, he says, "'I couldn't help it. I never got over it.'" His son tells him to be quiet and get in the car. The story ends with an image of a truck lugging a two-story house up a hill followed by this description of Conor: "He is beginning now to shiver, as the truck, carrying the burden it was made to carry, struggles up the next hill" (251). This ending suggests that far from comic, Conor's irrational obsession with Merilyn's appearance weighs down his life. He connects love and beauty in a way that even his seventeen-year-old son finds absurd and embarrassing. But Conor cannot outgrow this ideology.

Sherwood Anderson offers some hope that men can find salvation in relationships with women in *Winesburg, Ohio* although it depends not on a woman, but on the evolution of George Willard's attitude towards women. Throughout the book he has romantic escapades, including a sexual experience with Louise Trunion, which leaves him uncomfortable until he realizes "'she hasn't got anything on me. Nobody knows.'"[46] After amazing himself with his ability to think large thoughts and use big words, George thinks that the presence of an admiring woman would enhance his experience, so he asks Belle Carpenter to go for a walk; George has kissed her before, but did not feel completely in control. Now, he thinks, his power has grown so great that no one can use him. After George whispers, "'Lust and night and women'"(104) and falls to his knees before Belle, Ed Hanby, her boyfriend, appears and pushes George aside. George tries to go after Ed, who keeps shoving him out of the way until George hits his head on a root. In *Winesburg, Ohio*'s penultimate story, "Sophistication," George has gained humbling insight into his insignificance, and it frightens him. He wants company: "If he prefers that the other be a woman, that is because he believes that a woman will be gentle, that she will understand. He wants, most of all, understanding" (131). George seeks out Helen White, whom he has known and treated as an equal for years. Their time together satisfies him because his newfound humility allows him to enjoy a sense of connection with her: "Two oddly sensitive human atoms held each other tightly and waited. In the mind of each was the same thought, 'I have come to this lonely place and here is this other,' was the substance of the thing felt'" (135). George tries to build relationships with women on his sexual desires and then on his narcissistic needs, without success. Only after he develops some modesty and he and the woman respond to each other with reciprocal emotional generosity does the relationship work. In other words, those men who have learned to feel humility and empathy themselves have the best chance of understanding and connecting with the emotional richness that these authors consistently associate with women.

One such man is Nanapush in Louise Erdrich's *Tracks*. He admires women's ability to give birth and gladly seizes the opportunity to get a sense of how it may feel: "Many times in my life, as my children were born, I wondered what it was like to be a woman, able to invent a human from the extra materials of her own body." When Lulu suffers from frostbite, he sees bringing her feet back to life as similar to childbirth: "I gave birth in loss. I was like a woman in my suffering, but my children were all delivered into death.... Now I had a chance to put things in proper order."[47] In *Four Souls*, he puts on a dress Margaret has made, imitating one she sees in a dream, and winds up having to preside over a council meeting in it. He tells the group that wearing the dress has educated him: "'It wasn't that the dress spoke to me. It was that my ears were opened to hear all that I missed when I was arrayed like a man.'" With his opened ears, he heard Mother Earth pointing out that he owed everything to her and asking what he had given in return. The issue before the council was whether to sign over their land: after Nanapush's speech, they refuse. As Debra Holt points out, Erdrich's novels argue for "a world where men and women alike tap into the power of femininity."[48]

The protagonist of Saul Bellow's *Herzog* obsesses over his divorce from Madeline until it leads him to redemptive self-awareness. He worries that the demise of his relationship with Madeline has left him incapable of attracting another woman: "His sexual powers had been damaged by Madeleine. And without the ability to attract women, how was he to recover? It was in this respect that he felt most like a convalescent."[49] But he soon has a new love interest, Ramona, who believes fervently in the healing powers of sex. Herzog finds himself incapable of arguing with her, or even thinking: "And so he would suck in his belly and stand on aching feet—he, the captive professor, she the mature, successful, laughing, sexual woman. Quack, quack!" (34) Herzog realizes that in his submission to Ramona and other women he plays a feminine rather than a masculine role: "Amorous Herzog, seeking love, and embracing his Wandas, Zinkas, and Ramonas, one after another? But this is a female pursuit. This hugging and heartbreak is for women. The occupation of a man is in duty, in use, in civility, in politics in the Aristotelian sense" (119). Herzog tries to meet these more masculine obligations with his obsessive letter writing and theorizing, all attempts to discover and define patterns and orders. But Ramona interests him far more, for she offers him "metaphysical, transcendent pleasure—pleasure which answered the riddle of human existence" (186). And, finally, he sees much less value in theories than in relationships: "The world should love lovers; but not theoreticians. Never theoreticians! Show them the door. Ladies, throw out those gloomy bastards!" (211). Moreover, the callousness of the world has made loving and compassion rarities that deserve respect: "Reason itself, logic, urged you to kneel and give thanks for every small sign of true kindness" (246). So Herzog comes to see the relationships wherein he identifies with women as the most crucial aspect of modern life: "'The real and essential question is one of our employment by other human beings and their employment by us. Without this true employment you never dread death, you cultivate it. And consciousness when it doesn't clearly understand what to live for, what to die for, can only abuse and ridicule itself ... as I do by writing impertinent letters" (333). At the novel's conclusion, he abandons letter writing altogether: "At this time he had no messages for anyone. Nothing. Not a single word" (416).

Jim Harrison sees a similar movement towards the feminine in his work. He admits that his early work focused on tough guys, but he got tired of them: "I started writing fiction in my mid-to-late twenties, but I only could write inner versions of myself. Much of the content of male American fiction is nifty guys at loose ends and that's what I lost patience with: that narrowness of vision, 'I'm bad, but I'm really neat.' That kind of bullshit. That became so tiresome, I couldn't stand that kind of person either to read or write about." Harrison identifies *Sundog* as the first novel when he could successfully enter characters unlike himself. When he wrote *Dalva*, he focused on the character of a woman and found it very educational to write from the perspective of someone so different from himself. He even discovered that for the first time he could write in the morning while inhabiting her voice. He found the experience so absorbing that "when I finished the last sections, my doctor said both my eardrums were broken and I had no thyroid sign. I had just ignored everything. I'd had the flu and infections in my ears." He believes "the power comes from that androgyny, I'm sure, because traditionally, if you go back, a writer is a version of a priest or a shaman. And those are all somewhat androgynous professions."[50] James McClintock suggests that this move towards androgyny has enriched both Harrison's fiction and his life: "To thrive, Harrison had to acknowledge a masculinity of greater dimension symbolized by locating the 'twin sister' he had lost. She was, of course, within; Dalva is the outward sign that Harrison did, indeed, find her and extend in redemptive ways his understanding of masculinity."[51] Harrison has not only continued to write from the perspective of female characters, he has also traveled culturally, writing from the perspective of Ojibwe and of people in earlier generations. One can easily see the growing impact of Harrison's enthusiasm for engaging others' perspectives in his fiction.

Not only can Harrison lose himself in a variety of characters, he can make characters like Donald, in *Returning to Earth*, admirable and compelling. A good but completely ordinary and modest man, Donald helps the reader understand that kindness guarantees that he will have enduring impact on those who love him. Donald dies in the first chapter; the remaining chapters show the powerful influence of his decency on those who knew him best. When Donald proclaims that "love will carry you through the hard parts,"[52] he states the book's central theme. And here, Donald embraces, as Herzog would point out, a feminine perspective. Perhaps not accidentally, his aunt

Flower taught him these kinds of lessons when he lived with her. His wife, Cynthia, identifies them as "somewhat mystifying notions of people as interlocking and that to separate yourself is to be doomed" (50). Gerald Vizenor's *Heirs of Columbus* regrets the way women have been treated and describes a tribal world rife with gender crossing. Michael Hardin argues that this reflects the centrality of the trickster myth to this society: "Not only does the trickster represent a critique of the categories of race, but according to Vizenor, he/she also represents a critique of gender, sex, and species; ideally a space is created wherein none of these categories is privileged."[53] This means that in such a world feminine dispositions have the same value as masculine ones.

One can see the same movement towards feminine values even in the work of the notoriously macho Ernest Hemingway. The easy judgment that Ernest Hemingway suffered from terminal sexism makes it tempting to see the posthumously published *The Garden of Eden* as exposing his inability to ever understand or relate to women other than physically. His other novels' increasing emphasis on making connections with others calls this conclusion into serious question. Hemingway's first book, the interconnected stories composing *In Our Time*, offer a terminally cynical view of relationships. "Mr. and Mrs. Elliot" portrays a couple that clearly gets married to satisfy conventions: they have little interest in each other. The husband winds up staying up late at night writing poetry while his wife sleeps with her girlfriend. "A Very Short Story" portrays a wounded soldier falling in love with a nurse, getting jilted and consoling himself by having sex with a sales clerk in a taxicab traveling through Chicago's Lincoln Park; he comes away from this experience with gonorrhea. The couple in "Out of Season" fights its way through the tale.

The relationships improve little in *The Sun Also Rises*, as its protagonist, Jake Barnes, struggles repeatedly to achieve stoicism because the war has left him impotent. But he realizes that his wound merely provides an external manifestation of his problems with intimacy. When his friend Brett claims that if it were not for his physical problems, "'We could have had such a damned good time together,'" Jake replies "Isn't it pretty to think so?'"[54] In *A Farewell to Arms*, Hemingway again depicts a chaotic world, but allows two people who both reject society's platitudes to find each other, fall in love and briefly withdraw to a place that allows their love to develop before death cuts it down. *A Farewell to Arms* tacitly embraces the despairing attitude towards love made explicit in *Death in the Afternoon*: "Madame, all stories, if continued far enough, end in death, and he is no true-story teller who would keep that from you. Especially do all stories of monogamy end in death, and your man who is monogamous while he often lives most happily, dies in the most lonely fashion.... If two people love each other there can be no happy end to it."[55] Even if both survive the experience, after love passes, those who enjoyed it suffer because they realize the relative hollowness of their lives afterwards: "All those who have really experienced it are marked, after it is gone, by a quality of deadness" (122).

The narrator of *The Green Hills of Africa* adopts a more optimistic view, suggesting that the experience itself never dies even though the lover may pass away or simply leave: "You are not alone, because if you have really loved her happy and untragic, she loves you always."[56] Still, only the creation of art guarantees eternity: "People all die and none of them were of any importance permanently, except those who practiced the arts" (109).

But by the time Hemingway writes, *For Whom the Bell Tolls*, when Robert Jordan falls in love with Maria he knows it is "the most important thing that can happen to a human being,"[57] no matter how long it or Robert lasts. His relationship with Maria helps him develop compassion. Robert understands that fighting in a war requires detachment, but he fights for principle and the feelings of empathy from which those principles grow: "It was a feeling of consecration to a duty toward all of the oppressed of the world which would be as difficult and embarrassing to speak about as religious experience and yet it was authentic as the feeling you had when you heard Bach, or stood in the Chartres Cathedral or the Cathedral at Leon and saw the light coming through the great windows" (235). This book also implies that love creates eternity: anyone who has loved survives in the lover; Robert invokes this philosophy to convince Maria not to die with him. But the novel's title with its silent reference to John Donne's poem that asserts "No Man Is an Island," suggests that Robert not only continues to live through Maria, but through everyone: his war experiences connect him to all people. He will never write the book he planned, but he has found a more human way to defeat death: through his connections to others. Death is no longer a dirty trick visited on love; the lover outsmarts death.

Robert Crozier's analysis of the novel leads him to the same conclusion: "What should be clear now is how profoundly Hemingway, the supposedly *macho* author, is concerned about the nature, the meaning, and the complex but simple relationship of both the feminine and the masculine in universal terms, one cannot do without the other."[58] Marc Hewson agrees: "Hemingway makes a step forward in this book that indicates an increasing unease with the gender and sexual definitions available to men and women in a patriarchal society and suggests a desire to find an alternate means of self-definition through openness, commitment, and love."[59]

Islands in the Stream makes the shift in Hemingway's values clear. His early novels value discipline and locate immortality in art. Tolerating isolation poses the greatest difficulty for those who would create. But once Hemingway establishes that relationships can defeat death, he admits their value. With his characterization of Thomas Hudson, he concedes that withdrawal from others can show cowardice rather than courage. Thomas Hudson clearly uses the isolated, transcendent, disciplined ritual of his art to shut out loneliness. But immortality interests him much less than spending time with his noisy sons. When his sons die, he retreats to his work, painting only because he needs a palliative to distract him from the overwhelming pain he feels. He goes to war and, as he lies wounded, he vows to return home and do his greatest work. When a comrade tells Thomas that he loves him, Thomas realizes that he will soon die. He glances at the sky he has always adored and quietly accepts death. Hudson has searched for peace all his life. When his relationships failed to provide it, he turned to his painting. When he knows he will die, he regrets that he never produced immortal work, but he needs only one friend to say he loves him in order to make peace with death. Caring, not discipline, finally becomes the best defense against death in Hemingway's work.

Midwestern fiction finally recommends androgyny: before attempting to have relationships with each other, men and women would do well to understand each other's points of view. Huck's and Jim's cross-dressing seems almost prophetic. These authors stress the importance of men coming to understand women, more than the reverse, because men have traditionally had more cultural control, making it mandatory for women to understand their perspectives. These fiction writers suggest that women developing more of the strength and independence typically possessed by men, and men attending to and even cultivating women's compassion, would produce a kinder, gentler world with solid relationships between men and women.

Four

The African American Dimension

Although critics passionately debate the authenticity and fairness of Mark Twain's characterization of Jim in *Huckleberry Finn*, he clearly has presented African American experience more compassionately than the canonical authors from New England who preceded him. Despite their commitment to abolition, Ralph Waldo Emerson and Henry David Thoreau do not imaginatively engage African American life in their work. Nor does Nathaniel Hawthorne include significant African American characters in his fiction. In *Moby Dick*, Herman Melville presents Pip, a man who prays to "'Thou big white God aloft there somewhere in yon darkness, have mercy on this small black boy down here; preserve him from all men that have no bowels to feel fear.'"[1] Pip's prayers go unanswered: he gets accidentally tossed overboard and goes mad.

The distinguished African American novelist Ralph Ellison admires the ambiguity of *Huckleberry Finn*, an attitude that shapes his largely positive reaction to the book. For instance, in "Change the Joke and Slip the Yoke," he writes that Twain "fitted Jim into the outlines of the minstrel tradition, and it was from behind this stereotype mask that we see Jim's dignity and human capacity—and Twain's complexity—emerge."[2] Elliston regretted that those who commented on this passage emphasized his linking minstrel shows to Jim's characterization, overlooking the larger, more positive point he makes. In his essay "Twentieth-Century Fiction and the Black Mask of Humanity," Ellison once again celebrates the novel's rich characterization: "Jim was not only a slave but a human being ... who expressed his essential humanity in his desire for freedom, his will to possess his own labor, in his loyalty and capacity for friendship, and in his love for his wife and his child. Yet Twain ... does not idealize the slave. Jim is drawn in all his ignorance and superstition, with his good traits and his bad. He, like all men, is ambiguous."[3]

Toni Morrison argues with herself about Twain's novel. In *Playing in the Dark* (1992), she explains the admiration of others for *Huckleberry Finn* as a manifestation of unstated racism; or, of the enthusiasm for an "apparently limitless store of love and compassion the black man has for his white friend and white masters; and his assumption that the whites are indeed what they say they are, superior and adult." She sees this as "the yearning of whites for forgiveness and love, but the yearning is made possible only when it is understood that Jim has recognized his inferiority (not as slave, but as black) and despises it. Jim permits his persecutors to torment him, humiliate him, and responds to the torment and humiliation with boundless love." In this essay, she puts her praise of *Huckleberry Finn* in qualifying quotation marks: "In that sense the book may indeed be 'great' because in its structure, in the hell it puts its readers through at the end, the frontal debate it forces, it simulates and describes the parasitical nature of white freedom."[4] Yet her 1996 introduction to *Huckleberry Finn* concludes with an unqualified assertion of the book's worth: "For a hundred years, the argument that this novel is has been identified, reindentified, examined, waged and advanced. What it cannot be is dismissed. It is classic literature, which is to say it heaves, manifests and lasts."[5]

Like Morrison, Jane Smiley seems to change her mind about the book. In her 1996 essay "Say It Ain't So, Huck: Second Thoughts on Mark Twain's 'Masterpiece,'" she complains that Huck does not try to facilitate Jim's longing for freedom, suggesting that he does not take Jim or his desires seriously. To support this judgment, Smiley points out that Jim and Huck could have crossed the Mississippi into Illinois, which would automatically free Jim. Smiley condemns this failure as a product of the notion that "if Huck *feels* positive toward Jim, and *loves* him, and *thinks* of him as a man, then that's enough. He doesn't actually have to act in accordance with his feelings." Smiley argues that this celebration of the notion that positive feelings suffice excuses racist behavior: "To invest *Adventures of Huckleberry Finn* with 'greatness' is to underwrite a very simplistic and evasive theory of what racism is and to promulgate it, philosophically, in schools and the media as well as in academic journals."[6] Some critics, like Sanford Pinsker, find Smiley's position here more ideological than literary: "She sides with propaganda rather than with art."[7]

Later, when asked about the controversy this essay provoked, Smiley makes the bewildering claim that it amuses her because "my beef against *Huckleberry Finn* is a purely readerly beef: I think it's boring. It's hilarious to me that I've been so attacked for thinking it's boring. I've always thought taste is not a moral issue." She describes the ancestry of her novel *The All-True Travels and Adventures of Lidie Newton* as follows: "Twain is the dad, Harriet Beecher Stowe is the mom, and Catherine Beecher is the maiden aunt."[8] Jim O'Loughlin cites this statement when he argues that in the novel Smiley tries to improve on Twain's mistaken perspective and implicitly racist point of view in *Huckleberry Finn*. And, indeed, near the novel's end, Lidie attempts to help a slave named Lorna achieve her freedom, and fails. So, unlike Huck, she acts. On the other hand, she does not succeed and Lidie is a grown woman who only temporarily holds abolitionist views while Huck is a thirteen-year-old boy who thinks abolitionists will all go to hell. O'Loughlin admits that at the end of the novel Lidie "questions whether her actions did any good,"[9] but, in fact, at the end of the novel Lidie questions her earlier abolitionist views largely because of their absolutism. She no longer considers an ideology, even one as morally attractive as abolitionism, adequate to the truth: "I found myself increasingly unable to speak about any of these issues…. The very certainty of everyone around me drove all certainty out of me." She believes she can only articulate the truth through specific interactions with particular people, not through proclamations: "To say what was true, you had to look into the eyes of your interlocutor and see something that you recognized."[10] In other words, without acknowledging it, Jane Smiley seems to have abandoned the position she articulated in 1996, instead deferring to and even embracing the kind of nuance that Ralph Ellison sees and praises in *Huckleberry Finn*.

Despite all the critical discussion about the novel's handling of race, it not only unquestionably offers the first substantial portrayal of an African American character in classic American literature; it also characterizes Jim as the kindest, most decent person in the book, as Seymour Chwast notes: "At critical junctures Jim is Huck's adult guide and protector and throughout lives on a higher ethical level than anybody else in this book, including Huck."[11] Morrison points out that he not only becomes a loving as well as an appropriately reprimanding father to the orphaned Huck, he flees slavery because he fears for his own children's fates.

During the years before midwestern African American authors made it into print, other white midwestern writers besides Twain attempted to render the African American experience positively. Given these authors' persistent resistance and sensitivity to demeaning stereotypes that social codes impose on people, it makes sense that the treatment of African Americans would get their sympathetic attention. Despite their good intentions, it remains unclear whether a collection of white authors have the capacity to characterize African Americans with appropriate complexity and subtlety. Not surprisingly, they sometimes fell into the kinds of stereotypes that black authors would later condemn. Vachel Lindsay's poem "The Congo," subtitled "A Study of the Negro Race," intends to portray the salvation of an African American from the slums through his entrance into a world where "'mumbo-jumbo will hoo-doo you.'"[12] The poem seems embarrassingly racist and condescending today and complements the behavior of the Carraways in Langston Hughes's story "Slave on the Block": "They went in for the Art of Negroes—the dancing that had such jungle life about it, the songs that were so simple and fervent, the poetry that was so direct, so real."[13] Still, Langston Hughes named Lindsay an important influence on him and according to Robert Hayden: "It was Vachel Lindsay who helped the Afro-American poet Langston Hughes gain early recognition."[14] So apparently Hughes could look beyond the poem's insulting implications and honor Lindsay's good intentions.

The linking of blacks and primitivism that makes Lindsay's poem ludicrous today persists through Sherwood Anderson's novel *Dark Laughter* and Saul Bellow's *Henderson the Rain King* wherein both Anderson and Bellow suggest that blacks have a joyfulness whites lack. In *Dark Laughter*, Anderson writes: "Niggers like good things. Good big sweet words, flesh, corn, cane. Niggers like a free throat for song."[15] In a letter to his publisher Horace Liveright, Anderson describes the book as providing a contrast between "the neuroticism, the hurry and self-consciousness of modern life, and back of it the easy, strange laughter of the blacks."[16] Similarly, Bellow's Henderson in *Henderson the Rain King* adopts as a mentor an African king who rejects effort. As the King explains to Henderson: "Many, many nice people. Oh yes. Their will tells them to perform good and they do. How ordinary! Mere arithmetic.... My whole view is opposite or contrary, that good cannot be labor or conflict."[17] As Choki Ikeda reports, Henderson's "immersion in mid–Africa" helps him realize his passionate side, allowing "him to return to his home with joy and rediscovery of self."[18] Eugene Lesche, a white hustler in Hughes's story "Rejuvenation through Joy," profitably sells whites the same idea: "Look at the Negroes! The know how to move from their feet up, from the head down. Their centers live. They walk, they stand, they dance to their drum beats, their earth rhythms.... They live through motion, through movement, through music, through joy!" (72). Lesche particularly cherishes "the curative values of Negro Jazz" (76). But in his essay "The Negro Artist and the Racial Mountain," Hughes himself portrays jazz as a uniquely black art form that offers an antidote to white death: "Jazz to me is one of the inherent expressions of Negro life in America; the eternal tom-tom beating in the Negro soul—the tom tom of revolt against weariness in a white world, a world of subway trains, and work, work, work; the tom-tom of joy and laughter, and pain swallowed in a smile."[19] So Hughes seems to embrace this perspective himself, but still he objects to whites projecting it onto blacks. The projection also troubles Toni Morrison: "This new white male can now persuade himself that savagery is 'out there.'"[20]

Morrison complains about Willa Cather's *Sapphira and the Slave Girl* for portraying a slave as indifferent to her child's fate. She also offers extensive analyses of Hemingway's presentations of black characters only to conclude that she has no intention of portraying Hemingway as racist: "It would be irresponsible and unjustified to invest Hemingway with the thoughts of his characters. It is Harry who thinks a black woman is like a nurse shark, not Hemingway. An author is not personally accountable for the acts of his fictive creatures, although he is responsible for them. And there is no evidence I know of to persuade me that Hemingway shared Harry's views. In point of fact there is strong evidence to suggest the opposite."[21] One could also argue that Cather's characters do not necessarily represent her views. Moreover, other critics defend Cather's portrayal of racial issues, among them Angela M. Salas: "We can see that in *Sapphira and the Slave Girl* Cather does raise and face many of the complexities surrounding race, gender, authority, ethics and equality still facing our culture."[22] In other words, attempting to determine whether white midwestern authors attempting to depict black life fall into hopeless stereotyping or offer a valid glimpse of how the African American experience leads one into confusion. But that these authors, unlike earlier classic American writers, found African Americans a compelling subject for literature and attempted to render their lives sympathetically, rests beyond dispute.

William Dean Howells wrote a novel entitled *An Imperative Duty*, in which a young woman, Rhoda Algate, who always considered herself white discovers that she has black blood. After Mrs. Meredith, the aunt who raised Rhoda, tells her this news, Rhoda goes to the black section of town to familiarize herself with her new culture and finds the people ugly. While there, she runs into an extremely kind African American woman who, recognizing Rhoda's anguish, takes her to church where she hopes Rhoda can find comfort. Although the preacher has a voice "rich and tender, with those caressing notes in it which are the peculiar gift of his race," Rhoda can still think only of how unattractive she finds these people and, as a result, how much she despises them: "These poor people, whom their Creator has made so hideous by the standards of all his other creatures, roused a cruel loathing in her, which expressed itself in a frantic refusal of their claim upon her. In her heart she cast them off with vindictive hate."[23]

Her aunt dies as a result of accidentally taking too much sleeping medicine, and Miss Aldgate turns down her current beau without telling him of her background. Dr. Olney, whom Rhoda's aunt had made privy to Rhoda's situation, steps in. He has just returned from Europe and finds the separation of the races in America disturbing. Olney likes the blacks he encounters in Boston, although in a very condescending manner: "They all alike seemed shining with good-nature and good-will and the desire of peace on earth. Their barbaric taste in color, when it flamed out in a crimson necktie or a scarlet jersey, or when it subdued itself to a sable that left no gleam of white about them but a point or rim of shirt collar, was invariably delightful to him" (6). He develops a theory that blacks, because of their inferiority, will disappear into whites: "'I've been more and more struck with the fact that sooner or later our race must absorb the colored race; and I believe that it will obliterate not only its color, but its qualities. The tame man, the civilized man, is stronger than the wild man ... because vice is savage and virtue is civilized'" (38–39).

Although initially repulsed when he learns of Rhoda's black blood, Dr. Olney decides that "the impulse had to have its course; and then he mastered it, with an abiding compassion and a sort of tender indignation" (44). He happily proposes to Rhoda because he comes to believe that her black blood makes her beautiful: "It was like the grace of a limp, the occult, indefinable loveableness of a deformity, but transcending these by its allurement in infinite degree, and going for the reason of its effect deep into the mysterious places of being where the spirit and the animal meet and part in us." The narrator reports that Olney's "moral sense plays no role in this decision" because it has been "submerged and blotted out" (133). This may help explain why, when Olney notes signs of Rhoda's unkindness, they disturb him only mildly. For instance, when meeting the man she expected to marry, Olney notes his "unselfish frankness" and judges him "noble" (119). Olney guesses that Rhoda turns him down to avoid revealing her black blood, but he learns she simply disliked him. When the aunt who raised her dies, Olney finds the shallowness of Rhoda's grief bewildering: "He was puzzled, if not shocked, that she seemed forgetful of the woman, so recently gone forever, who had been in all effects a mother to her, and who had sacrificed and borne more than most mothers do for her sake" (130).

Rhoda argues that she has an obligation to spend her life elevating blacks because she persuades herself that "'I can endure them if I love them, and I shall love them if I try to help them'" (95). Mr. Olney says she would have a duty to serve only "'if you had ever consented to be of their kind.... The way to elevate them is to elevate us, to begin with. It will be an easy matter to deal with those simple-hearted folks after we've got into the right way ourselves'" (143). And so these two superficial, fundamentally racist characters marry and settle in Rome, far from possible questions about Rhoda's background. Not surprisingly, given their shared insensitivity, Mr. Olney and Rhoda do not enjoy wedded bliss: "It could not be pretended that Olney found more than the common share of happiness in the lot he chose; but then it could be said honestly enough that he did not consider either life or love valuable for the happiness they could yield." His wife seems equally unhappy: "When he saw that even his love failed at times to make life happy for his wife, he pitied her, and he did not blame her." He suspects that a little more black blood may have redeemed her: "If Olney had any regret it was that the sunny-natured antitypes of her mother's race had not endowed her with more of the heaven born cheerfulness with which it meets contumely and injustice. His struggle was with that hypochondria of the soul into which the Puritanism of her father's race had sickened in her, and which so often seems to satisfy its crazy claim upon conscience by enforcing some aimless act of self-sacrifice" (148–49).

Critics seem to take this novel's surface at face value. Jeffory Clymer, M. Giulia Fabi, and Henry B. Wonham accuse Howells of racial insensitivity; Paul Petrie and Julie Carey Nerad defend him by claiming he simply faces racism's complexity. But no critic argues that Howells intends readers to mistrust his central characters, although his most anthologized story, "Editha," demonstrates that Howells was capable of composing a work ironic from start to finish. Presumably Howells, the man who introduced Paul Lawrence Dunbar to the public emphasizing his excellence as a poet, not as an African American poet, had the sophistication to understand the shallowness of his "heroine's" concern with appearance, especially when the blacks she encounters so persistently manifest kindness, generosity, and joy—all qualities Rhoda lacks. Dr. Olney has little more depth: he barely knows her, yet aspires to marry her, apparently attracted primarily by her black flavoring; he only regrets that her black racial history had made a stronger impression on her. And their anxiety to avoid sensitive questions from others leads them to spend their lives together, not especially happily, in exile. Why would two superficial creatures like this have rich lives? Intentionally or not, William Dean Howells has produced a novel that makes whites look trivial and benighted; blacks, openhearted and wise.

Sinclair Lewis and Sherwood Anderson expand on this characterization in *Kingsblood Royal* and *Dark Laughter*, respectively. Perhaps African Americans may find Sherwood Anderson's *Dark Laughter* offensive because of its stereotyping blacks as joyous and singing, but at the same time, the black laughter referred to in the title relates to black women who work for Fred and Aline Grey laughing about the affair between Aline and Bruce Dudley of which Fred remains ignorant: "The older negro woman tried to quiet the younger, blacker woman, but she kept laughing the high shrill laughter of the negress. 'I knowed it, I knowed it, all the time I knowed it,' she cried, and the high shrill laughter ran through the garden and into the room where Fred sat upright and rigid in bed" (318). Aline's lover Bruce realizes earlier in the affair that the black woman working in Aline's house probably understands what's going on between them because "negro women have an instinctive understanding. They say nothing, being wise in woman-lore" (233). Anderson's novel mirrors Toni Morrison's novel *Tar Baby*, wherein the black servant knows that the white woman for whom she works abuses her child while the white woman's husband has no clue to this activity. Both novels argue that in terms of insight, black underlings have a more acute awareness than their white bosses.

In *Kingsblood Royal*, Sinclair Lewis suggests that all blacks have a deeper grasp of reality than whites because of their repeated confrontation with the discrimination that whites ignore, blinded by a not-so-secret sense of innate superiority. Neil Kingsblood is a thirty-one-year-old man who discovers that he has a black ancestor. This new knowledge makes him sharply sensitive to race. But unlike Rhoda in *An Imperative Duty*, instead of rejecting the way blacks look, he finds himself totally taken by their intelligence and kindness. His black friends understand why he wants to keep the new information about his background quiet, so they protect his secret. But his fresh realization guarantees that acts of casual racism now sting him. He repeatedly retreats to the comforting company and insights of his African American friends when the thoughtless racism of whites unnerves him. After spending a career lambasting conformity, in this book Lewis attributes this destructive behavior to whites, not blacks. As an African American train porter explains, mindless acceptance of the social norms sustaining their sense of superiority keeps whites stupid:

"'White folks are awful nice, but of course they're all babies and have to be taken care of. They never look things over real sharp, way we colored folks have, since we were knee-high to a traveling-man. They're like some Delta colored fellows that we all know—believe what the preachers and the law tell 'em. You can't blame 'em, poor things.'"[24] After Neil makes his race public, he tries to eat at the same club he did when officially white and gets advice from a black waiter: "'We Negroes have to know everything, in order to get along in a mean white world. So get wise to yourself, boy, and stay where you belong'" (264). Lewis's novel validates the claim of the African American writer Clarence Major that discrimination has given blacks a profound understanding of the social structure's dangers: "We are in a position to know at first hand the social and political machinery that is threatening to destroy the earth and we can use creative and intellectual black criteria on it."[25]

But Neil Kingsblood also comes to see that the blacks' exclusion from social norms has given them a freedom whites lack, so he declares Winthrop Brewster, the son of the Reverend Evan Brewster, a brilliant black minister, lucky because "he would not be sent in a plush-lined coffin through Princeton and the officers' club; he could honorably be independent and poor" (154). While attending a black church, Kingsblood sees Emerson Wollcape, an African American former classmate and recalls feeling jealous of their obvious happiness when he once saw the Wollcape family picnicking: "They had all been singing, and he had enviously thought that they were having more fun than his family ever had" (93). Understanding the meaninglessness of the social codes that have shaped Kingsblood's life helps him grasp that this contentment comes from a far more honest awareness of life's realities and their situation in it than the delusory, self-congratulatory view held by whites.

Similarly, Tillie Olsen's story "O Yes" describes the emotional support members of the African American community give each other. It focuses on a friendship between an African American girl named Parry and a white girl named Carol, which deteriorates as they grow up and assume the roles society assigns them, but not before Carol attends Parry's baptism. The intense emotion expressed on this occasion, especially through music, makes Carol feel so ill that she has to leave the service early. Her mother tries to explain to her that the church offers a sanctuary to African Americans where they can articulate what they feel "'so they can go on.'"[26] As the story ends, Carol wishes that she could feel indifferent about the end of her relationship with Parry and could also forget about her experience in Parry's church, but both memories haunt her. Her mother thinks of trying to explain, but stops herself because she knows her perspective will strike Carol as incomprehensible. Carol's mother understands too well the emotional release the African American church provides and wishes she could find a similar refuge for herself: "Her own need leapt and plunged for the place of strength that was not—where one could scream or sorrow while all knew and accepted, and gloved and loving hands waited to support and understand" (55). But her daughter has not experienced enough of life's challenges to genuinely grasp the need for such solace. Rose Kamel believes that, in fact, Helen remains silent because she distances "herself from the immediacy of passion, and remains static." Kamel contrasts her with Parry's mother, Alva, who "allows communal celebration to temper her and thus sets her spirit free."[27] Joann Frye believes that Helen simply acts like a responsible mother: "A mother must find a way to facilitate the child's growth in conscience and social responsibility without wrenching the child by a responsibility beyond the child's own current capacities and understandings."[28] No matter which view one takes of Helen, Olsen, like Lewis and Anderson, suggests that African American culture provides far greater support for emotional integrity than the social norms pervading white society.

As shown by the inclusion of African American writers in earlier chapters about recurrent themes in midwestern literature, white and black midwestern writers find themselves drawn to the same issues. The African American author Willard Motley makes the identification of black and white concerns explicit in his novel *Knock on Any Door* by giving his book a white protagonist, Nick Romano. The book's central plot seems reminiscent of novels by James Farrell and Nelson Algren: a boy from the lower classes sees only a future in petty crime for himself. But in Motley's version of this story, he meets and falls in love with a gentle woman named Emma. Unlike Farrell's and Algren's lost youths, Motley marries her, but finds himself lured away from his commitment to her by gang activity. Emma commits suicide and Nick winds up in jail, where he is executed.

In his introduction to Algren's *Never Come Morning*, Richard Wright also states that race distinguishes people far less than class. Wright explains that Algren's novel "portrays what actually exists in the nerve, brain, and blood of our boys on the street, be they black, white, native or foreign born."[29] In "How Bigger Was Born," Wright describes his own novel, *Native Son*, as a characterization of modern personalities "whose existence ignored racial and national lines of demarcation." Wright sees all of his contemporaries, no matter what race, as products of a world that has lost all sense of higher purpose, where "men could no longer retain their faith in an ultimate hereafter.... It was a world in which millions of men lived and behaved like drunkards, taking a stiff drink of hard life to lift them up for a thrilling moment, to give them a quivering sense of wild exultation and fulfillment that soon faded."[30] As Ian Peddie explains, Wright's comments complement Algren's novel: "Time and time again in *Never Come Morning* Algren draws the reader to questions of ethnic and racial identity in ways that openly reflect the deep influence class issues have on those who share an economic position that is hopeless but who maintain hierarchies based on questions of interethnic distinctions."[31] James G. Kennedy suggests "that the working class character of [*Native Son*] can help white working class people to recognize and relate to class-and-race conscious blacks."[32] And Benjamin Appel describes Lefty, the central character of Algren's *Never Come Morning* as "a sort of Polish-American Bigger Thomas."[33] James Saunders agrees, writing that *Native Son* "tells about the plight of blacks in general and others who compose the lower classes."[34] The novels of Chester Himes, like Jack Conroy's *The Disinherited*, see labor unions as offering some hope to the lower classes. So even African American authors explicitly suggest that they share fundamentally the same concerns about the destructive impact of social norms as whites.

But it seems important to acknowledge that African American writers also offer a distinctive take on these topics. Although both white and black midwestern authors complain of convention's distorting influence, when midwestern African American writers complain about the social structure, they tend to single out white people as perpetrators, even while acknowledging that many kind whites have and do exist. Also, black authors create no characters like Nick Carraway who rest in ambivalence, both attracted and repulsed by the displays of wealth and power. African American writers fully understand the connection between money, power, and slavery which makes aspiring to the American Dream of, at best, ambiguous value. They know that greed makes people cruel. In *A Mercy*, Toni Morrison describes a decent white man opposed to slavery who accepts a slave girl only because she is the only restitution offered him for a debt. But as the novel continues, he becomes infected with greed and puts the construction of a huge house at the center of his life. His attachment persists after death: he haunts it. Jacob Varrk's mad commitment to this project helps demonstrate how "slaves [are] freer than free men" for "it is the withering inside that enslaves."[35] Justine Tally agrees that Vaark's ambitious project destroys him: "Jacob Vaark, tantalized by the grandiose project of his American Dream, a house that used up fifty trees 'without asking their permission' (44) loses his life in the process and provides us with striking imagery of the American Dream gone amuck."[36] Geneva Cobb Moore says that Vaark's return to his house "can be read as a demonic parody of his wandering, soulless atrophy."[37] Cathy Waegner concludes that "Morrison's novel serves as a tough counterpoise to any unreflective patriotism which glorifies the American project while neglecting the ruthless exploitation based on ethnicity, gender, and class."[38] Susan Strehle adds that the novel's disconnected structure "marries theme with form to represent the devastating effects on community of the exceptionalist logic that separates chosen people from their Others."[39]

And despite Richard Wright's proclamation that his book's issues transcend race, *Native Son* deals extensively with the black experience, but like his counterparts in the novels of Farrell and Algren, Bigger Thomas's personality seems largely a reaction to a social structure that shuts him out. If anything, Bigger has more opportunities than do James Farrell's Studs Lonigan or Nelson Algren's Lefty: no one offers them a comfortable existence in a nice home and an elegant car to drive for people who, although white, do their best to treat Bigger kindly. Still, convention carries so much weight with Bigger that interacting with these essentially decent people terrifies him. He struggles to understand and supply what they want from him. He fears them so passionately that Wright entitles Book One, which deals with Bigger's sojourn in the Dalton household, "Fear."

Terror of the white social structure completely controls Bigger's actions. He accidentally kills Mary while trying to keep her quiet so Mrs. Dalton will not discover him in her room. As Ira Wells notes, "That slaying was an automatic response to Bigger's desperation, a desperation that was in turn produced by engrained patterns of structural oppression"[40] He kills his girlfriend, Bessie, because he can neither leave her, since he has told her that he killed Mary, nor can he flee with her. But he persuades himself that these two killings, both precipitated by terror of whites, demonstrate that he has taken control of his life. Some critics seem to agree, among them Lale Demiturk: "He has taken on the role of oppressor in determining and destroying the image-formation of the whites by the dynamics of his own blackness."[41] All of his life, his situation as a black man in a white world has made him angry and now, he reasons, he has finally acted on these feelings. Bigger tells himself a convincing story here, but his craving for acceptance undergirds the anger: "Why should not the cold white world rise up as a beautiful dream in which he could walk and be at home" (241). But his deep sense that this is impossible pushes him back into the rage he embraces because it gives him delusory energy and focus.

That's why Bigger appalls his lawyer, Max, at the end of the novel when he claims that the murders he commits express his fundamental nature: "What I killed for, I *am*! It must've been pretty deep in me to make me kill! I must have felt it awful hard to murder...." (429). In fact, Bigger killed primarily out of a desire to feel comfortable in a world that has shut him out because of his race.

Chester Himes's novel *If He Hollers Let Him Go* goes into much greater detail than *Native Son* about the ways confrontations with white prejudice shape the thinking of its African American protagonist, Bob Jones. At the start of the novel, he declares his determination to rise above racism: "Race was a handicap, sure, I'd reasoned. But hell, I didn't have to marry it."[42] Despite this vow, he thinks constantly about race. But it would require his complete detachment from reality to avoid considering it since whites constantly abuse him. At one point, he vows to kill a white man, even going so far as to follow the man to his home. Bob also goes to the residence of a white woman named Madge who complained about him at work and got him demoted. But unlike Bigger, Bob has the ability to see his behavior as self-destructive: "The whole idea of going to bed with her to get even with Kelly and Mac and the other peckerwoods out at the yard seemed silly now. She wasn't nothing but trouble any way you looked at it, I told myself; and I'd always figured myself too smart to let the white folks catch me out there on their own hunting grounds" (140).

Bob considers his black girlfriend, Alice, the best thing in his life and she urges him to focus on cultivating the aspects of his life whites do not and cannot control, like his relationship with her. She tells him, "All of life is not commercial. The best parts of it are not commercial. Love and marriage, children and homes. Those we control. Our physical beings, our personal integrity, our private property—we have as much protection for these as anyone." Bob knows that Alice's advice makes good sense: "No matter what the white folks did to me, or made me do just in order to live, Alice and I could have a life of our own, inside of all the pressure, away from it, separate from it, that no white person could ever touch" (169). But Madge accuses him of rape, he loses his job and, as the novel ends, a judge allows him to avoid jail if he enlists in the armed services and promises to "'stay away from white women and keep out of trouble'" (203). Bob complies because he has no choice. So at the end of *If He Hollers Let Him Go*, Bob Jones loses everything in his life he cares about and winds up even more profoundly trapped by the white power structure. Robert Bone dislikes the choice Himes has Jones make: "We feel put upon for we have been following Jones' inner conflict as if it mattered. Suddenly it is revealed as meaningless—no matter what Jones decides, society will dispose of his future." Bone has seen this kind of futility before: "The novel is Wrightian to the core."[43]

Chester Himes's *The Lonely Crusade* focuses on a black labor organizer named Lee Gordon who has even more awareness and a better job than Bob Jones. He also suffers milder and more indirect abuse than Bob and reacts to it in a cooler, more controlled way, but racism threatens to ruin his life all the same. Lee's new job thrills him because it offers "vindication of his conviction that a man did not have to accept employment beneath his qualifications because he was black."[44] But his joy quickly fades as he recalls that because of racism, his job will attract mistreatment: "He had once again crossed into the competitive white world where he would be subjected to every abuse concocted in the minds of white people to harass and intimidate Negroes" (4). His wife, Ruth, also knows she will pay for his success. Unable to retaliate against whites for their hostile treatment, he will attack her. She has taken his mistreatment for six years because she understands and accepts her husband's need for it: "She had not minded absorbing his brutality, allowing him to assert his manhood in this queer, perverted way, because all the rest of the world denied it" (7). But she has grown understandably weary of this mistreatment.

His new job does, in fact, expose Lee to a variety of racial obstacles and his wife pays, once again, for his difficulties. But Ruth comes to the depressing understanding that absorbing the pain for her husband serves no purpose. No matter what she does, the white power structure defeats them both: "She could see how she had lost to white values in a white world the man she had married—and how he had lost his wife. There had been nothing she could have done about it" (293).

Lee persistently decides that no matter what the consequences, he has to behave with integrity and while realizing its probable futility, he has to fight for improved working conditions, to "face his duty to the end" (365). As the novel concludes, Lee takes up the union banner from "Joe Ptak, lying there unconscious in the sun, who had done the best he could for the thing in which he most believed" (397) and starts marching, holding it high, while the police level guns at him. Although he may well lose his life, Lee symbolically defeats the white power structure by refusing to resign his integrity. And although his wife does not enjoy his putting himself in danger's way, she admires his choice. Robert Skinner argues that "changing attitudes" call for re-evaluation of these two Himes novels, claiming that they "deserve to be considered in the front rank of the literature of labor."[45]

In *Maud Martha*, Gwendolyn Brooks describes a series of smaller, more mundane racial slights that still rankle. Maud thinks she overhears a white woman trying to sell a product to a black beauty salon operator use the word "Nigger" and sees no reaction. She asks the salon owner about her silence and she replies, "Why make enemies?" In response, "Maud Martha stared steadily into Sonia Johnson's irises. She said nothing. She kept on staring into Sonia Johnson's irises."[46] When Maud wanders into a hat store the white sales woman flatters her while thinking insults to herself like this one: "Oh, not today would she cater to these nigger women who tried on every hat in her shop, who used no telling what concoctions of smelly grease on the heads" (155). Maud points out the woman's spoken dishonesties and leaves without a purchase. Harry B. Shaw sees this episode as an event in Brooks's "psychological war with beauty or with those who are considered beautiful.... Because for Maud white women fall into this category, she uses every opportunity to claim little victories at their expense."[47] Maud Martha arrives at the front door of the home she will clean and is told to use the back door in the future. She mentally reviews her finances and concludes: "I can't find a filing job in a hurry. I'll smile at Mrs. Burns-Cooper and hate her just some" (159). But as Maud leaves, she decides to never come back even though it will bewilder Mrs. Burns-Cooper, who pays her good wages. She tries to think of an excuse and then concludes: "One was a human being" (163).

Because blacks know that whites attempt to play them, they respond in kind. As a result, whites and blacks cannot have open relationships with each other. As Mrs. Teenie Thompson, someone who has cleaned for a woman living on Chicago's elegant north shore for years, explains to Maud Martha: "'These old whi' folks, They jive you, honey. Well, I jive 'em just like they jive me. They can't beat me jivin'. They'll have to jive much, to come anywhere near my mark in jivin'"" (119). But like Bigger, Bob, and Lee, Maud Martha yearns for easy interactions with whites. She and her husband attend a film along with an all-white audience: "When the picture was over, and the lights revealed them for what they were, the Negroes stood up among the furs and the good cloth and faint perfume, looked about them eagerly. They hoped they would meet no cruel eyes. They hoped no one would look intruded upon. They had enjoyed the picture so, they were so happy, they wanted to laugh, to say warmly to the other outgoers, 'Good, huh? Wasn't it swell?' This, of course, they could not do. But if only no one would look intruded upon" (78). Despite Maud Martha's discouragements, Patricia H. Lattin and Wernon E. Lattin see the book as hopeful: "In *Maud Martha* Brooks suggests a positive way of life that can help one maintain one's self respect and creativity in the face of the racism and death which surround one. One can create in spite of the deadening realities of life."[48]

On occasion black writers offer accounts of an African American person adopted by a white, either formally or informally; no matter how well intentioned the white, escape persistently offers the best outcome for the African American. In Langston Hughes's story "The Blues I'm Playing," Mrs. Ellsworth, a white woman, supports a young black woman named Oceola Jones to study classical piano, even sending her to Paris, where Oceola becomes seduced by the blues. She plays them for Mrs. Ellsworth, who responds, "'Is this what I spent thousands of dollars to teach you?'" Oceola replies: "This is mine.... Listen! ... How sad and gay it is. Blue and happy—laughing and crying.... How white like you and black like Me.... How much like a man.... And how like a woman.... Warm as Pete's mouth.... These are the blues ... I'm playing."[49] In other words, playing the blues brings her to life by engaging her in a culture truly hers.

In Langston Hughes's story "Poor Little Black Fellow," the Pembertons adopt Arnie, the child of their maid, Amanda Lee, and her husband, Arnold, both deceased. The Pembertons do their best, sending him to fine schools and taking him to Europe with them. But Arnie feels lonely because the whites he lives among don't truly accept him and their different histories make the blacks he encounters foreign to him, until he travels with the Pembertons to Paris: "Paris and music and cocktails made you forget what color people were—and what color you were yourself. Here it didn't matter—color."[50] Here, he discovers an interracial group among whom he feels comfortable and accepted. Not surprisingly, he chooses to stay in Paris. Hughes also writes a complementary story, "Home," about an African American who becomes an accomplished musician according to Euro-American standards, with fatal results. After receiving a sophisticated musical education, a young man returns to where he grew up to no job and, finally, death at the hands of whites.

In Toni Morrison's *Tar Baby*, Jadine, an African American woman, lives with her aunt and uncle who work for a white man named Valerian Street and his wife, Margaret, whom Ralph Reckley appropriately characterizes as "people who have given up the spiritual for the material."[51] When Street and his wife offer to educate Jadine, her guardians eagerly accept and Jadine becomes an art historian and model totally comfortable traveling through sophisticated circles in Paris and New York. But then she becomes involved with a black fugitive named Son despite her initial revulsion to him; he has similarly ambivalent feelings about her. They have a relationship which both enjoy for a time, but their differences push them apart. Still, Son attempts to reconnect with Jadine as the novel ends. Margaret Street's abuse of her child along with Valerian Street's habit of spending his mornings escaping reality in a greenhouse, listening to Bach, call into question the human value of the cultural opportunities they make available to Jadine. The novel seems to validate the conclusion drawn about the Streets by another servant, this one named Therese: "She thought they felt nothing at all."[52] Critics like Judylyn S. Ryan believe that by embracing white culture, Jadine has acquired a "materialist and self-alienating consciousness which recommends selling one's cultural inheritance and birthright for a mess of pottage."[53] Lothar Bredella agrees that *Tar Baby* "confirms the need for decolonizing the mind."[54] So, in all this fiction, white saviors of blacks inflict harm. However well-intentioned, whites cannot understand or accept black culture, making them dangerous mentors.

Midwestern African American writers suggest that rather than trying to get whites to help them, they prefer to rely on their own considerable resources.

Malin Walther Pereira sees Morrison's first four books, *The Bluest Eye*, *Sula*, *Song of Solomon*, and *Tar Baby*, centering initially on white oppression and then moving into a validation of black culture: "With *Tar Baby*'s explicit identification of colonization as a central issue, Morrison finally breaks free from the need to focus primarily on white ideas." The books that followed, *Beloved* and *Jazz*, concentrated "on black history and [were] written primarily within an African American perspective."[55]

The singing, which in the work of other midwestern authors signals that those at the lower rungs of society survive just fine in spite of their mistreatment, reaches a crescendo in the work of African American writers. In Rita Dove's *Through the Ivory Gate*, one of her characters traces the importance of singing back to Africa, commenting, "'Did you know that some African tribes believe that the mark of a healthy soul is its ability to sing?'" But then she continues to universalize the positive significance of song: "'And the French have a wonderful expression—mechant—which means "wicked" but comes from two other words meaning "no song" and "bad song."'"[56] Langston Hughes creates musical poetry, which sometimes includes musical transcriptions. Hughes acknowledges Carl Sandburg as an important influence, and Sandburg would certainly understand this emphasis on song. But Hughes's writing obviously rests on and expresses African American culture. Margaret A. Reid explains: "Hughes borrowed his language from the Negro folk idiom, his poetic form from the spiritual and blues tradition and his themes from the life and experiences of the common Negro. Using the blues form, Hughes wrote of the social tragedies in ways that would allow the Negro to see himself and laugh to keep from crying."[57]

Like Toni Morrison's *Jazz*, the structure of Clarence Major's novel *Dirty Bird Blues* reflects the musical form in its title, but in Major's novel, unlike Morrison's, this results from the inability of its major character, Manfred Banks, to stop mentally singing the blues—not that its intrusion annoys him. Throughout the book, the blues move through Manfred's mind, cheering both him and his readers despite all his struggles. After his wife's boyfriend shoots him, the blues in his head lift him out of pain as he hurries to the hospital: "Running through the snow, he felt like he's been embalmed, weightless, without pain. Just like singing the blues. Lord have mercy."[58] When he's in the hospital emergency room getting buckshot removed after a three-hour wait, he serenades the woman dressing his wounds. When the nurse compliments him on his singing, he tells her that he tries to make a living with his music and that despite the difficulties, "'ain't nothing gon stop me'" (7). Craig Werner describes the impact of the blues on *Native Son*, saying it "resounds with a painful blues laughter, echoing through a modernist waste land which may or may not respond."[59] William Ferris argues that Richard "Wright understood that blues are intimately associated with alienation and flight, themes that are central to his fiction. The lone bluesman, constantly singing and traveling, is an appropriate metaphor for Wright's life as a writer."[60]

But although the singing comforts black characters, it does not quiet the anxiety African American midwestern writers, like other midwestern writers, feel about the damage the social structure may inflict on their children. Thanks to slavery and racism, cultural norms particularly menace black children; after all, Jim flees slavery to save his children. Toni Morrison's *Beloved* tells the story of a woman who kills her child to spare her daughter the pain she has endured as a slave. Even after slavery ends, the abuse continues. In *A Mercy*, the enslaved girl Florens never recovers from the early separation from her mother. As Jean Wyatt notes, "Without her mother to teach her essential lessons, Florens cannot learn; she can only repeat."[61] Langston Hughes's novel, *Not Without Laughter*, narrated from the point of view of a young black child, makes clear how often racism impacts his life and how furious it makes those attempting to protect him. When a new amusement park opens and children are promised free admission with coupons clipped from the newspaper, the young boy, Sandy Roger, and all the other African American children are refused admittance, despite their coupons. When he returns home, Sister Johnson becomes enraged: "'Dey ain't nary hell hot 'nough to burn ole white folks, 'cause day's devils deyselves,'" but his grandmother takes a more compassionate and condescending stance: "'They's po' trash owns that park what don't know no better, hurtin' chillens' feelin's, but we'll forgive 'em!'"[62] Later, when Sandy hypothesizes that Kansas, where they live, has become as racist as the South, his grandmother comforts him with song and tradition: "And Sandy, as he stood beside his grandmother on the porch, heard a great chorus out of the black past—singing generations of toil-worn Negroes, echoing Hager's voice as it deepened and grew in volume: 'There's a star fo' you an' me, /Stars beyond!'" (143). Eventually, Sandy comes to see black singing, dancing, and laughing as a product of living in a racist world: "Dancers because of their poverty; singers because they suffered; laughing all the time because they must forget.... It's more like that, thought Sandy." Then Sandy comes to understand this response as evidence of spiritual vitality: "Black dancers—captured in a white world.... Dancers of the spirit, too. Each black dreamer a captured dancer of the spirit" (211). Joan Stone points out that, for Hughes, dance generally becomes an expression of psychic wholeness: "Thus Hughes presents dance as moving people closer to earth and stars; as bringing together the truth of the physical and the mental, as protecting and permitting the effort to exorcise, liberate, and to explain; and, therefore, as fundamental to an ethos of wholeness."[63] As the novel closes, Sandy vows to achieve the greatness his grandmother urged him towards, buoyed by African American tradition.

In this literature, African American mothers persistently attempt to protect their children from awareness of racism. In the Hughes story "One Christmas Eve," a mother discourages her son from trying to visit an advertised Santa Claus, but he goes anyway and gets frightened away by Santa shaking a loud rattle and laughing at him. When he reports his experience to his mother, she replies, "'That wasn't no Santa Claus.... If it was, he wouldn't a-treated you like that.... He's just an old white man.'"[64] When Maud Martha takes her child Paulette to see Santa Claus, he ignores her. The mother tries to reassure the child but worries that she has experienced enough to begin to understand racism: "She hoped there hadn't been enough for that. She wasn't up to coping with—.... Keep her that land of blue! Keep her those fairies with witches always killed at the end" (176). Maud Martha prays that her child will avoid the reality of racism as long as possible, or at least until she has a greater capacity to protect herself.

Black children like Pecola in Morrison's *The Bluest Eye* who suffer abuse carry an even greater burden than a white child who suffers the same fate because racist culture inflicts her with a sense of innate inferiority. Even another child, Claudia, recognizes when Pecola comes to stay with them because she has nowhere else to go, that their guest has profound problems: "Being a minority in both caste and class, we moved about anyway on the hem of life, struggling to consolidate our weaknesses and hang on, or to creep singly up into the major folds of the garment. Our peripheral existence, however, was something we had learned to deal with—probably because it was abstract. But the concreteness of being outdoors was another matter."[65] Moreover, Claudia's mother's singing the blues helps Claudia understand and believe in a life beyond suffering. Her song "took all of the grief out of the words and left me with a conviction that pain was not only endurable, it was sweet" (26). Pecola's house offers no such protection to her. Her father terrorizes her with his rages and Pecola comes to believe that if she had blue eyes, he would stop; so she prays for blue eyes every night and eats Mary Janes, with blue-eyed, blonde girls on the wrappers: "To eat the candy is to somehow to eat the eyes, eat Mary Jane, Love Mary Jane, Be Mary Jane" (50). When her father impregnates her, she has no reservoir of self-trust to sustain her. She goes mad: "The damage done was total. She spent her days, her tendril, sap-green days, walking up and down, up and down, her head jerking to the beat of a drummer so distant only she could hear" (204). African American literature also includes testimonials to blacks who love and protect white children mistreated by their own parents. In Langston Hughes's story "Cora Unashamed," Cora protects her white employer's daughter Jessie all her life: "It was always Cora who stood like a calm and sheltering tree for Jessie to run to in her troubles."[66] Cora recognizes that the constant spankings and criticisms wound the child, so she welcomes Jessie in the kitchen, where she blossoms. When Jessie dies as a result of the abortion her parents force on her, Cora shouts out the truth at the girl's funeral, even though she loses her livelihood as a result.

When African American young men go off to war, they endure the same agonies as white soldiers, with the added insult that the culture they fight and die for treats them as inferiors. Toni Morrison's novel *Home* delineates the nature of the change participation in a war produces through its description of Frank Money after his return from the Korean War. Like the soldier in Willa Cather's novel *One of Ours*, he looked forward to the war as an escape from his boring life in Lotus, Georgia: "In Lotus ... there was no goal other than breathing, nothing to win and, save for somebody else's quiet death, nothing to survive or worth surviving for."[67] He and his two best friends can't wait to go to war together, "disbelieving the unbelievable malignance of strangers"

(98). Like the soldiers in Hemingway's *In Our Time*, Frank experiences some exhilaration in battle: "*Battle is scary, yeah, but it's alive. Orders, gut-quickening, covering buddies, killing—clear, no deep thinking needed*" (93). But only Frank survives this experience. He witnesses his friends' deaths; as a result, for months "only alcohol dispersed his best friends, the hovering dead he could no longer hear, talk to, or laugh with" (99). Like Harold Krebs, after he leaves the army, he sits around listlessly, frightening his girlfriend, Lily. And his murder of a Korean girl persistently haunts him. After getting himself into and out of trouble repeatedly, he returns home determined to save his sister Cee, to make up for failing to save the friends who went to war with him. And like Nick Adams in "The Big Two-Hearted River," he finds peace in a place connected with his childhood: "Waving occasionally at passing neighbors or those doing chores on their porches, he could not believe how much he had once hated this place. Now it seemed both fresh and ancient, safe and demanding" (132).

While at home, Frank recalls when he and his sister as children witnessed the hasty disposal of a black man's body. He learns that men had forced a child to kill his father, or die himself. His father urged his child to kill him so that the child could live. Frank and his sister Cee return to the grave and give the man, yet another black parent attempting to protect his child from social realities as long as possible, a real burial under a tree where Frank nails a board painted with the words "Here Stands a Man." And like Hemingway's story "The Big Two-Hearted River" from *In Our Time*, the novel concludes with the suggestion that returning to the past will heal Frank. Nature also plays an important role in this restitution in both works. After he marks the man's grave with a sign acknowledging his courage, Frank thinks the tree under which he buries the man approves: "He could have sworn the sweet bay was pleased to agree. Its olive-green leaves went wild in the glow of the fat cherry-red sun" (145).

Just as hostile social codes have made life more difficult for black children and young men than for white youth, Toni Morrison argues that they have also created a fundamental difference between black women and white women. Because African Americans traditionally get paid less than whites, black men frequently could not support their wives forcing them to work themselves. Since black women have often worked while white women stayed home, the feeling that men interfere with their freedom to, say, develop a career, strikes them as foreign: "In a way black women have known something of the freedom white women are now beginning to crave. But oddly, freedom is only sweet when it is won. When it is forced, it is called responsibility. The black woman's needs shrank to the level of her responsibility; her man's expanded in proportion to the obstacles that prevented him from assuming his. White women, on the other hand, have had too little responsibility, white men too much. It's a wonder the sexes of either race even speak to each other."[68]

In Toni Morrison's novel *Song of Solomon*, First Corinthians Dead received a white woman's elite education at Bryn Mawr College, but cannot find a black mate because she lacks the grit African American men know their wives will need to get ahead in an inhospitable world: "These men wanted wives who could manage, who were not so well accustomed to middle-class life that they had no ambition, no hunger, no hustle in them. They wanted their wives to like the climbing, the acquiring, and the work it took to maintain status once it was achieved. They wanted wives who would sacrifice themselves and appreciate the hard work and sacrifice of their husbands. Corinthians was a little too elegant."[69] Morrison cites Ida Lewis's comment: "The Women's Liberation Movement is basically a family quarrel between white women and white men.... The role of black women is to continue the struggle in concert with black men for the liberation and self-determination of blacks."[70] As Morrison explains in an interview with Claudia Tate, "Black women seem able to combine the nest and the adventure. They don't see conflicts in certain areas as do white women."[71] On the other hand, D.H. Milhem sees in Brooks's Maud Martha "the pre-women's liberation either-or choice between domestic duties and self-fulfillment.... Maud has learned to adapt, while maintaining ego-strength that permits change and preserves dreams."[72]

Black women authors and their black female characters complain less about men than white women, even when they misbehave. In *Jazz*, Violet stays with her husband after he has an affair and kills his lover. This reinforces Dorothy Randall Tsuruta's claim that "a self-sustaining legacy position Black women to 'bring noble understanding' ... to the shortcomings of others who figure importantly in their lives."[73] It also explains the apparently bottomless patience of Lee Gordon's wife, Ruth, in Chester Himes's *Lonely Crusade*. As much as Lee's treatment of her injures her, she understands its dynamic too completely to protect herself rather than him. And she finally does not regret this choice. When she sees him after he has betrayed her with a white woman, "they crossed the River Jordan into togetherness again.... And they were safe again; they were in each other's arms, and her heart was singing thanks" (351).

While white men squeezed by the social structure in the novels of Farrell and Algren fantasize about relationships with women that they never achieve, in the fiction of Morrison, Motley, and Himes, all the protagonists not only have solid relationships with real women, they understand that this bond has greater value than anything else in their lives.

Many critics comment on the negative characterization of women in Richard Wright's *Native Son*, among them Farah Griffin, who complains, "Just as Bigger sacrifices the lives of Mary and Bessie for his fear and freedom, so does Wright. Neither woman is given the complexity or depth of Bigger; they exist only to demonstrate Bigger's aspirations and inhibitions."[74] But it seems inappropriate to infer Wright's view of women from Bigger's behavior: Wright does not present Bigger as a model of mental health. As Masaya Takeuchi notes, "*Native Son* recounts how the assertive, masculine side of Bigger is constructed in opposition to his family's plight and to the white racism that oppresses them all."[75] Kimberly S. Drake blames Wright's portraits of women on his "obsessive interest with false rape charges which serve in his mind as the predominant symbol of black male existence in America."[76] Amanda Putnam believes that much the same dynamic explains the violent women in Toni Morrison's work: "Violence itself can become an act of rebellion, a form of resistance to oppressive power."[77] Some critics are ambivalent about Wright's characterization of black women. Butler Brewton claims, "Wright is saying that the black woman cannot offer aspiration and courage or life of the human spirit to the black boys or to the black community."[78] But Kathleen Ochshorn sees a positive dimension to *Native Son*'s characterization of black women: "The black women in particular do represent a community."[79]

And kinder men appear in the literature of African American women than in writings by white women, wherein men frequently put women down. In Toni Morrison's *Beloved*, for instance, black men not only show amazing compassion for women, they help these women become their best selves. Baby Suggs achieves freedom only through the efforts of her son, Halle. She thinks it will matter little to her, but when she actually becomes free, she finds the experience completely transformative, as her son presumably had the sensitivity and thoughtfulness to understand:

> What does a sixty-odd-year-old slavewoman who walks like a three-legged dog need freedom for? And when she stepped foot on free ground she could not believe that Halle knew what she didn't; that Halle, who had never drawn one free breath, knew that there was nothing like it in this world. It scared her.... Suddenly she saw her hands and thought with a clarity as simple as it was dazzling, "These hands belong to me. These are my hands." Next she felt a knocking in her chest and discovered something else new: her own heartbeat.[80]

Full of self-hate for killing her child, even though she did it to spare her daughter a life in servitude like her own, Sethe finds herself validated by Paul D as the book ends. She cannot believe it:

> "Sethe," he says, "me and you, we got more yesterday than anybody. We need some kind of tomorrow."
>
> He leans over and takes her hand. With the other he touches her face. "You your best thing, Sethe. You are." His holding fingers are holding hers.
>
> "Me? Me?" [273].

In Thylias Moss's memoir *Tale of a Sky-Blue Dress*, her husband literally saves her from self-doubt: "I believed that I could, from then on, face my challenges without completely surrendering, for if I fell, I would fall into Wesley's arms."[81]

In *Home*, Frank Money saves himself by rescuing his sick sister. She knows that he cares about her, but she must learn to live independently: "Frank alone valued her. While his devotion shielded her, it did not strengthen her. Should it have? Why was that his job and not her own?" (129). And, indeed, during her recovery she becomes so strong that she no longer needs him to take care of her, but nonetheless wants to be with him: "Meantime her brother was there with her, which was very comforting, but she didn't need him as she had before. He had literally saved her life, but she neither missed nor wanted his fingers at the nape of her neck telling her not to cry, that everything would be all right" (131). And although the protagonists of *Knock on Any Door*, *If He Hollers Let Him Go*, and *Lonely Crusade* have difficulty showing it through their behavior, they all understand that despite their inability to do so, nurturing their relationships with the good women who share their lives would be the most valuable activity they could pursue.

Given this generally positive view of heterosexual relationships, it makes sense that black women writers not only own sexual experiences, they celebrate them. Thylias Moss reports that to her, sex has a kind of divinity: "Sex first was pernicious, but sex also was a gateway to numinous rapture with a man; when we make love, we form a chrysalis where we transform our feelings, our commitment, our love, our energy, reaching the more we can't hold on to, but we reach it again and again; we always return to the numinous and want to return; it is worth the work to enter that place of such concentration and transcendence that we forget where we are, time, our separate identities" (254–55). Toni Morrison actively aspires to produce convincing sexual descriptions that will encourage readers to acknowledge the importance of sex in their lives: "To describe sexual scenes in such a way that they are not clinical, not even explicit—so that the reader brings his own sexuality to the scene and thereby participates in it in a very personal way. And owns it."[82]

Just as black women authors generally characterize men and their relationships with them respectfully, sometimes even reverently, male authors often return this admiration. Clarence Major seems to know from the start of his career that women have something important to teach him. In his first novel, *All-Night Visitors*, his protagonist, Eli Bolton, initially has a meaningless sexual relationship with a woman named Cathy. The novel suggests that Eli's inability to truly care about others derives from his brutal youth in an orphanage and from his service in the Vietnam War. Still, he manages to establish a more substantive connection with Eunice because they both care about art. By the end of the novel, he has acquired enough empathy to take in a Puerto Rican woman and her children. Afterwards, his elation sends him into the street where he stands admiring his surroundings until dawn.

Major's next three novels have male protagonists who struggle with identity issues, but after writing them, Major told Alan Katz that since his sense of himself seemed firm, at last, he was beginning to lose himself in the perspectives of characters who differed from himself: "I think I'm in transition.... The complexity of my early poetry and fiction is a result of my own struggle mentally."[83] Still, one of these works, *Emergency Exit*, makes clear his reverence for women with its testimony to women's mythic power.

But just as he predicted to Katz, his next two novels, *Such Was the Season* and *Painted Turtle: Woman with Guitar*, focus on female characters. Major has said that Annie Eliza's voice in *Such Was the Season* came naturally to him because he "grew up in a house full of women." His mother and his aunt resemble Annie Eliza, so in the process of producing the book, he "discovered how well" he knew his mother: "She came out as a convincing character because of that inarticulate experience."[84] Both books validate relationships. Annie Eliza in *Such Was the Season*, although naïve about a number of subjects, not only understands and cares intensely about them, she manifests a deep decency herself. In *Painted Turtle*, Baldy and Painted Turtle have spent their lives as outsiders, but they have established an honest and loving bond with each other. So Major not only loses himself in the perspective of women when he writes these books, his subject shifts from how a man finds his way in the world to how people can connect with each other constructively.

Then Major completely inhabits his mother's point of view in *Come by Here*: he writes her autobiography in her own voice, relying heavily on their taped talks. Although his mother comes across as caring, she also has incredible strength: raised as the unacknowledged daughter of a white man in the small town where she grew up, she found the courage to marry and move to Atlanta, leave her husband when he turned abusive, move to Chicago and make enough money to bring and raise her children there, and eventually start her own dry-cleaning business. She told Clarence he could do anything and he believed her: as a boy, he aspired to become another Leonardo Di Vinci. Major's willingness to tackle poetry as well as fiction writing, nonfiction writing, painting, dictionary making, and anthologizing makes sense after reading about his formidable mother.

Major's most recent novel, *One Flesh*, expands on the issues he considered in earlier work: the male protagonist, John Canoe, worries that marriage will inhibit his individuality; instead, he discovers it nurtures it. And John feels connection not just with his wife, Susie Chang, but with all people, even someone who insults them on the street; John pities the man because he sees his cruelty as a confession of pain.

African American midwestern writers turn to the same issues as their white and native counterparts and, in many respects, take much the same positions on them. But their history of enduring cruelty inflicted by a racist (primarily white) culture gives them a much sharper sense of conformity's dangers than whites possess. They do not bother even to consider pursuing wealth, which they link to slavery and cruelty. They consider their children enormously valuable and try to protect them from damaging interactions with racism. These authors, like white writers, validate the strength and wisdom of women. But the criticism of male oppression that appears in the work of white midwestern women writers seems mostly absent in this work perhaps because African American writers see men and women facing and dealing with the same problem: the delusional judgments of a bigoted society. The shared dilemma of African American women and men seems to make them more interested in caring for each other than in blaming each other.

Five

Surrendering to Nature

Like the New Englanders who wrote before him, Mark Twain and the midwestern writers who follow him portray nature as a place to escape social pressures; as Huck puts it: "I was powerful glad to get away from the feuds, and so was Jim to get away from the swamp. We said there wasn't no home like a raft, after all. Other places do seem so cramped up and smothery, but a raft don't. You feel mighty free and easy and comfortable on a raft."[1] But other than the avoidance of normal social interaction, Huck and Jim's experiences in nature have little in common with Thoreau's. Thoreau goes to the woods to realize his spiritual side; Jim and Huck have no larger agenda than escape. Thoreau wanted to enjoy nature without any human interference; Huck and Jim find deep solace in each other's company and become frantic when separated. And while Thoreau realizes his individuality at Walden, Jim and Huck intensify their connection to each other. Thoreau's *Walden* sets out general conclusions about how people should live, which his time in nature taught him; nature touches Jim and Huck so deeply that it renders them speechless: "It was kind of solemn, drifting down the big still river, laying on our backs looking up at the stars, and we didn't even feel like talking loud" (94). Finally, while Thoreau busily draws human analogies to the activities of nature and issues human truths based on his experiences, seeing, for instance, human warfare reflected in ant activity, Huck and Jim find themselves imitating the river: "We would watch the lonesomeness of the river, and kind of lazy along, and by-and-by lazy off to sleep.... So we would put in the day, lazying around, listening to the stillness" (158). Any suggestion that Huck and Jim's thinking resembles Thoreau's would appall the man who concluded: "Why level downward to our dullest perception always, and praise that as common sense? The commonest sense is the sense of men asleep, which they express by snoring."[2]

In his book *The Midwestern Pastoral*, William Barillas suggests a link between New England writers like Thoreau and Emerson and midwestern authors when he discusses Willa Cather, Aldo Leopold, Theodore Roethke, James Wright, and Jim Harrison as pastoral writers who convey a "Romantic spirit," intuit "a spiritual essence within nature" and "emphasize imagination and the individual's need for direct contact with wild nature." Certainly this transcendental strain exists in many midwestern writers, including those Barillas discusses. But, as in *Huckleberry Finn*, another, more realistic stance towards nature also emerges in midwestern literature. Barillas offers a telling distinction when he writes, "Contemporary pastoralists like Sanders and Harrison are philosophical idealists, intuiting a spiritual essence within nature, which the regionalists often portray as indifferent or even antagonistic to human concerns."[3] As Barillas points out, a regional attitude coexists with the romantic strain he identifies in midwestern nature writing. And in his book *The Environmental Imagination*, Lawrence Buell suggests that the stance Barillas describes as "regional" may be more progressive and less problematic than the pastoral attitude. After all, Barillas essentially considers the authors he discusses descendants of Thoreau and Emerson rather than innovators. And, as Lawrence Buell explains: "Thoreau's canonicity has, in a way, exercised a restricting influence, reinforcing for example the notion of andocentric pastoral escape as the great tradition within American literary naturalism."[4] Buell believes pastoralism, although flawed, can play an important transitional role in a healthier attitude towards the environment: "Even if, as is clear, pastoralism interposes some major stumbling blocks in the way of developing a mature environmental aesthetic, it cannot but play a major role in that endeavor" (32). And the general difference between the rendering of nature in the literature of New England versus that in the Midwest suggests movement towards this healthier attitude along with the lingering pastoralism Barillas discusses. While the New Englanders look for themselves in nature, some midwestern writers find nature strikingly different from themselves. Like Huck and Jim, they see nature as a mentor that can never be fully understood or even rendered in language. So they observe it intensely, and when things go well, lose themselves in nature too completely to contemplate moralizing about the event. Buell sees this movement as natural and constructive: "As this ecocentric repossession of pastoral has gathered force, its center of energy has begun to shift from representation of nature as a theatre for human events to representation in the sense of advocacy of nature as a presence for its own sake" (52).

Buell further explains that the kind of natural sublimity central to the pastoralism Barillas analyzes has come to be seen as "an arm of American manifest destiny" and thus associated with white males. Since four of the five authors Barillas considers are white males, and all five authors are white, his work does not seem to challenge this judgment. Buell concludes: "Hence the theory of American idealization of nature and wilderness has acted as a kind of moral tonic or social conscience has come to seem increasingly suspect" (35). Indeed, Buell believes this old-fashioned view of nature comes linked to the traditional dismissal of precisely those social groups midwestern authors have repeatedly identified as particularly powerful sources of the vitality American society needs: "The natural environment as empirical reality has been made to subserve human interests, and one of these interests has been to make it serve as a symbolic reinforcement of the subservience of disempowered groups: nonwhites, women, and children" (21). Thus, ability of midwestern authors to see nature not as a reflection of themselves but also as other as well as a refuge from convention, presumably finds its root in the same tolerance that allows them to acknowledge the positive cultural value of children, women, and African Americans.

Midwestern fiction primarily addresses social issues, so the discussion of nature does not play a central role. For instance, no one who has read it would describe *Huckleberry Finn* as primarily a novel about nature. So the midwestern shift in nature's representation easily escapes notice since it stands in the background of most midwestern work. But a reader watching for the renditions of nature in this fiction will see certain patterns that reflect ideas set out most clearly in the nonfiction of midwestern nature writers Aldo Leopold and John Muir.

First, both Leopold and Muir see nature not as a reflection of themselves but as something beyond their comprehension. In the opening entry of *A Sand County Almanac*, Aldo Leopold follows a skunk trail: "I follow curious to deduce his state of mind and appetite, and destination, if any." Making guesses along the way, Leopold follows the skunk to some driftwood, where he hears the sound of water. Then he gives up: "I turn homeward, still wondering."[5] Throughout his book, Leopold poses many such questions about nature; often they remain unanswered. Similarly, John Muir tells of asking an "eminent ornithologist" what jays did with their eggs while their nests were being built. "He didn't know; neither do I to this day. A specimen of the many puzzling problems presented to the naturalist."[6]

Because Leopold and Muir admit that they can never understand nature, they often simply observe it, carefully, drawing few conclusions. When Thoreau watches nature closely, as he does when the water coaxes the sand to form leaf shapes in the spring, he cannot resist imposing large human meanings on the activities he records. He writes this about the sand leaves: "I am affected as if in a peculiar sense I stood in the laboratory of the Artist who made the world and me,—had come to where he was still at work, sporting on this bank, and with excess of energy strewing his fresh designs about" (247). Compare this to Aldo Leopold's entering into the carp's point of view during his spring encounter with water: "The enthusiasm of carp is obvious and unmistakable. No sooner has the rising flood wetted the grass roots than here they come, rooting and wallowing with the prodigious zest of pigs turned out to pasture, flashing red tails and yellow bellies, cruising the wagon tracks and cow-paths, and shaking the reeds and bushes in their haste to explore what to them is an expanding universe" (26). Sherman Paul explains the central difference between Thoreau and Leopold: "Thoreau went to the woods to find *himself* in relation to nature, to the end of self-culture, soul-making. More than a century later, Leopold went to the farm as a trained scientist in order to recover a relationship to the land and further its health."[7] John Tallmadge sees a similar distinction between Muir and Emerson; he notes that although Muir "embraced Emerson's desire to make the study of natural history a tool of religion ... his attention was always directed outward, toward the creatures and things of this world."[8] Because of Leopold's respectful stance towards nature, Tim B. Rodgers argues that his work, like much of midwestern fiction, offers an important corrective to our culture's individualism: "We begin to see an alternative view of the individual which does not automatically imply a self-contained, separated entity, but rather one that is fully enmeshed in the natural world in which it lives."[9]

Muir and Leopold suggest nature not only differs from human nature, it is superior to it. Humanizing nature as Thoreau does may demean it since nature outpaces human abilities in multiple ways. They often note that natural creatures outsmart people. John Muir admires clever nighthawks who, when a nest is discovered, pretend injury to lure the human away from the eggs and then circle back once the intruding person has been led off track. Aldo Leopold wishes human beings could function together as smoothly, productively, and beautifully as geese: "By this international commerce of geese, the waste corn of Illinois is carried through the clouds of the Arctic tundras, there to combine with the waste sunlight of a nightless June to grow goslings for all the lands between. And in this annual barter for food for light, and winter warmth for summer solitude, the whole continent receives as net profit a wild poem dropped from the murky skies upon the muds of March" (25). As a result, Leopold cheerfully identifies himself with nature rather than with people. He comments that most hunters fail to realize that woodcocks and partridges hide under briars and, as a result, wear "themselves out in briarless scrub, and, returning home birdless, leave the rest of us in peace." Then Leopold quickly identifies "us": "the birds, the stream, the dog, and myself." He even sees the stream as a role model that has much the same impact on him as the Mississippi has on Jim and Huck: "The stream is a lazy one; he winds through the alders as if he would rather stay here than reach the river. So would I" (67).

And because Muir and Leopold respect nature so thoroughly, the way human beings abuse it, upsets them profoundly. It disgusts John Muir that humans so casually destroy these amazing creatures: "None of our fellow mortals is safe who eats what we eat, who in any way interferes with our pleasures, or who may be used for work or food, clothing or ornament, or mere cruel, sportish amusement" (144). They see the natural order suffering as a result of the same greedy arrogance that contaminates human society. Aldo Leopold explains that human beings should begin to cure the damage done by their egotism and cultivate humility: "Ability to see the cultural value of wilderness boils down, in the last analysis, to a question of intellectual humility" (279). The harm done by the thoughtless recreational use of the wilderness has only one solution: "building receptivity into the still unlovely human mind" (295). Certainly most midwestern fiction validates Leopold's view that modesty and decency serve humanity's ends far more effectively than arrogant appropriation.

And just as midwestern novelists lament their contemporaries' determination to use rather than respect one another, the attitude towards nature that Leopole and Muir most treasure is one of admiration and love: John Muir enjoys such a moment when he and his brother first see the Wisconsin wilderness they will soon call home:

> This sudden plash into pure wildness—baptism in Nature's warm heart—how utterly happy it made us! Nature streaming into us, wooing teaching her wonderful glowing lessons, so unlike the dismal grammar ashes and cinders so long thrashed into us. Here without knowing it we still were at school; every wild lesson a love lesson! [34].

Because Muir and Leopold value connection rather than transcendence, they do not share Thoreau's contempt for practical interactions with nature, such as farming, or Thoreau's adulation of wild rather than domesticated nature. Muir argues that farm life gives people the advantage of establishing enduring relationships with creatures which allow them to understand just how many traits they share with animals, the most notable of these being affection: "Thus godlike sympathy grows and thrives and spreads far beyond the teachings of churches and schools, where too often the mean, blinding, loveless doctrine is taught that animals have neither mind nor soul, have no rights that we are bound to respect, and were made only for man, to be petted, spoiled, slaughtered, or enslaved" (56). Leopold and Muir also both love their dogs with unadulterated passion. Aldo Leopold aspires to become as wise as his hunting dog, who "persists in tutoring me, with the calm patience of a professor of logic" (67). John Muir's dog not only has more facility at interpreting smells than he, it "was a good judge of character, always knew what was going on and what we were about to do, and liked to help us" (42–43). Muir also has high moral praise for the first horse he owned as a child: "He was the stoutest, gentlest, bravest little horse I ever saw" (53). Although he also admires his family-owned horse named Nob: "She was the most faithful, intelligent, playful, affectionate, human-like horse I ever knew, and she won all our hearts" (56).

The attitudes Muir and Leopold define quietly shape most of the renditions of nature that appear in midwestern writing. But some characters in this fiction do not enjoy the revitalizing connection with nature that Muir and Leopold celebrate and find themselves too shaped by social norms to enjoy even a momentary escape from convention into nature. Bigger Thomas, in *Native Son*, for instance, does not enjoy the snow which he sees only as a symbol of the white power structure that robs him of the ability to even formulate his own thoughts. The snow, therefore, strikes Bigger simply as cold: "It was too stark, not redeemed, not made real with the reality that was the warm blood of life." He has a sense that if he could have followed a different path through life, the snow could help him experience a feeling of peace: "He felt that there was something missing, some road which, if he had once found it, would have led him to a sure and quiet knowledge."[10] Instead, it serves as the frigid environment for his capture by the whites: "They let go of his feet; he was in the snow, lying flat on his back. Round him surged a sea of noise. He opened his eyes a little and saw an array of faces, white and looming." Rather than providing solace, Bigger Thomas's nature, like the white power structure, engulfs him: "Two men stretched his arms out; as though about to crucify him; they placed a foot on each of his wrists, making them sink deep down in the snow. His eyes closed, slowly, and he was swallowed in darkness" (270).

Bob Jones, the protagonist of Chester Himes's *If He Hollers Let Him Go*. realizes that his obsession with the racism that haunts his life puts the beauty of nature out of reach for him: "It was a bright June morning. The sun was already high. If I'd been a white boy I might have enjoyed the scramble in the early morning sun, the tight competition for a twenty-foot lead on a thirty-mile highway. But to me it was racial.... The sharp, pungent smell of exhaust that used to send me driving clear across Ohio on a sunny summer morning, and the snow-capped mountains in the background, like picture post-cards, didn't mean a thing to me. I didn't even see them; all I wanted in the world was to push my Buick Roadmaster over some peckerwood's face."[11] While Bob's black colleagues object to Wright's characterization of Bigger Thomas in *Native Son*, claiming, "'It just proved what the white Southerner has always said about us,'" Jones argues, "'You couldn't pick a better person than Bigger Thomas to prove the point'" (88). That the burden of racism makes it impossible for the protagonists of *Native Son* and *If He Hollers Let Him Go* to savor nature helps explain Lawrence Buell's observation that "African American interest to date in environmentalist causes" is "tepid" (17). But Buell also sees this situation improving along with the situations of African Americans.

The white characters in Nelson Algren's *Man with the Golden* Arm also live in a world of bars and neon, completely unrelieved by nature of any kind: "There was only a long line of faces that had passed straight from the noseless embryo into the running nose of senility. And had seen no birch tree at all."[12] James Farrell's Studs Lonigan also finds his life determined by social forces beyond his control, but he experiences brief but important moments of respite in nature. When he first feels love, he sits in a tree in a park with Lucy. He later discovers that floating in Lake Michigan liberates him. Just as Muir and Leopold would recommend, Studs does not try to understand nature; he just rests in it, becoming part of it as best he can: "He just floated and didn't have anything to think about. He looked up at the drifting clouds. He felt like a cloud that didn't have any bothers and just sailed across the sky." And after becoming like a cloud and letting go of social judgments, Studs discovers that for the moment he accepts himself: "He floated, and suddenly he liked himself a lot. Sometimes he was ashamed of his body.... Now he liked his body, and wasn't at all ashamed of it." He dives under the water and feels as though he has entered a dream world: "He felt far away from all the world now, and he didn't care. He came up, choking for air, and it was like coming out of a goofy dream." And when he lies on the beach afterwards, he feels uncharacteristically at peace as the social norms that usually shape his life melt away. Like Huck and Jim, he finds that his experience rests beyond articulation: "It was too good to talk.... He just lay there and pretended that he wasn't Studs or anybody at all, and he let his thoughts take care of themselves. He was far away from himself, and the slap of the waves on the shore, the splash of people in the water, and all the noise and shouts of the beach were not in the same world with him."[13] Edgar Branch argues that "Farrell uses water imagery to reveal the inner Studs: not the 'iron man,' but the unique, unknown individual in need of love. Fluidity is constantly associated with Studs's deepest feelings and desires, with his ideal moments and dreams, and with important maturing experiences." After noting that another critic associates water with death, Branch continues: "If he gave in to his feelings death indeed would be the fate of Studs Lonigan, the tough guy; but to Studs the man of feeling, death subconsciously appeals as a release from his hell on earth."[14] But these moments of natural freedom occur rarely in Studs's life and he soon finds himself once more overwhelmed by social codes.

From the opening of *A World I Never Made*, Danny O'Neill, who flourishes in the same urban environment that traps Studs, finds himself powerfully attracted by the park across the street from the house where he lives. As Robert Butler notes, although Danny can manipulate the environment, Studs usually falls victim to it, and Bigger always does: "Farrell's experience, therefore, led him to portray Chicago's South Side as an ethnic neighborhood that contained two basic alternatives for his central characters. Although it becomes a trap for Studs Lonigan, whose limited consciousness never allows him to grasp the options available to him, it also helps to liberate Danny O'Neill.... Wright, in order to portray the more extreme and stark world his central character is forced to confront, described Chicago's South Side in Gothic terms as a racial ghetto that became for him a terrifying revelation of a racist society intent on destroying blacks systematically depriving them of adequate 'warmth' and 'light.'"[15] And, as Butler points out, the characterization of nature in all these works plays a subtle but important role in the distinctions between these three characters' shaping by urban forces. The resignation to nature that brings persistent peace to Danny, and brief relief to Studs, totally evades Bigger, who can see the world only in terms of oppressive social codes.

Thanks, in part, to its execution of Dan Burnham's plan, Chicago has given nature a central place, making its lake shore a centerpiece and attempting to protect and even extend park land since its founding in the nineteenth century, but nature plays an even larger role in the rest of the middle west, where large numbers of the immigrants who settled it built farms. Early settlers would probably find Leopold's and Muir's enthusiasm for resigning themselves to nature somewhat bewildering since most of them, like the denizens of Hamlin Garland's fiction, found themselves struggling to survive by taming it, but they would completely concur with the view that nature has a power and complexity far beyond human comprehension, an insight presumably less available to an inhabitant of the well-settled village of Concord, Massachusetts, than to a pioneer attempting to cut out a life on the plains. Just as Huck marvels at the Mississippi's size, a number of midwesterners agree that nature's enormity puts it beyond human influence. In Willa Cather's *My Antonia*, the grass threatens to overrun everything, just as the wind threatens to blast away all the inhabitants and their homes in *O Pioneers!*: "The little town of Hanover, anchored on a windy Nebraska tableland, was trying not to be blown away."[16] Although now largely settled, nature survives in most sections of the Midwest, and midwesterners continue to see it as free of man-made orders. In Jonathan Franzen's *The Corrections*, when Chip arrives at his Missouri home after sojourns in New York City and in Vilnius, the environment easily draws him into something larger than himself: "The light in the wood-framed windows, though gray, had a prairie optimism.... And the posture of the older oak trees reaching towards this sky had a jut, a wildness and entitlement, predating permanent settlement, memoirs of an unfenced world were written in the cursive of their branches. Chip apprehended it all in a heartbeat. The continent, his homeland."[17]

Indeed, how would human beings know nature? Our systems of measures do not coordinate with it, as Lulu Lamartine explains in Louise Erdrich's *Love Medicine*: "All through my life I never did believe in human measurement. Numbers, time, inches, feet. All are just ploys for cutting nature down to size. I know the grand scheme of the world is beyond our brains to fathom, so I don't try, just let it in."[18] In Louise Erdrich's *The Painted Drum*, the narrator asserts that all natural activity remains finally mysterious to people: "There is nothing human in the least about it and its source is unknowable, as are the hearts of all things wild."[19]

But the incomprehensibility of nature does not mean that people cannot benefit from submitting to it. In Saul Bellow's *Henderson the Rain King*, Henderson finds salvation in imitating a lion. Louise Erdrich aspires to function as successfully as spiders: "I watch each spider closely, admire its curved and tapered legs. They are black with hot yellow death's heads on their bellies. They are patient with the gravity of their intent. Of their means of survival they've made these elegant webs, their beauty a by-product of their purpose.

Which causes me to wonder, my own purpose on so many days as humble as the spider's, what is beautiful that I make? What is elegant? What feeds the world?"[20]

While Thoreau and Emerson believe nature and humans participate in the same ethical universe, some midwestern writers admire the superior morals of creatures. Santiago, in Ernest Hemingway's *The Old Man and the Sea*, considers human beings smarter than fish, which "are more noble and more able."[21] Leo Gurko explains engaging the fish helps Santiago become a more honorable human being: "To be true to oneself makes a return to the lost world of Nature categorically imperative. And that lost world, as *The Old Man and the Sea* reveals, has its own responsibilities, disciplines, moralities, and all-embracing meaning quite the equivalent of anything present in society and of much greater value because it makes possible a total response to the demands of the self."[22]

The narrator of Sherwood Anderson's story "The Man Who Became a Woman" contrasts animals' easy acceptance of their achievements with human egotism: "Let's say Pick-it-boy had won his race that day.... Well, he was neither proud, like I would have been in his place, or mean in one part of the inside of him either. He was just himself, doing something with a kind of simplicity."[23] Human arrogance, unlike nature's modest efficiency, does great damage, generating a world full of the industrial odors Charles Baxter notes in *The Feast of Love*: "There was a smell in the air of slightly rancid cooking oil mixed with the odor emanating from the paper plant near the river, an odor of cardboard and vanilla, a numbing upsurge of profitmaking industrial aerosols."[24] Charles Baxter's entire novel *Shadow Play* focuses on human damage to the environment as does Jonathan Franzen's novel *Strong Motion*. In Toni Morrison's *Tar Baby*, Son sees the whole process of making candy from sugar, which has made Valerian a rich man as an example of the waste of natural and human resources produced by modern greed:

> That was the sole lesson of their world: how to make waste, how to make machines that made more waste, how to make wasteful products, how to talk waste, how to study waste, how to design waste, how to cure people who were sickened by waste so that they could be well enough to endure it, how to mobilize waste, legalize waste and how to despise the culture that lived in cloth houses and shit on the ground far away from where they ate. And it would drown them one day, they would all sink into their own waste and the waste they had made of the world and then, finally they would know true peace and the happiness they had been looking for all along.[25]

Barbara Christian sees nature's destruction as a persistent theme in Morrison's work: "There is an admonition in these fables, which inevitably leads us back to the inherent desire for growth in each human being, an admonition that this desire will manifest itself either in natural terms or in derangement. And because Nature is a part of each human being, it is too complex to be categorized or wiped away. Thus society's perennial attempts to ignore the relationship between human beings and Nature result in waste, pain, and often death."[26]

And midwestern authors echo Muir in arguing that learning to respect nature can teach us how to love. Jonathan Franzen suggests that through caring about nature, we learn to care for one another, just as he did when he became interested in birds: "My love of birds became a portal to an important, less self-centered part of myself that I'd never even known existed."[27] In *O Pioneers!* it takes time for Alexandra to sort out her relationships with people, but her affection for the land is instant and entire: "The chirping of the insects down in the long grass had been like the sweetest music. She had felt as if her heart were hiding down there, somewhere, with the quail and the plover and all the little wild things that crooned or buzzed in the sun."[28] This empathy lays the groundwork for her compassionate treatment of others. In Toni Morrison's *Song of Solomon*, spending time in the woods transforms Milkman Dead from a narcissist to a loving person. When he finds himself alone in the forest, Milkman comes to understand that he has behaved arrogantly. His new humility allows him to enter a universe where the separation between man and nature vanishes: "Language in the time when men and animals did talk to one another, when a man could sit down with an ape and the two converse; when a tiger and man could share the same tree, and each understood the other; when men ran *with* wolves, not from or after them." In the woods, the self-centered Milkman not only comes to understand and regret how selfishly he has behaved with others, he also cares intensely for other people, even for the strangers with whom he hunts: "He felt a sudden rush of affection for them all."[29]

While Thoreau yearns for the wilderness and has a contempt for farmers, many midwestern authors, like Muir and Leopold, have an intense attachment to domesticated elements of nature. For instance, Antonia in Willa Cather's *My Antonia* loves the trees she planted: "'I love them as if they were people,' she said, rubbing her hand over the bark. There wasn't a tree here when we first came. We planted every one, and used to carry water for them, too—after we'd been working in the fields all day.... They were on my mind like children.'"[30] Father Joseph in Cather's *Death Comes for the Archbishop* especially admires the Tamarisk tree "because it was the tree of the people, and was like one of the family in every Mexican household."[31]

These authors also love and admire domesticated animals. When Jim Harrison hunts, he aspires to the same focus as his dog and when he achieves it, finds it liberating: "Hopefully your concentration on what you are doing is close to that of the dog and after a couple of hours, when you both are quite tired, you find that you have been so immersed in this creaturely behavior that you haven't had a worrisome or contemporary thought since you got out of the car."[32] But it frustrates Harrison that he cannot realize his dog's wholeheartedness: "Desire and intensity mean a lot in bird dogs and with them come no recognizable limits. In the morning we hunted in a gale and I couldn't have become more wet if I had drowned but Rose was very happy with a completeness I deeply envied."[33] Not surprisingly, David Burkett, an important character in Harrison's *Returning to Earth* and *True North*, has trouble with human ties, but adores his dog so passionately that when told he cannot bring him into the United States because he lacks vaccination papers for the animal, "I had to be restrained, after standing there fifteen minutes bellowing, sobbing and cursing."[34] Confidence in dog judgment causes a woman in Charles Baxter's story "Kiss Away" to use her boyfriend's dog to evaluate the veracity of claims made about him by another woman. After she notes how completely the dog trusts him, looking at him "with straightforward dog love," she concludes that "she believes this dog more than the woman."[35]

A number of midwestern authors share Muir's attachment to horses. In Sherwood Anderson's story, "I Want to Know Why," a young boy falls in love with horses and the racetrack, declaring the rest of the world relatively corrupt: "If you've never been crazy about thoroughbreds, it's because you're never been around where they are much and don't know any better. They're beautiful. There isn't anything so lovely and clean and full of spunk and honest and everything as some race horses."[36] After writing a number of books that involve horses, Jane Smiley gives her passion for horses full and complicated voice in *Horse Heaven*, which offers personality sketches of various horses. It presents the horse Justa Bob reflecting on life and concluding that "he could find no precedents for either the place he now found himself or the people he found himself with."[37] The horse Limitless is a prodigy that needs to run: "For him, as for all geniuses, the aim was insistent, the prompt was immediate and strong. The three-year-old never forgot that he wanted to move." Other "activities only momentarily distracted his attention from his real aim, which he felt in his body, his mind, his heart—move move move" (456). That race horses spend their lives in unconflicted pursuit of what their DNA shapes them to do helps explain their kindness. Horses definitely love: "There were horses that died for love." Even geldings, although castrated, form passionate attachments: "Geldings had a culture among themselves, didn't they, and it was a culture based on affection, love, passion, whatever you wanted to call it. Geldings were the proof that love was not an instinct but a choice, a learned behavior, something you developed a capacity for over the years" (346).

Some of these midwesterners single out farmers for praise. Vachel Lindsay suggests that farming keeps one alive: even eating while harvesting wakes one up: "Every nerve in the famished body calls frantically for reinforcements. And the nerves and soul of a man are strangely alert together.... I sing of the body and of the eternal soul."[38] Their closeness to the earth causes farmers to "increase in stature and strength." This means that they produce strong children who "will make our land lovely" (215–16). The good bishop in Cather's *Death Comes for the Archbishop* chooses to spend his final days quietly farming, growing exotic fruits and beautiful wild flowers. The most admirable character in Sinclair Lewis's *Main Street* is Miles Bjornstam, a farmer with socialist tendencies. The townspeople suspect him, but Carol Kennicott's child worships him: "To Hugh, the Red Swede was the most heroic and powerful person in the world. With unrestrained adoration he trotted after while Miles fed the cows, chased his one pig—an animal of lax and migratory instincts—or dramatically slaughtered a chicken."[39] During a rare moment of good feeling in *If He Hollers Let Him Go*, the thoroughly urban Bob Jones feels as though he has defeated racism: "Big tough world, but I got you beat now." He thinks that he and his girlfriend should settle down in the country and tend to plants: "I noticed the fields of young corn beside the road and resolved right then to get some place where we could have a victory garden. It'd be fun growing things." This short-lived fantasy brings him "*Peace, Father.*" Jones declares this moment "*truly wonderful*" (172). In Tillie Olsen's *Yonnondio*, Mazie enjoys sustained happiness when her family's attempt to farm brings her into contact with nature. She escapes to it when she can no longer bear the difficulties in her home: "Light, weightless, she walked out to the yard, the earth under her feet like air, and turned her face to the heavens. Pale, half drowned, blurred like through tears, the stars."[40] When her family leaves the farm, her mother Anna has trouble pulling herself away from the sweet-smelling hay. Even Ginny Cook Smith, the major character in Jane Smiley's *A Thousand Acres*, who happily leaves behind the farm where her father abused her, admits that farm life had a density of significance that her urban existence lacks: "My life passed in a blur, that blessing of urban routine. The sense of distinct events that is so inescapable on a farm, where every rainstorm is thick with odor and color, and usefulness and timing, where omens of prosperity or ruin to come are sought in every change, where any of the world's details may contain the one thing that above all else you will regret not knowing, this sense lifted off me. Maybe another way of saying it is that I forgot I was still alive."[41]

No wonder people in search of restoration seek out nature, just as Huck and Jim flee to the raft from the turmoil on shore. Exhausted from having their work shaped by social norms, Martin Arrowsmith and Terry Wickett in Sinclair Lewis' novel *Arrowsmith* enthusiastically pursue their scientific research in the safety of the woods. In Jonathan Franzen's *Freedom*, after his marriage falls apart and his lover dies in a car crash, Walter Berglund settles into the cottage where his family stayed during his childhood and concentrates on birds. After six years, his wife returns and Walter has recovered enough of his emotional vitality to reunite with her. So the two of them leave, after turning the area around his cabin into a bird sanctuary. Similarly, nature soothes the broken heart of the young boy in Hemingway's story "Ten Indians": "When he awoke in the night he heard the wind in the hemlock trees outside the cottage and the waves of the lake coming in on the shore, and he went back to sleep. In the morning there was a big wind blowing and the waves were running high up on the beach and he was awake a long time before he remembered that his heart was broken."[42] Even mean townspeople from Sinclair Lewis's *Main Street*, relax into pleasant human beings at their summer cabins: "Here the matron forgot social jealousies, and sat gossiping in gingham; or, in old bathing-suits."[43] When Neil Kingsblood can no longer take the turmoil of his inner debate about acknowledging his black blood, he finds relief in the country: "Two weeks can do an extensive healing, in a Northern magic of gray rocks and orange lichens and sweet pines and sliding red canoes and blade-blue distances across the tremendous lake."[44] David, in Harrison's *Returning to Earth*, finds that leaving his futile historical studies which he describes as "trying to force my puny logic on the sprawl of history," and stepping on the porch of his cabin in the woods delivers him to sanity by freeing him from his deadening thoughts: "My emotional life has squeezed out the edges of this effort so that when I wake up from my books and notes I'm disgusted. I walk out on the cabin porch and suddenly a mere mosquito, the last one of the fall, seems far more interesting than any of my thinking, and the presence of the river is so overwhelming that my sense leave my thoughts well behind where I'm beginning to think they belong."[45] In *Death Comes for the Archbishop*, the power of his New Mexican environment always makes the Bishop see the world with young eyes: "His first consciousness was a sense of the light dry wind blowing in through the windows, with the fragrance of hot sun and sage-brush and sweet clover; a wind that made one's body feel light and one's heart cry 'Today, today,' like a child's."[46]

Nick Adams in Ernest Hemingway's story "The Big Two-Hearted River" goes to the country after the war leaves him on edge. When he arrives, he discovers that fire has damaged the place where he fished before the war, but he keeps walking, confident that although "the country was burned over and changed, ... it did not matter. It could not all be burned. He knew that."[47] And further along, he finds peace: 'He was settled. Nothing could touch him. It was a good place to camp. He was there, in the good place. He was in his home where he had made it."[48] Luchen Li explains that Nick finds tranquility "by submerging the dramatic human emotions deeply in the landscape. The landscape in the story ... is vast, solid, stable, serene."[49]

Jakes Barnes in Hemingway's *The Sun Also Rises* also leaves behind his exhausting friends to enjoy a fishing trip in the country: "We stayed five days at Burguete and had good fishing. The nights were cold and the days were hot, and there was always a breeze even in the heat of the day. It was hot enough so that it felt good to wade in a cold stream, and the sun dried you when you came out and sat on the bank. We found a stream with a pool deep enough to swim in.... There was no word from Robert Cohn, not from Brett and Mike."[50] Mark Spilka sees a similarity between Jakes Barnes's experiences and Nick Adams's: "As with Nick Adams, it brings him health, pleasure, beauty and order, and helps to wipe out the damage of his troubled life in Paris."[51] But Spilka thinks the *Sun Also Rises*' epigraph suggests that both Jake and Nick also lose themselves in something larger than themselves: "According to the opening epigraphs, if one generation is lost and another comes, the earth abides forever, and according to Hemingway himself the abiding earth is the novel's hero" (44).

As William Barillas points out, the vitality nature can evoke in these authors shares important characteristics with the spirituality New England writers enjoy in nature. But nature more often speaks to these authors of connection rather than transcendence which helps explain why areas of nature touched and shaped by human concerns draw them rather than repulse them they way they do Thoreau. Louise Erdrich asserts that Emerson notwithstanding, certain aspects of reality do not elevate people to the eternal: "Dim wings will close over our conniving brains no matter what and so we lose ourselves most happily in tasks that partake of the eternal. And once we realize that nothing really does, anything can—pulling weeds, picking apples, putting children to bed."[52] The Bishop in *Death Comes for the Archbishop* identifies the essential symbolic significance of rocks as not timelessness, but relation: "The rock when one came to think of it, was the utmost expression of human need; even mere feeling yearned for it; it was the highest comparison of loyalty in love and friendship" (69).

Not everyone feels a bond with nature and its import and power can make nature frightening to those not in tune with it, like the narrator of Charles Baxter's novel *The Feast of Love* who climbs the Porcupine Mountains and finds them terrifying: "It's a moody landscape given to early morning fogs and indescribable forest sounds.... Tree branches snap and fall in front of you. These seemingly harmless nature scenes fill you with premonitions of bucolic doom."[53] Early in his Western sojourn, Archbishop Latour from Cather's *Death Comes for the Archbishop* feels fearful of a cave that saved his life: "It flashed into his mind from time to time, and always with a shudder of repugnance quite unjustified by anything he had experienced there" (105). Sometimes nature proves fatally inhospitable as when greedy people go into the woods in Louise Erdrich's *Tracks* and simply vanish: "Every year there are more who come looking for profit, who draw lines across the land with their strings and yellow flags. They disappear sometimes, and now there are so many betting with sticks and dice out near Matchimanito at night that you wonder how Fleur sleeps, or if she sleeps at all."[54] All these people suffer for their lack of empathy with nature. Lipsha admits in Erdrich's *The Bingo Palace* that Matchimanito Lake, a "spirit place," punishes those who are bad like himself. So when an old woman leads him into the woods, he cannot escape: "The trunks are dense, twisting against me, and the leaves seem to wrap around me so I can't keep the springtime flash of her dress in my line of vision. I keep edging forward, easing under dead falls and squeezing through crossed tangles. The air grows dense, buzzing, and smells of ripped green wood and heavy sunlight. I try backing up once but the twigs and leaves have closed behind me in sharp knots. This is a one-way woods."[55]

These writers retain the sense that they come from a different order of being, but they cherish those moments when they escape into nature. This relocation does not always allow them entry into a spiritual world, but does persistently let them move into a larger, kinder, and more ancient mode of being. Henderson, in Saul Bellow's *Henderson the Rain King*, who finds relief from his sadness by roaring like a lion: "And so I was the beast. I gave myself to it, and all my sorrow came out in the roaring. My lungs supplied the air but the note came from my soul."[56] Donald W. Markos argues that Bellow's novel challenges "the dualistic view of the universe which makes death unacceptable and nature hostile and alien, the novel has posed the possibility of ... an organic universe in which man can feel more at home, more related to sun and earth, to childhood, animals, death, and his own body."[57] Perhaps his analysis applies to all this midwestern writing where authors inhabit nature as completely as possible.

Louise Erdrich's *The Painted Drum* details the process of giving oneself over to nature. The character Faye Travers points out that when a person must travel without a trail, or abandon himself or herself to nature, he or she must leave something of themselves behind: "It is that sudden loss, I think, even more than the difficulty of walking through undergrowth that keeps people firmly fixed to paths. In the woods, there is no right way to go, of course, no trail to follow but the law of growth. You must leave behind the notion that things are right."[58] She takes the plunge and later leaves the woods torn by the brambles, but feeling good: "I'm slick with sweat and gritty with scrapings of bark and wood rot, and I'm peaceful. I have reached an understanding with the woods, as I always do" (78). But she loses this equipoise when she hears wolves. When an old man explains to her that "the wolves accept the lives they are given.... They deal with what they encounter and go on" (120–21) and she comes to see even the wisdom of wolves. In *The Blue Jay's Dance*, Erdrich reports that if she could become any animal it would be a skunk because, like the wolf, it accepts its life: "live fearlessly, eat anything, gestate my young in just two months, and fall into a state of dreaming torpor when the cold hit hard. Wherever I went, I'd leave my sloppy tracks. I wouldn't walk so much as putter, destinationless, in a serene belligerence—past hunters, past death overhead, past death all around."[59]

Some midwestern authors suggest that this apparent abandonment of themselves brings about a deep homecoming: through nature they connect with their unconscious. In Saul Bellow's *The Dean's December*, Albert Corde associates dreams and cyclamens: "Someone had once suggested to him that these green beings produced their leaves and flowers in a state of sleep, perfection devoid of consciousness, design without nerves.... Brooding over the cyclamens on the table, he often dozed; he felt too hazy to remember anything. He thought, if you had enough of these plants in a room and watered them with a Nembutal solution, they might cure insomnia, make a dream atmosphere."[60] Louise Erdrich directly asserts the connection between wilderness and dreams: "What are dreams but an internal wilderness and what is desire but a wildness of the soul?"⁶¹ And like nature, those dreams restore us: "When every inch of the world is known, sleep may be the only wilderness that we have left. In sleep's preserve, the body repairs itself, talks to itself, leads a separate life we cannot know.... Some days, when my body wakes, it seems wider than the consciousness that inhabits it. Unhampered by the beams of my thoughts, it performs its necessary tasks and by morning usually manages to have accomplished an active rest. While I am not there to impede its work, the body takes lessons on how to save me."⁶² Charles Citrine, in Bellow's *Humboldt's Gift,* makes an explicit connection between nature and the unconscious: "I had the strange hunch that nature was not *out there*, an object world eternally separated from subjects, but that everything external corresponded vividly with something internal, that the two were identical and interchangeable and that nature was my own unconscious being."⁶³ And so this connection to nature does not elevate human beings to a higher realm, but ties them more profoundly to themselves. It helps make them whole. And by losing themselves in the endlessly fertile and enduring natural order, human beings may also evade death.

Louise Erdrich makes a direct link between nature and overcoming death in *The Last Report on the Miracles at Little No Horse*. As Father Damien dies, she becomes more responsive to and connected to nature: "The constant murmur of the pines, her beloved music, now became comprehensible to her in the same way that flows of Ojibwe language first began to make sense—a word here, a word there, a few connections, then the shape of ideas. Instead of growing duller, shutting down her senses, turning away from life, she found to her joy and consternation that she was growing keener. Her understanding was more intense, her vision wary and her hearing razor sharp. The roar and whisper of the pine needles intensified and she fell into a reverie of nostalgia."⁶⁴ Also as Erdich's novel *The Birchbark House* ends, Omakayas, the book's protagonist, rests in nature, listening to the singing of sparrows. Then she hears the voice of the infant brother she could not save from death in their songs. "She heard him tell her to cheer up and live. I'm all right, his voice was saying, I'm in a peaceful place. You can depend on me. I'm always here to help you, my sister. Omakayas tucked her hands behind her head, lay back, closed her eyes, and smiled as the song of the white-throated sparrow sank again and again through the air like a shining needle, and sewed up her broken heart."⁶⁵ Some midwestern authors admire Native American culture for giving nature the central role it deserves in daily life. Of course, this orientation plays a role in all of Louise Erdrich's novels. As her Ojibwe character Nanapush says at the end of *The Last Report on the Miracles at Little No Horse*: "Every feature of the land around us spoke its name to an ancestor. Perhaps, in the end, that is all we are. We Anishinaabeg are the keepers of the names of the earth."[66] The Bishop in Cather's *Death Comes for the Archbishop*, finds the natives "reptilian" at the start of his mission work among them.[67] Then he comes to find them mysterious: "He was already convinced that neither the white men nor the Mexicans in Santa Fe understood anything about Indian beliefs or the workings of the Indian mind" (105). Eventually, he comes to understand that just as white men aspired to leave their marks on the landscape, "It was the Indian's way to pass through a country without disturbing anything; to pass and leave no trace, like fish through water or birds through air" (185). By the time he dies, he admires them and feels grateful that he has lived long enough to see the natives begin to get the decent treatment they deserve: "'God has been very good to let me live to see a happy issue to those old wrongs. I do not believe, as I once did, that the Indian will perish. I believe that God will preserve him'" (236). Carol Steinhagen points out that "what distinguishes this novel in Cather's oeuvre is its acknowledgement of an environment that cannot be landscaped and of the integrity of the Native Americans who preserve that environment."[68]

In *Heirs of Columbus*, Gerald Vizenor explains that Columbus, or the Europeans, brought a distorted view of nature with them to the new world where they imposed it on the inhabitants, to everyone's detriment. In this novel, the natives are Anishinaabe, Vizenor's people, and in their mythology, nature and humans are one, but far from transcendent: "The compassionate tribal trickster who created the earth, had a brother who was a stone: a bear stone, a human stone, a shaman stone, a stone, a stone, a stone."[69] The stones of this native culture "heal and remember the blue radiance of creations and resurrections" (13), but were stolen, at first by missionaries. The stories that surrounded the stones nourished people's imaginations until "humans lost their humor over land, gold, slaves, and time" (16). Memphis, the panther, explains that shamans are animals disguised as humans and that "the animals are stories in our blood, and the stories have power to heal, and the power to heal is comic and has never been sacred." Those who hear this explanation "who imagined animals in their blood could see the panther, but those who were cowed by their disguises as human lived in mortal fear of wild animals in a wilderness that was human" (71). In other words, those people who accept their bond to nature, as do the natives, feel comfortable with it. Those who deny this link, fear it and feel compelled to conquer it. Most dread nature and its stories, but Doctor Pir Cantrip "and other scientists" have found a way to cure them: they "had isolated the genetic code of tribal survivance and radiance, that native signature of seventeen mitochondrial genes that could reverse human mutations, nurture shamanic resurrection, heal wounded children, and incite parthenogenesis in separatist women" (132). And they heal "women and children, those wounded by men" (146).

Here Vizenor joins those midwestern authors who complain of the damage inflicted by the patriarchal order and link it to a view of nature as something that needs domination. This stance towards nature has left the world polluted by chemicals. The native group Vizenor describes seeks to reverse the damage these chemicals have done to children: "'They come by the thousands to be healed, abandoned children, the tribal mutants who bear the curse of a chemical civilization'" (170).

In the book's epilogue, Vizenor explains that "Columbus arises in tribal stories that heal with humor the world he wounded; he is loathed, but he is not a separation in tribal consciousness" (185). In other words, Vizenor's novel, *The Heirs of Columbus* not only explores the positive consequences of the connection with rather than the transcendence of nature a number of midwestern authors espouse, he links the damaged natural bond to the conquering of native cultures by European ones and to the blindness to the value of women and children which other midwestern authors have also protested.

Other midwestern authors also see healing potential in native cultures. From childhood, Jim Harrison identifies with natives: "Because of my familiarity with the natural world I identified strongly with those who until recently had depended on such familiarity for their existence. I had also long understood that my most intense pleasures came in activities such as hunting, fishing, and studying wild country that were the same for any Pleistocene biped." Harrison sees the exploitation of the natives as the largest difference between him and them: "My people never got the rawest of deals."[70] Harrison believes this interest in Native Americans has served him well, allowing him to learn multiple truths from them, most importantly "that we have failed our Natives should urge us on, on both their behalf and that of the earth we share. If we can't comprehend that the reality of life is an aggregate of the perceptions and nature of all species we are doomed with the earth we are already murdering" (166). Thus it makes complete sense that Harrison produce *Returning to Earth* with a half–Ojibwe protagonist and hero named Donald who finds giving himself over to nature so satisfying that he asks his family to bury him in the ground at the place he spent three days alone, looking at the world from the perspective of birds and animals. In "The River Swimmer," a young man named Thad briefly explores a glamorous life in Chicago but then happily returns to Michigan, where he can swim with water babies pointed out to him by native women. His reaction to this discovery may explain why this intense engagement with nature on its own terms happens so rarely, at least for whites: going out of themselves requires energy. Thad's engagement with happiness wears him out: "He felt mentally victimized by the miraculous. Life would have been easier without the water babies. The world lost its top with their appearance."[71]

Willa Cather's *The Professor's House* includes the story of Tom Outland, whose discovery and exploration of an abandoned and ancient native village causes him to spend every day there bursting with joy partly because of the incredible natural beauty surrounding this place the natives chose to live. He withdraws from it when his surroundings seem to indicate the appropriateness of this choice: "I stood outside the cabin until the gold light went blue and a few stars came out, hardly brighter than the bright sky they twinkled in and the swallows came flying over us, on their way to their nests in the cliffs."[72] Tom's description of his adventures inspires the professor to join him at this gorgeous place and the professor's memory of this trip inspires him to put his genuine desires at the center of his life instead of passively accepting what life presents to him.

And so, to these authors, although nature can serve as an entry into a higher reality, it also has its own eternality. One cannot count on achieving a spiritual experience through nature, but one can usually find peace by resigning oneself to it. And since nature always has more power, acumen, and beauty than people, wise human beings happily seek it out and surrender to it. If they have trouble achieving this or understanding its value, native stories may help them find their way back to the healthy bond with nature; the attempt to shape it so that it answers to human terms has broken.

Six

Relaxing into Compassion

Writers from New England, incluidng Thoreau, Emerson, and Hawthorne, advocate for intellectual and spiritual growth; for instance, Hawthorne identifies "adding wisdom to wisdom throughout Eternity" as the activity that distinguishes human beings from animals.[1] Thoreau repeatedly urges spiritual evolution in a manner suggesting contempt for those who content themselves with ordinary lives: "The millions are awake enough for physical labor; but only one in a million is awake enough for effective intellectual exertion, only one in a hundred millions to a poetic or divine life."[2] But Huck and Jim, the most admirable characters in *Huckleberry Finn*, achieve their status by accepting rather than improving themselves. The flawed characters in the novel, like Tom Sawyer and the King and the Duke, differ from Huck and Jim in that they have and act upon grand aspirations. Similarly, midwestern writers admire children, women, African Americans, and nature insofar as they challenge the wisdom of obeying social norms that encourage energetic efforts to transform oneself. Louise Erdrich says in *The Antelope Wife* that resisting this kind of exertion lays the groundwork for beauty: "The lack of trying is what makes them lovely. We all try too hard. Striving wears down our edges, dulls the best of us."[3] On the other hand, identifying with and appreciating these often overlooked groups and realities provides a way to "light out for the Territory"[4] with Huck and live in terms of one's innate sense of decency and wonder. People who stop trying to shape their lives into something impressive often discover that abandoning their noble goals brings joy because it allows space for their feelings to emerge. One midwestern writer after another describes a life grounded in whole-hearted authenticity, rather than a performance that garners praise from society, as highly desirable. Although Thoreau does not favor conventional behavior, the spiritual growth he advocates can just as surely lead to alienating arrogance, as Hawthorne recognizes when he makes The Giant Transcendentalist one of the sights encountered when smug citizens mistake a train to Hell for one to Heaven in "The Celestial Railroad." And certainly Thoreau's designation of philanthropy as an overrated virtue does little to establish his compassion. In "Ethan Brand," Hawthorne also acknowledges the alienating potential of a life devoted to intellectual cultivation, but his renditions of the common folk reveal little faith in them. They, after all, kill people whom they declare witches on spurious grounds, believe so mindlessly in progress that they think the invention of a train makes it easier for them to get to heaven, torture poor Hester Prynne, and somehow manage to overlook their sainted minister's confession to the same sin they spend decades abusing Hester for committing. One of the few characters with a job to receive any significant development in Hawthorne's fiction, the hardware store owner Mr. Lindsay in "The Snow Image," gets described as one who takes "what is called the common-sense view of all matters that came under his consideration." As a result, he "had a head as hard and impenetrable, and therefore perhaps as empty, as one of the iron-pots which it was a part of his business to sell."[5] And Hawthorne characterizes the lime burner who rejects Brand as little better than the tale's supposed villain. "Ethan Brand" opens by describing him as "a rough, heavy-looking man, begrimed with charcoal" (11: 83). It closes with the image of him shattering what remains of Brand so he can put the pieces in a bushel and sell them: "The rude lime-burner lifted his pole, and letting it fall upon the skeleton, the relics of Ethan Brand were crumbled into fragments" (11:102).

On the other hand, midwestern authors repeatedly value the perspectives of ordinary people and fret over the damage done to both their hearts and minds by a competitive social structure. Those midwestern authors like Meridel Le Sueur, Chester Himes, Jack Conroy, Tillie Olsen, Willard Motley, Nelson Algren, James Farrell, and Richard Wright, whose works call attention to the decency and mistreatment of the lower classes, would find little to identify with in the writings of the authors from New England who preceded them. Midwestern fiction not only focuses on common lives, it advocates for the people who live them, suggesting that if they inhabited a society less hostile to their functioning authentically, it would improve not only their lives, but everyone's. The earlier chapters on children, women, African Americans, and nature expose the reality that those shut outside of the mainstream sometimes have an easier time moving towards integrity than those the social structure rewards. But these writers also argue that one can remain true to oneself and still win community approval as long as one's aspirations grow naturally from one's passions rather than from society's dictates. And just as in this fiction, alienating forces tend to move into the midwest from other regions and inauthentic individuals tend to flee the Midwest for one of the coasts. Chicago, the same city that thwarts Richard Wright's Bigger Thomas, James Farrell's Stud Lonigan, and most characters in Nelson Algren's novels, often serves as the site of fruitful self-realization in midwestern fiction.

Even in Wright's *Native Son*, Algren's *Never Come Morning*, and *Man with the Golden Arm*, Chicago's negative power is not absolute. One can easily imagine Lefty from Algren's *Never Come Morning* not turning the woman he genuinely loves over to his friends for them to rape if he could develop real courage, or Frankie Machine in *The Man with the Golden Arm* building a rich emotional life if not hampered by the drug addiction he acquired in the service. Even Bigger's isolation results from his inability to own that he wants connection with the whites and the fear that prevents him from understanding that many whites wish him well. And James Farrell spares his readers the trouble of imagining Studs honoring his "soft feelings" and saving himself, by writing novels about Danny O'Neill, who grows up in the same environment as Studs but builds the foundation for a life of integrity there rather than moving rapidly towards death, like Studs. When midwestern authors portray Chicago as a place that nourishes rather than squelches wholehearted self-development, they undermine the literary cliché that cities oppress integrity.

Theodore Dreiser is one of many midwestern writers who characterize Chicago as a place that aids self-realization. Inspired by the possibilities she sees there, Carrie Meeber in Theodore Dreiser's *Sister Carrie* begins developing into a fuller person the moment she arrives. At first the changes seem trivial: awed by the stylish women she sees on the street, she begins dressing better. After her first paramour, Charles Drouet, tactlessly comments on women who strike him as attractive, rather than getting angry, Carrie learns to imitate them. When Drouet introduces her to George Hurstwood, she immediately recognizes that Hurstwood's more elegant clothing indicates his superiority to Drouet. Simultaneously, Carrie savors the new feelings that emerge when she enjoys the piano music that drifts into her apartment from a neighbor's. When Hurstwood makes clear he cares for her, Carrie responds with new emotional depth of her own: "Several times their eyes accidentally met, and then there poured into hers such a flood of feeling as she had never before experienced."[6] And she discovers that she can actually change her circumstances in terms of her growing priorities rather than submitting to them. Carrie's acting career follows naturally from her emerging emotional life, refining tastes, talent for mimicry, and growing ability to understand and lose herself in the feelings of others. The narrator points out that "Carrie was possessed of that sympathetic, impressionable nature which, even in the most developed form, has been the glory of the drama" (110). As Ames explains to her: "'Most people are not capable of voicing their feelings. They depend upon others. That is what genius is for.... Sometimes nature ... makes the face representative of all desire. That's what has happened in your case.'" He warns her: "'If you turn away from it and live to satisfy yourself alone, it will go fast enough'" (339). Even though Carrie eventually moves to New York, there she merely profits from the self-realization that took place when exposed to the possibilities Chicago offered her. Moreover, she stops learning from others in New York: she finds her social life there empty because of its inauthenticity. Thus, although Chicago changes Carrie, the way it does so delivers her to a life that eventually feels empty and lonely to her. As *Sister Carrie* concludes, Carrie has tired of adulation and wants to discover a life of greater meaning. The novel hints that Ames's remarks about the poor have pointed her in a new direction, but asserts unambiguously that changes lie ahead for Carrie: "Though often disillusioned, she was still waiting for that halcyon day when she would be led forth among dreams become real. Ames had pointed out a farther step, but on and on beyond that, if accomplished, would lie others for her" (351–52).

Similarly, Thea Kronberg in Willa Cather's *Song of the Lark* fulfills her potential only after leaving Nebraska for Chicago to study piano. She not only learns from her instructor that her natural ability for singing far outpaces her piano performance, she discovers that she feels most completely herself when she sings beautifully before an audience: "While she was on the stage she was conscious that every movement was the right movement, that her body was absolutely the instrument of her idea. Not for nothing had she kept it so severely, kept it filled with such energy and fire. All that deep-rooted vitality flowered into her voice, her face, her very finger-tips. She felt like a tree busting into bloom."[7] Perhaps this discovery brings Thea greater joy than it does Carrie because it grows from rather than transforms the young girl who arrived in Chicago from the country and because it emerges naturally from her own soul rather than from the traits of others that she has imitated.

Six. Relaxing into Compassion

The novel's narrator claims that Thea has an advantage coming from Nebraska, a place where "the important thing was that one should not pretend to be what one was not." As a result, Thea develops into an adult who hates lack of integrity. Thea vehemently explains: "If you love the good thing vitally, enough to give up for it all that one must give up, then you must hate the cheap thing just as hard" (383). Art, the novel's narrator maintains, comes from authenticity: becoming an artist is essentially a process of honest self-realization: "Artistic growth is, more than it is anything else, a refining of the sense of truthfulness. The stupid believe that to be truthful is easy; only the artist, the great artist, knows how difficult it is" (398).

Even though Nebraska's emphasis on honesty helps make Thea an artist, she must leave for a larger cultural center in order to develop her singing. For instance, she had never attended a symphony before her arrival in Chicago. Moreover, the people she grew up with in Nebraska have no way of comprehending her commitment to music; indeed, to them, her artistic aspirations may well seem pretentious. When Thea tells her sister that she enjoys singing with Mexicans because she finds them talented, her sister snarls at her: "'Talented!' Anna made the word sound like escaping steam. 'I suppose you think it's smart to come home and throw that at your family!'" (207). While it helps an artist to grow up in a place that shuns pretense, it becomes a disadvantage when he or she tries to achieve something large. For one thing, he or she has no models. For another, he or she abandons the unspoken promise not to attempt anything outstanding. So, like Thea, midwestern artists tend to find themselves leaving not only their home towns, but even Chicago for other cities, often on one coast or another. But by the time they move away, they have absorbed midwestern values: "Thea was glad that this was her country, even if one did not learn to speak elegantly there. It was, somehow, an honest country, and there was a new song in that blue air that had never been sung in the world before" (192). Chicago serves as an intermediary between the simple honesty of rural life and the glitter of the larger world on the coasts and in Europe.

Lucy Gayheart, in Cather's novel with the same name, follows Thea to Chicago and also realizes her musical potential there. But Lucy has a clearer understanding of her desires and capacities when she arrives, so her transformation into a distinguished musician takes place quickly and painlessly. She goes to musical performances immediately and they expose her to an educative sublimity: "In its calmness and serenity there was a kind of large enlightenment, like daybreak" (25). She loves the freedom the city offers her to "come and go like a boy; no one fussing about, no one hovering over her" (22). Dashing around the city, exploring one pleasant option after another, leaves her in a state of perpetual joy. She wakes each day, excited to discover what her experiences will unfold for her; knowing that despite their newness, they will always take her further towards herself: "She had changed so much in her thoughts, in her ways, even in her looks, that she might wonder she knew herself—except that the changes were all in the direction of becoming more and more herself" (79).

Born in Chicago, Saul Bellow's eponymous character Augie March finds himself drowning in its possibilities. Although designated as "reality instructors," the master manipulators Grandma Lausch and William Einhorn, in fact, teach Augie that one can always bend circumstances to one's advantage. His brother Simon marries well above his station, showing Augie the path to upward mobility. And throughout his life, Augie has people adopting him and educating him in various trades: clothing sales, book thievery, union organizing, and bird training. Because he likes people and hates disappointing them, Augie happily adopts all of these occupations, even though he claims to strive to fulfill something he calls the axial lines, which allow one to find one's center and live joyously. He believes his axial lines would consist of running a home for foster children and, indeed, Augie does love all people, especially his mentally handicapped brother, Georgie. But Augie's wife has other plans for him and he loves her, too, so he does what pleases her. *The Adventures of Augie March* suggests Augie cannot resist exploring Chicago's bountiful possibilities, something he does with unbridled enthusiasm. This trait makes Augie an enormously attractive character, but also encourage doubts that he will ever find a focus. Still, if Chicago bears any blame, it's for introducing so much richness into Augie's life that when the novel closes, he has yet to tear himself away from exploring his multiple options and realizing his axial lines.

Herzog, the protagonist in Bellow's novel of the same name, does, in fact, face reality in Chicago. An academic supposedly working on an endless manuscript he seems doomed to never finish, Moses Herzog has no time for his real work because he repeatedly loses himself in a variety of unhealthy obsessions. One of his passions is writing authoritative letters theorizing about the shortcomings of modern life. These grandiose epistles briefly elevate him above the person whom his ex-wife, Madeline, left for a colleague, but do not save him from fixating on his broken marriage as well. His sexually expert new girlfriend, Ramona, supplies Herzog with a happier third obsession: he gladly turns his chaotic emotional life over to her for therapeutic escape. Instead of fleeing from one frantic "solution" to another, Herzog needs to stop running and face that whatever messes modern society generates pale next to the emotional frenzy of his life. And he does precisely this in Chicago.

Armed with an ancient gun, Herzog leaves New York to confront his ex-wife and her new husband, Gersbach, in Chicago and winds up confronting himself. As he peers through a window and sees Gersbach gently bathing his child, Moses Herzog begins to realize that his angry emotions have carried him into an alternate reality that has little to do with the world he shares with others. When he has an accident on Chicago's Outer Drive with his child in the car, Herzog comes to understand that indulging in lunatic anger not only solves nothing, it could hurt the child he claims he wants to protect. Charles Citrine of Saul Bellow's novel *Humboldt's Gift*, provides a clear analysis of Herzog's dilemma when he argues that academics doing their jobs will suck the vitality from their lives with egocentric reflection: "The educated speak of the disenchanted (a boring) world. But it is not the world, it is my own head that is disenchanted.... For me, the self-conscious ego is the seat of boredom." For the "independently conscious" self stands "proud of its detachment and its absolute immunity, its stability and its power to remain unaffected by anything whatsoever," so it resists the influence of its environment and other people.[8] Citrine calls busyness slothful, for it "drives off the wonderful rest or balance without which there can be no poetry or art or thought." He believes that one achieves true knowledge by listening: "The old philosophy distinguished between knowledge achieved by effort (*ratio*) and knowledge received (*intellectus*) by the listening soul that can hear the essence of things and comes to understand the marvelous" (306).

Herzog makes this transition from *ratio* to *intellectus*. He only finds serenity when he lets go of all this theorizing, stops trying to correct and shape the universe, moves into his cabin and follows his impulses, doing whatever appeals to him, whether painting the piano green or sharing his house with owls. He discovers his capacity for joy in by allowing himself to become vulnerable to life: "*I am willing without further exercise in pain to open my heart. And this needs no doctrine or theology of suffering. We love apocalypses too much, and crisis ethics and florid extremism with its thrilling language.*"[9] As Nathan A. Scott points out, in *Herzog*, as in other Bellow novels, when "striving stops, there is the infinitely poignant fullness and beauty of the very miracle of life itself."[10]

When Herzog finally gives up his aspirations and rests in peace, he takes in the details of his environment: "He lay stretched in the lawn chair, facing south. As soon as the sun lost its main strength the hermit thrushes began, and while they sang their sweet fierce music threatening trespassers, the blackbirds would begin to gather in flocks for the night, and just toward sunset they would break from these trees in waves, wave after wave, three or four miles in one flight to their waterside nests" (413–14). He worries for a moment about his girlfriend Ramona's arrival, then relaxes back into an awareness of the unimportance of this event and virtually all others: "*I will do no more to enact the peculiarities of life. This is well done, without my special assistance.*" This decision allows him to resume enjoying his surroundings: "Now on one side the hills lost the sun and began to put on a more intense blue color; on the other, they were still green and white. The birds were very loud" (414). Martin Corner identifies Herzog's turning towards the world as the central event in his development, claiming that the novel presents "different stages in a history of outward movement away from the self-enclosure of discursively constructed consciousness to the otherness of the world." Thus, Herzog achieves "at least the possibility of moral action" because he has moved beyond self-absorption. Corner admits that the conclusion of Herzog offers only "a slender bridge thrown across the gulf": "It does not assure us of everything: but if we refuse the outward movement, we shall have nothing at all."[11]

Chicago also awakens characters from Jim Harrison's fiction to the central realities of their lives. Jim Harrison's novella "The River Swimmer" from the book with the same name portrays a young man named Thad who loves to swim, especially with water babies pointed out to him by an Ojibwe woman. He decides to swim from Michigan to Chicago and, on the way, meets a glamorous and rich young woman from Chicago named Emily. Drawn by her, he tries to begin a life in the city, but finally gives up and heads home because, after briefly sharing the lives of wealthy Chicagoans, he decides he prefers swimming with water babies. Cynthia, the wife of Donald who passes away in Harrison's novel *Returning to Earth*, thinks that she deals with his death very well, until she travels from Marquette, Michigan, where she lives, to Chicago, where she collapses sobbing on the street. Afterwards, she returns to Marquette and an existence awash in the grief she had previously evaded. Traveling through this sadness eventually delivers her to new, more solid choices for the life ahead of her. Thus, a wide range of midwestern authors see Chicago not as a symbol of urban oppression but as a place that nudges people towards authenticity, whether by giving them the opportunity to realize previously undeveloped gifts or by forcing them to face their evasive ways. Even when protagonists flee Chicago, as does Manfred Banks in Clarence Major's *Dirty Bird Blues*, the knowledge of what he most needs and wants in his life follows him. He had planned to give up his hope of becoming a blues musician and live an ordinary life with a nine-to-five job in Kansas City. But at the novel's end, he happily picks up his Chicago dreams again.

Finding integrity becomes especially challenging for those who have succeeded in society's norms. How can they renounce lives that bring them so much admiration—and money? But in the work of several midwestern fiction writers, as improbable as it may seem, characters come to understand, again and again, that they must choose between the appearance of success and genuine contentment; they choose rectitude.

Businessmen in Sherwood Anderson's novels often realize they can no longer stand their work and quit to explore their worlds and their feelings about them. Sam McPherson in *Windy McPherson's Son* meets and marries Sue Rainey, who introduces him to "six weeks of readjustment and freedom, during which he learned to sail a boat, to shoot, and to get the fine taste of that life into his being."[12] Unable to handle so much pleasure, Sam leaves his wife and returns to money-making, but as the novel ends he goes back to Sue. John Webster of the novel *Many Marriages* stops working and stares at the life around him as though he just entered it. Eventually, he feels a strong connection to the rest of the world: "He himself was a man standing, clad in ordinary clothes, but within his clothes, and within his body too there was something, well perhaps not vast in itself, but vaguely indefinitely connected with some vast thing."[13]

At the conclusion of Sinclair Lewis's *Arrowsmith*, Martin Arrowsmith and Terry Wickett retreat into the woods to supposedly do important scientific research, but as the novel ends, they sit out on a lake in a boat, presumably fishing, while Martin confesses that their experiments may well fail. These two men learn in the woods that achievement does not matter as long as one lives wholeheartedly. Martin and Terry not only work with enthusiasm, it seems to Martin "this was the first spring he had ever seen and tasted." This new life brings him enormous joy: "Martin felt sun-soaked and deep of chest, and always he hummed."[14]

Willa Cather's *The Professor's House* shows the elderly Professor Godfrey St. Peter discovering as he and his wife move into a new house that he longs to spend time in his office at the top of his old house. There, he enjoys retreating into a dreamlike state where he encounters a boy he knew as a child, whom he recognizes as his essential self. He bears little resemblance to the Professor: "The Kansas boy who had come back to St. Peter this summer was not a scholar. He was a primitive. He was only interested in earth and woods and water. Whenever sun sunned and rain rained and snow snowed, wherever life sprouted and decayed, places were alike to him.... He seemed to be at the root of the matter; Desire under all desires, Truth under all truths. He seemed to know, among other things, that he was solitary and must always be so; he had never married, never been a father. He was earth, and would return to earth."[15] St. Peter knows he must trust and embrace this child's way of life: "He loved his family, he would make any sacrifice for them, but just now he couldn't live with them. He must be alone" (274). As Stephen L. Tanner notes, "His family will neither understand his epiphany nor realize he is not the same man. His qualified contentment must remain private and solitary."[16] Fortunately, St. Peter's relationships with his family have become so attenuated that they barely notice his change, so he can continue to lose himself in reverie almost entirely undisturbed.

In Toni Morrison's *Song of Solomon*, Pilate, who consistently does what she feels, inspires Milkman, who initially chooses to imitate his father's life and work in real estate. Bored, but successful, Milkman asks for time off to find gold his father believes his aunt Pilate left in the South. On this trip, Milkman finds no gold, but becomes involved in constructing a family history, fixating on a male ancestor who reportedly could fly. Through his travels, Milkman learns how to relate to people, listen to others, and obey his own passions. As a result, when he catches sight of his reflection in a picture window, he realizes he is happier than he has ever been. And those who encounter him after this journey meet a Milkman far kinder and more alive than the one who set out from Michigan.

In Jim Harrison's novella "The Land of Unlikeness," a sixty-year-old, successful art historian must leave New York to take care of his mother in the Michigan home where she raised him. This break in the normal pattern of his life causes him to rediscover his love of painting and gives him space to act on it, as well as on his long-term fantasy of painting his next door neighbor in the nude. During this period of good feeling, he also heals the relationship with his daughter that broke years before. At the novella's end, he gives himself permission to simply enjoy what remains of his life. He will begin now: "He had had his dream of the world's idea of success but it was surprisingly easy to give up for his first love."[17]

For people intensely involved in seeking success, leaving behind their accomplished lives proves too difficult. So, they realize their genuine lives only when their triumphant progress falls apart. They simply cannot continue to embrace achievement for reasons sometimes mysterious to them except, per-

Six. Relaxing into Compassion   161

haps, in retrospect. This happens to Willa Cather's Alexandra in *O Pioneers!* who, after decades of functioning with miraculous efficiency and insight, collapses in bed, heartbroken over her brother Emil's murder. While there, she becomes aware of an illusion she has harbored all her life "of being lifted and carried lightly by some one very strong." This time she sees the man in her doorway, and "knew at last for whom it was she had waited, and where he would carry her."[18] She has concluded that he represents the death which will bring her relief. But when her friend Carl returns, she confesses to him that, thanks to his love, her dream "'will never come true, now, in the way I thought it might.'" She realizes that Carl is the man whose strength will sustain her. So when the agony of Emil's death incapacitates her, independent, competent Alexandra must acknowledge that she needs to rely on Carl: "She leaned heavily on his shoulder. 'I am tired,' she murmured. 'I have been very lonely, Carl.'" Despite her nephew's death and the sadness of so many of Alexandra's years, at the novel's conclusion, Alexandra tells Carl: "'I think we shall be very happy'" because, at last, she owns and can attempt to nourish the emotional life she put aside in order to focus on successfully managing the land her father left her and her brothers.[19] Warren Motley notes that because "Alexandra's own emotional resources are depleted ... her rescue must be initiated from outside the self. In a sense this represents progress for Alexandra; her willingness to accept help to speak directly from her feelings, to admit her weakness, implies an end to her isolation."[20]

Jonathan Franzen's novel *Freedom* shows that one can move through apparently self-destructive passionate abandon to stronger connections with others. Patty and Walter Berglund marry after childhoods they both spend struggling to win approval. Patty in particular works at becoming a good wife and overcoming her long-standing attraction to Walter's irresponsible friend, Richard Katz. Richard lures her because during an early conversation with him, she finally feels free to be herself: "She wanted to take a road trip with Richard and, what's more, she was going to do it. The sad truth was that their talk in the car had been a tremendous excitement and relief to her—an excitement because Richard was exciting and a relief because, finally, after months of trying to be somebody she wasn't or wasn't quite, she'd felt and sounded like her unpretended true self."[21] Richard ignores her on the trip, so she returns to Walter with whom she has a good marriage and two children. But, eventually, Patty has an affair with Richard, and Walter becomes involved with his assistant, Lalitha, who understands and shares his fondness for birds. Patty and Richard inevitably split and Patty winds up teaching children, a job she loves. Lalitha dies in a car accident and Walter becomes an eccentric, living alone at what had been his family's summer cabin. He knows that beneath his social efforts on behalf of the environment he has always yearned for solitude: "The love he felt for the creatures whose habitat he was protecting was founded on projection: an identification of their own wish to be left alone by noisy human beings" (457). He now enjoys isolation in abundance.

After Walter plays out his suppressed desire to spend time alone and Patty gives vent to her attraction to Richard, they reconcile and rebuild what looks like a happy marriage between two people who have learned the importance of trusting and being themselves, no matter what detours this decision creates for them. When they meet, Walter

> stopped looking at her eyes and started looking into them, returning their look before it was too late, before this connection between life and what came after life was lost, and let her see all the vileness inside him, all the hatreds of two thousand solitary nights, while the two of them were still in touch with the void in which the sum of everything they'd ever said or done, every pain they'd inflicted, every joy they'd shared, would weigh less than the smallest feather on the wind.

She responds to this look by calling him back to normalcy: "'It's me... Just me'" (559).

Similarly, in midwestern fiction, people who stumble often use this event as an opportunity to rethink their orientation towards life and shape an existence more consonant with their values and needs. In Chester Himes's *Lonely Crusade*, his protagonist Lee Gordon persists in attempting to do the right thing. His white employer attempts to co-opt Lee's efforts on behalf of the union by offering him another, better-paying job. Lee refuses even though it irritates his wife because she thinks it would require so little compromise on his part for him to make more money and vastly improve the physical circumstances of their lives. He tries to persuade himself to do the clever thing, take the job, and believe "that honor never was and never would be for the Negro, and integrity was only for a fool; that from then on he would believe in the almighty dollar, the cowardice of Negroes, and the hypocrisy of whites, and he would never go wrong."[22] But Gordon finds himself incapable of fulfilling this vow. At the novel's end, when it becomes clear that his honest efforts have delivered him to a wall, he refuses to give up; instead, he grabs a union banner from a wounded comrade and carries it down the street as the police take aim.

All the women who collect at the Convent in Toni Morrison's novel *Paradise* have disastrous histories, but they now live in a place run by a woman who gives them total acceptance. After their disappointing pasts, these women wonder at "this sweet, unthreatening old lady who seemed to love each one of them best; who never criticized, who shared everything but needed little or no care; required no emotional investment; who listened; who locked no doors and accepted each as she was. What was she talking about, this ideal parent, friend, companion in whose company they were safe from harm?"[23] They resist, but she eventually convinces them to try loud dreaming, which consists of lying on the ground and talking out their memories and pains. Through this process of owning their experiences and their reactions, they become stronger people: "The Convent women are no longer haunted" (266). And then they dance in the rain: "There are great rivers in the world and on their banks and the edges of oceans children thrill to water. In places where rain is light the thrill is almost erotic. But those sensations bow to the rapture of holy women dancing in hot sweet rain. They would have laughed, had enchantment not been so deep" (283).

In Louise Erdrich's *Four Souls*, Fleur goes to Minneapolis to execute elaborate revenge on John Mauser, the man who took her land: she seduces and marries him, intending to kill him, but she keeps procrastinating. Then she has a child with him whom the doctors declare slow. And so she drinks. Eventually, she returns to her Ojibwe community with her son: "Her spirit was still longing for her old place, her land, her scraped-bare home that had nothing on it but kind popple, raspberry bushes, and a cabin caved in from last year's snow."[24] Fleur's deterioration saddens everyone who once admired her: "She was the last of the Pillagers, and to see her as a common drunk would take something out of every one of us" (194). Her son wins her land back by besting the Indian agent in a card game, but this triumph brings Fleur little genuine joy: "The pleasure in her voice was wild. Her movements were jerky, her face stark with exhaustion. She looked older and almost sick, yellow showed under the smooth sheen of her skin" (200). Then Margaret, an elder woman in the tribe, dresses Fleur in a medicine dress and orders her to cleanse herself by "fasting on the dark rock eight days and eight nights with all of her memories and her ghosts" (205). Afterwards, Fleur "lives quiet in the woods" (210). Nanapush closes the book saying that everyone needs to accept change gracefully because "all things familiar dissolve into strangeness" (209–10). And this mandate includes the Ojibwe: "Even our bones nourish change, and even a people who lived so close to the bone and were saved for thousands of generations by a practical philosophy, even such people as we, the Anishinnaabeg, can sometimes die, or change, and or change and become" (210).

Some characters in this fiction are wise or lucky enough to live persistently in quiet acceptance of their lives without the aid of Chicago or breakdowns or failure. They come to understand what Delphine in Louise Erdrich's *The Master Butcher's Singing Club* knows: society's interest in drama can make it hard to acknowledge the quiet life's pleasures: "It was a routine, she later thought, she didn't treasure enough. An even life, without any jumps or starts. No stalls either. It was the kind of life you didn't know at the time you were living it was a happy life."[25] Eventually, she cherishes her calm existence but she must resist fanciful "truisms" to do so: "She hadn't exactly feared the word *contentment*, but had always associated it with vague sense of failure. To be discontented always seemed much richer a thing. To be restless, striving. That view was romantic. In truth, she was finding out, life was better lived in a tranquil pattern" (302).

In *Death Comes for the Archbishop*, Will Cather does a magnificent job of presenting the serene life of someone who has mastered the midwestern philosophy of accepting himself and enjoying ordinary existence: Archbishop Latour, a European sophisticate, comes to love the people and the environment of his simple western desert mission. Cather describes his experiences in understated language that makes the novel a testimony to the impact of small, apparently insignificant events, if one has the composure to acknowledge them. In the following passage, Latour savors the air in uncultivated regions: "He did not know just when it had become so necessary to him, but he had come back to die in exile for the sake of it. Something soft and wild and free, something that whispered to the ear on the pillow, lightened the heart, softly, softly, picked the lock, slid the bolts, and released the prisoned spirit of man into the wind, into the blue and gold into the morning, into the morning!"[26] Cather set out consciously to write such a work, confessing about the novel that "I had all my life wanted to do something in the style of legend, which is absolutely the reverse of dramatic treatment." In such writing, she continues, it "is as though all human experiences, measured against one supreme spiritual standard, were of the same importance."[27] Mundane materials have as important roles to play as those with large impact and meaning. And, indeed, through the simple rendering of his experiences, Cather gives a sense of the Archbishop's tranquility. In the following passage, the Bishop returns to his mission and reflects on how isolated he finds himself, especially compared to the life he would lead in Europe: "But when he entered his study, he seemed to come back to reality, to the sense of a Presence awaiting him. The curtain of the arched doorway had scarcely fallen behind him when that feeling of personal loneliness was gone, and a sense of loss was replaced by a sense of restoration. He sat down before his desk, deep in reflection. It was just this solitariness of love in which a priest's life could be like his Master's. It was not a solitude of atrophy, of negation, but of perpetual flowering."[28]

Latour's simple but resonant vision causes Marilyn Arnold to observe that the book affirms "that the physical and the spiritual are not separate essences, that in fact the spiritual resides in the physical, though it takes a special kind of sensibility to see it there."[29] Christina Murphy agrees: "Willa Cather has created one of the most striking and unusual novels of modern American literature—a novel that takes us into the 'life-world' of Latour's consciousness and that enables us to go with Latour forever 'into the morning, into the morning!' (277) in pursuit of a phenomenological awareness that enables us to experience as one the existence of meaning and the meaning of existence."[30]

This ability to savor the ordinary indicates psychological serenity. In Ernest Hemingway's "The Big Two-Hearted River," Nick Adams especially relishes the moment when he finally does nothing except luxuriate in his experience: "Nick was happy as he crawled inside the tent. He had not been unhappy all day. This was different though. Now things were done. There had been this to do. Now it was done. It had been a hard trip. He was very tired. That was done. He had made his camp. He was settled. Nothing could touch him. It was a good place to camp. He was there, in the good place. He was in his home where he had made it."[31] As Fredrik Brogger notes, this relaxed moment bodes well for Nick's recovery from the trauma of war: "However pleasant it is for Nick to master the simpler tasks of outdoor life, his mental health depends on his capacity to move beyond this impasse, to relinquish his need for control."[32]

By relaxing into his impulses, Charles Citrine, the central character of Bellow's *Humboldt's Gift*, finds himself connected to others. He cannot understand why he stays in crude Chicago; neither can his ex-wife, who complains that he not only insists on remaining in this backwater, he even avoids all the town's intellectuals. Citrine happily acknowledges that he evades such people because he believes theorists specialize in robbing the world of its magic, something best understood and accepted through emotional wholeness rather than intellectual labor. Citrine believes in the reality of the individual soul and follows his own inner sense of spirituality, even though he lives surrounded by people who distrust such matters, but try to avoid noticing their souls by keeping themselves frantically busy. They cannot relax into their spirituality because it will connect them to others and to the world. Instead, they fight to protect their individuality even though the exclusivity they defend so fiercely leaves them morally, spiritually, and emotionally empty: "You have the single self, independently conscious, proud of its detachment and its absolute immunity, its stability and its power to remain unaffected by anything whatsoever—by the sufferings of others or by society or by politics or by external chaos" (203). Citrine himself has long since lost his simple heart and joined the morally tangled masses, but his desire to recover simplicity distinguishes him. And the book he dominates offers much evidence that he has achieved this goal. He settles so easily in his soul that he not only cares about others, even loves them; inanimate objects move him. And he convinces himself that by relaxing into such feelings human beings achieve experiences confirmed as significant by their intensity. Citrine thoroughly enjoys his ride in the world to which trusting his spiritual impulses delivers him: "One life with its love affairs, its operatic ambitions, its dollars and horse races and marriage-designs and old people's homes is, after all, only a tin dipperful of this superabundance. It rushes up also from within" (331). Citrine's move from self-acceptance to affection for others and for the world seems typical in this literature. Those who learn to relax into a genuine sense of themselves simultaneously seem to learn to care for others.

Much the same thing happens to Lee Gordon in Chester Himes's *Lonely Crusade* after he lets go of his ambivalence about living with integrity. Suddenly he sees the world more kindly: "He saw the ravages of dissipation in the faces of the winos and the reeking ruins of syphilis in the bodies of the whores. Yet everything he saw was with compassion and all he heard was with a prayer. And the odor of garbage from the uncleaned gutters gave place to a fragrance of friendliness in this living world. Just life itself was pretty wonderful" (385).

And, indeed, in the work of one midwestern fiction writer after another, characters who rest in self-acceptance find their way to compassion. This begins with *Huckleberry Finn*. Arguably the most discussed passage in American literature occurs in Mark Twain's *Huckleberry Finn*, when Huck debates whether or not to turn in his enslaved companion, Jim. Although critics have disputed whether Huck helps Jim as much as he could or should, no one suggests that Huck makes the wrong decision when he declares, "'All right, then, I'll *go* to hell'" (292) while tearing up his letter to Jim's owner. Huck reaches this conclusion after reviewing instances of kindness between him and Jim, making his treatment of Jim consistent with the sympathy for others Huck repeatedly displays in the novel. For instance, he feels great sadness when his friend Buck dies in a feud. He protects the Wilks' girls from the King and the

Six. Relaxing into Compassion

Duke. And, the most frequent complaints about the novel involve Huck's uncharacteristic insensitivity to Jim's humiliating treatment when he and Tom Sawyer force Jim to perform tasks that will supposedly free him. But in these episodes, Huck simply subordinates himself to someone who enjoys more community approval than he does. Alone with Jim, Huck can do the right thing. Back in society, like most people, he lacks the courage and, probably, the awareness to behave morally. Huck's behavior offers a prime example of the kindness of relatively powerless members of society towards one another that constitutes the novel's central value as well as everyone's vulnerability to the power of social codes.

Ten years after the appearance of *Huckleberry Finn*, in 1894, Hamlin Garland argues that compassion and fellowship will play central roles in the new literature of the Midwest: "If the past celebrated lust and greed and love of power, the future will celebrate continence and humility and altruism. If the past was the history of a few titled personalities riding high on obscure waves of nameless, suffering humanity, the future will be the day of high average personality, the abolition of all privilege, the peaceful walking together of brethren, equals before nature and before the law. And fiction will celebrate this life."[33] As Garland predicted, implicit pleas for empathy pervade the literature produced by writers who grew up in the Middle West from the time of Garland's statement up to the present. Thus, *Huckleberry Finn* serves as the first example of a long stream of novels from this region suggesting that, first and foremost, people need to treat each other kindly.

The psychological development of Carrie in Theodore Dreiser's *Sister Carrie* consists primarily of her acquiring sympathy for others. At the book's start, she has little concern for other people. She leaves her sister's home without regret and virtually never alludes to her family in Wisconsin. When she finds herself attracted to George Hurstwood, it "was the first time her sympathies had ever been thoroughly aroused" (93). Carrie subsequently feels sad when she sees poor people on the Chicago streets: "Sorrow in her was aroused by many a spectacle—an uncritical upswelling of grief for the weak and the helpless." She finds people who endure the hard factory work she has escaped particularly moving: "Her sympathies were ever with that under-world of toil from which she had so recently sprung, and which she best understood" (102). This empathy allows Carrie to become a powerful actress, as well as to understand that this career alone will not redeem a life empty of compassion, thanks in large part to the advice of another midwesterner, Ames. As the novel closes, she understands the importance of actively helping others.

Alexandra Bergson in Willa Cather's *O Pioneers!*, like Carrie, begins the novel with a defective understanding of other people because keeping her family and their investments afloat financially has consumed her energy and attention. But, still, she comes to care intensely about the young women who work for her and vows to protect Ivar when others want to institutionalize him because he doesn't wear shoes and has visions. Despite the busy and demanding activity that dominates her life, Alexandra makes time for Ivar to pour out his concerns to her because she "had found that she could often break his fasts and long penances by talking to him and letting him pour out the thoughts that troubled him. Sympathy always cleared his mind, and ridicule was poison to him" (36). Indeed, Alexandra's profitable choices rest finally on her sympathy: Ivar helps her understand animals and her connection with the land allows her to anticipate its future: "She had never known before how much the country meant to her.... Under the long shaggy ridges, she felt the future stirring" (28). At novel's end, she finally realizes that she needs to take her attachment to others seriously enough to put it at the center of her life, and plans to marry Carl.

Although this concern for others seems natural in women characters, in the work of midwestern fiction writers, male characters often share it. George Willard in Sherwood Anderson's *Winesburg, Ohio* cares enough about the outcasts of his town to seek them out and listen to their stories. At the end of the book, when he plans to leave Winesburg behind, he feels enormous loneliness, but then realizes that his sympathy for the people of the town has enriched his life immeasurably. Anderson's narrator describes this experience in a way that suggests connections to others redeem and give meaning to the lives of all people: "One shudders at the thought of the meaninglessness of life while at the same instant, and if the people of the town are his people, one loves life so intensely that tears come into the eyes."[34]

The displaced midwesterner Nick Carraway in F. Scott Fitzgerald's *The Great Gatsby*, unlike virtually everyone else who has anything to do with Gatsby, actually cares about him. When Gatsby dies, the throngs who attended his lavish parties disappear and Nick joins the tiny collection of mourners at Gatsby's funeral. Meanwhile, the Buchanans' cruel treatment of everyone they encounter causes Nick to condemn them as "careless people" who "smashed up things and creatures and then retreated back into their money or their vast carelessness, or whatever it was that kept them together and let other people clean up the mess they had made"(180–81). Nick links his judgment of the Buchanans to his midwestern background when, after a brief confrontation with Tom, Nick sarcastically remarks that Tom is "rid of my provincial squeamishness forever" (181). *The Great Gatsby*'s conclusion all but overtly states that midwesterners care about each other more intensely than do easterners. Nick describes returning home for Christmas and calling greetings to old friends in Chicago's Union Station, explaining that he is perhaps "a little complacent from growing up in the Caraway house in a city where dwellings are still called through decades by a family's name" (177). This sense of community contrasts with his image of the East: four well-dressed men carrying an inebriated woman in a white silk dress on a stretcher: "Her hand, which dangles over the side, sparkles cold with jewels. Gravely the men turn in at a house— the wrong house. But no one knows the woman's name, and no one cares" (178).

Ernest Hemingway's *In Our Time* explains the stoicism that much of Hemingway's work recommends as an attempt to protect one's vulnerability. As a child, Hemingway's Nick Adams feels great sympathy. In "Indian Camp," when his father tries to tell him that the cries of the Indian woman he operates on do not matter, Nick tries to achieve the detachment his father recommends, but finally gives into his compassion, calling out to his father, "'Oh, Daddy, can't you give her something to make her stop screaming?'" (16). When Nick goes to war, he has to distance himself from others: "We waited till he got one leg over and then potted him.... Then three more came over further down the wall. We shot them. They all came just like that" (29). Naturally enough, when Harold Krebs returns home from the war in "Soldier's Home," he doesn't care about anyone, including his family. His mother asks him if he loves anyone and he replies, "'I don't love anybody'" (76). But when she begins to weep, he walks over to her and claims that he was just kidding. But, in fact, he resents his mother for making demands of him before he feels ready to engage in normalcy. In "The Big Two-Hearted River," Nick Adams, who, like Krebs, has returned from war, resuscitates his emotional life with a fishing trip. As he studies trout in a stream, "Nick's heart tightened as the trout moved. He felt all the old feeling" (134). And his healing begins. So even the coldness in Hemingway's work reflects not a lack of empathy, but a need to bury it until life makes it safe to allow it full play.

Compassion and kindness serve as the consistent standards of behavior in Willa Cather's masterpiece, *Death Comes for the Archbishop*. The Catholic prelates that precede Archbishop Latour and his friend Father Valliant, Friar Baltazar, and Padre Martinez, cynically use the natives. Bishop Latour finds these men repugnant, preferring to surround himself with people like Father

Valliant, whose "countenance had little to recommend it but kindliness and vivacity" (31) and Kit Carson, who has "a compassionate heart" (61). Latour interprets the Acoma attachment to their rock as a sign they see it as representing "the highest comparison of loyalty in love and friendship" (77). After Valliant declares that others need him more than LaTour because "down there it is work for the heart, for a particular sympathy" (166), La Tour tells his friend, "'Your feeling must be your guide in this matter'" (166).

One evening, when depression interrupts his sleep, LaTour goes to pray in church. There, he encounters Sada. After attempting to sleep in the cold woodshed where her Protestant owners sent her to spend the night, she decided to attempt to pray in a Catholic church, although her owners have forbidden it. She and LaTour go into the church to pray and she weeps "tears of ecstasy" (170). The experience restores the intense religious sense LaTour enjoyed as a young man: "He seemed to feel all it meant to her to know that there was a Kind Woman in Heaven, though there were such cruel ones on earth.... The beautiful concept of Mary pierced the priest's heart like a sword" (173). He gives Sada a small medal bearing the Virgin's likeness that had been blessed by the pope, thinking "now she would have a treasure to hide and guard, to adore while her watchers slept. Ah, he thought, for one who cannot read—or think—the Image, the physical form of Love!" (174). As his life ends, La Tour congratulates himself on surviving long enough to see at least some of the cruelty he has witnessed mitigated: "'I have lived to see two great wrongs righted; I have seen the end of black slavery, and I have seen the Navajos restored to their own country" (231). One could argue, therefore, that a celebration of empathy constitutes the heart of *Death Comes for the Archbishop*.

This valuing of compassion above all transcends any racial divides in midwestern literature. Pecola, in Toni Morrison's *The Bluest Eye*, goes mad because of the indifference she encounters from virtually everyone she meets. On the other hand, Pilate, the central character of Toni Morrison's *Song of Solomon*, easily sympathizes with others after spending her life as an outcast. Healing becomes her primary role: "She gave up, apparently, all interest in table manners or hygiene, but acquired a deep concern for and about human relationships."[35] As a result, "She was a natural healer, and among quarreling drunks and fighting women she could hold her own, and sometimes mediated a peace that lasted a good bit longer than it should have" (150). This ability rests on her decision to trust what she feels: "She tackled the problem of trying to decide how she wanted to live and what was valuable to her. When am I happy and when am I sad and what is the difference?" (149). Pilate's remark as she dies—"'I wish I'd a knowed more people. I would of loved 'em all. If I'd a knowed more, I would a loved more'" (336)—clearly demonstrates her profound attachment to others. Shortly after her death, her nephew Milkman validates that her loving nature makes Pilate more than mortal, declaring that "without ever leaving the ground, she could fly" (336).

In Louise Erdrich's *Four Souls*, another character explains Fleur Pillager's failed attempt to exact revenge on James Mauser, the man who stole her land as a product of her empathy: she notes that Fleur "had a heart, no matter how she tried to hide it from her husband, a heart that stood both fast and passionate when it came to defending those she loved" (122). Fleur returns to the reservation and to the influence of Margaret, who loves Nanapush, and likens this experience to "trying to remember the tune and words to a song that the spirits have given you in your sleep. Some days, I knew exactly how the song went and some days I couldn't even hum the first line. Then there were times we both knew the song and love was effortless" (182). Margaret urges Fleur to forget her strength and once more cultivate her empathy so that her children can love her: "'How can they love a woman who forgot to guard their tenderness, and her own?'" (206). At the novel's end, Fleur has quietly reassumed her old life on the reservation and seems also to have reestablished ties to the spirits animating her culture.

In two recent midwestern novels, Jim Harrison's *Returning to Earth* and Charles Baxter's *The Soul Thief*, the value of kindness comprises the books' thematic centers. *Returning to Earth* consists almost entirely of a celebration of sympathy. The book focuses on the death of an extremely kind part–Ojibwe man named Donald, who loves with such probity that another character declares that he never knew anyone else who was as completely himself. As the book begins, he attempts to enlighten his children of their history by dictating the story of his ancestors to his wife. He descends from a line of emotionally generous people and he retains their sensitivity to the plights of others. As he tells the story of his grandfather Clarence's decent treatment of his horse, Sally, and even of a thief, he worries about how badly his grandfather must have suffered. He also frets about his son Herald's loneliness, but likes his daughter Clare's enthusiasm for relationships because, as he tells her, "Love will carry you through the hard parts."[36] He even worries about the man he seeks out to kill because the man had kicked Donald's dog to death. When he sees just how pathetic his intended victim's life is, Donald offers to buy him groceries. Donald has no spectacular achievements other than supporting and loving his family, but his generosity nourishes and sustains those around him.

As a result, his nephew, K, describes him as "a tugboat, their dense weight and immense power, slow to achieve speed but with an irresistible surge of power" (78). Donald's imminent death convinces K simultaneously of everyone's mortality and of life's richness: "To care for Donald in his present state is to finally understand that there are no miracles except that we exist" (78).

The novel shows that Donald's kindness continues to shape the lives of those he leaves behind after his passing. K had taken Donald to a low-slung birch branch on the Lake Superior shore, where Donald rested and found serenity by losing himself in nature: "It was a miracle of sorts but there was no breeze until I laid out on the limb and my body calmed down. Within minutes there was no inside or outside to the world…. There was a spirit in the place that gave my body some peace" (16–17). After Donald's death, K feels a new connection with nature that allows him to consider, for instance, how he would look at a bird or talk to a skunk.

Donald's brother-in-law, David, tries to deny his sexuality because he fears resembling his father; he particularly dismisses his attraction to Vera, a woman his father raped when she was a girl. Although others tease David about his resemblance to his father, Donald assures David that there are striking differences between the two and ridicules David when he pretends that he does not care about sex. After Donald's death, David trusts himself enough to seek out a relationship with Vera. Donald's daughter Clare finds solace in the spiritual connection with nature her father enjoyed. Although this worries her mother, Cynthia, at first, she comes to share it. Moreover, Cynthia decides that she will begin work in a reservation school, a place she feels Donald has led her. And so Harrison's *Returning to Earth* argues for the large, persistent impact of kindness.

Charles Baxter's *The Soul Thief* opens by describing Jerome Coolberg as "insufferable, one of those boy geniuses, all nerve and brain."[37] Coolberg invents a character named Nathaniel Mason, an intellectual like Coolberg, whose academic career disintegrates when he breaks down on a seminar room floor. Mason's sister, who lived in a halfway house before his crisis, brings him back to normalcy by reading him novels. As Mason notes: "By saving me she saved herself" (153). Mason believes this event testifies to the power of compassion: "Though a prejudice exists in our culture against compassion, there being little profit in it, the emotion itself is ineradicable" (153). Mason marries a woman named Laura because her decency attracts him: "What I had always loved about Laura had been her kindness and innocence in the face of the world's sophisticated cruelty" (158). Meanwhile, Coolberg becomes the moderator of a successful radio show called *American Evenings* and invites Mason to California where, he explains, he invented Mason. But Mason has moved beyond Coolberg. Coolberg lives a lonely life built largely on contempt; his home reflects this choice: "The place had retained its ability to project a human solitude and loneliness, as did Coolberg, who gazed at his dominion with a resigned expression of deadened appetite" (202). While Coolberg values power, the book's narrator asserts the value of empathy: "Although love may die, what is said on its behalf cannot be consumed by the passage of time, and forgiveness is everything" (203). Mason happily returns home to his family and thinks, "Blessings ... on my family, on the poor and helpless, the brokenhearted, on the victims of violence and on its perpetrators. May they all be undestroyed. Blessings on everyone. Blessings without limit" (210).

And so Huck's kindness towards Jim represents but the first of many incidents of decency that not only pervade the novels produced by midwestern authors, but becomes a central theme as the decades pass. And consistent with Hamlin Garland's predictions, this empathy comes most naturally to those with enormous integrity and little power.

Indeed, critics frequently praise midwestern authors for producing works that invite their readers to view their subjects sympathetically. Claude Simpson commends this characteristic of Dreiser's work, claiming that "Dreiser's power of evoking sympathy, especially for his weak characters, is accompanied by a dramatic quality tune that has not much dimmed."[38] Robert Bone believes Algren's *Never Comes Morning* renders the complexity of people usually seen through stereotypes: "The unique triumph of the novel is that Algren, while portraying the world of Damen and Division in all its sordid crumminess, still communicates the complex humanity of his character. He does so by utilizing a narrative voice that reaches out to and identifies with his creations."[39] Carla Cappetti agrees: "Through their voices the criminal and the prostitute who inhabit *Never Comes Morning* challenge the objectification of which they are the victims. More important, they challenge the sustaining epistemology that condemns them to stereotypicality and denies them the privilege of individuality and typicality."[40] Barbara Cantalupo thanks Tillie Olsen for making audiences aware of issues that stifle women's lives, explaining that "*Yonnondio*, holding all that is possible and all that must be pursued, strikes a resonance with those issues of silencing, anxiety, fear, and resistance that affect women and women writers."[41] Heidi MacPherson argues that Olsen helps readers understand the traps that limit the working class: "*Yonnondio* remains a painful text, one that resists being read as escapism. It asks for new definitions of escape and reveals how working-class escape is as problematic as the more frequently studied middle-class escape."[42] Stephanie Li praises Morrison for writing novels that allow her readers to feel love towards her characters: "As lovers, reader, and text are united in a dynamic process of intimate creation that exists both within the continued reinterpretation of the novel and in the larger changes wrought within the reader by this new kind of love."[43] Karl Precoda and P.S. Polanah claim *Native Son*'s ability to help audiences understand the black experience makes it an important work: "Thus, *Native Son* exists in specific relation to its readers, to imprint this blackness upon them in an irreversible act of writing that forever rends the veil of their blindness, an achievement that, we have tried to suggest, whether we then classify the novel as modernist, naturalist or any combination of genres, fully justifies, in fact demands, its foremost place among American radical novels."[44] Stephen George says that even the violence in *Native Son* serves a compassionate purpose: "Wright's use of violence, language and sex—while shocking—are in fact meant to shock.... The contemporary reader of *Native Son* is invited to look up from the book's pages to see the morally and psychologically disfiguring effects of racism on both blacks and whites."[45]

All these testimonies to the emotional power of their work would probably please these authors because, to them, it finally does not matter how one achieves the capacity to enjoy the emotional richness of daily life, whether through choice, luck, or disaster. Once people have tasted freedom from struggling to measure up to society's standards, they have no desire to pursue those norms again. So, midwestern writers recommend replacing ambition with a humble sense of one's insignificance which allows one to relish the world and others rather than attempting to conquer them. Letting go like this makes room for the emotional honesty which allows one to savor the richness of their environment and other people. They suggest that this peaceful resignation not only offers the only genuine path to happiness, it also frequently allows people to feel and express their innate empathy for one another.

Chapter Notes

Preface

1. This study defines the Midwest as a dozen states in the center of the country, including Illinois, Indiana, Iowa, Kansas, Michigan, Minnesota, Missouri, Nebraska, North Dakota, Ohio, South Dakota, and Wisconsin.

Introduction

1. Lawrence Buell, *The Dream of the Great American Novel* (Cambridge: Harvard University Press, 2014), 19.
2. Wallace Stegner, "Yarn-Spinner in the American Vein," in *The Mark Twain Anthology*, ed. Shelley Fisher Fishkin (New York: Library of America, 2010), 272.
3. Ernest Hemingway, *Green Hills of Africa* (New York: Scribner's, 1963), 22.
4. Ronald Weber, *The Midwestern Ascendency in American Writing* (Bloomington: Indiana University Press, 1992), 15.
5. Kenneth S. Lynn, *Mark Twain and Southwestern Humor* (Boston: Little, Brown, 1959), 143–44.
6. Marcia Noe, "Midwestern Literature in Historical and Cultural Context," in *Midwestern Literature*, ed. Ronald Primeau (Ipswich, MA: Salem Press, 2013), 16.
7. Sara Kosiba, "What is 'Middlewestishness'? the Evolution of Midwestern Literary Studies" in *Midwestern Literature*, ed. Ronald Primeau (Ipswich, MA: Salem Press, 2013), 28.
8. Toni Morrison, *What Moves at the Margin: Selected Nonfiction*, ed. Carolyn C. Denard (Jackson: University Press of Mississippi, 2008), 64.
9. Nelson Algren, *Chicago City on the Make* (Chicago: University of Chicago Press, 2011), 81.
10. Scott Turow, "Review of *Yonnondio*: From the Thirties in *The Critical Response to Tillie Olsen*, ed. Kay Holye Nelson and Nancy Huse (Westport, CT: Greenwood, 1994), 30–31.
11. James Farrell, *The Fate of Writing in America* (New York: New Directions, 1946), 35.
12. Joseph Epstein, *The New York Times Book Review*, December 5, 1976, 92.
13. Richard Wright, *Black Boy* (New York: HarperPerennial, 1993), 250.
14. Gerald Vizenor, *The Heirs of Columbus* (Hanover: University Press of New England, 1991), 5.
15. Hamlin Garland, *Crumbling Idols: Twelve Essays on Art, Dealing Chiefly with Literature, Painting and the Drama* (Chicago and Cambridge: Stone and Kimball, 1894), 45–46.
16. Theodore Roethke, *Straw for the Fire*, ed. David Wagoner (Port Townsend: Copper Canyon Press, 2006), 161.
17. Nancy Bunge, *Master Class: Lessons from Leading Writers* (Iowa City: University of Iowa Press, 2005), 71.

18. Bob Dylan, *Chronicles, Volume One* (New York: Simon & Schuster, 2004), 292.

Chapter One

1. Henry David Thoreau, *The Variorum Walden*, ed. Walter Harding (New York: Twayne, 1962), 99–100.
2. Ralph Waldo Emerson, *Essays & Lectures* (New York: Library of America, 1983), 76.
3. Hamlin Hill and Walter Blair, *The Art of Huckleberry Finn* (San Francisco: Chandler, 1962), 27. All future quotations from *Huckleberry Finn* are taken from this book and appear in the text.
4. Mark Twain, "James Fenimore Cooper's Literary Offenses," *North American Review* 161 (July 1895): 3.
5. Nathaniel Hawthorne, *The Centenary Edition of the Works of Nathaniel Hawthorne* (Columbus: Ohio State University Press, 1974), 10:403.
6. F. Scott Fitzgerald, *The Beautiful and Damned* (New York: The Modern Library, 2002), 378.
7. F. Scott Fitzgerald, *The Great Gatsby* (New York: Scribner's, 1953), 13.
8. F. Scott Fitzgerald, *Tender Is the Night* (New York: Scribner, 1962), 201.
9. Sinclair Lewis, *Elmer Gantry* (New York: New American Library, 1970), 53–54.
10. Julia Eichelberger, "Renouncing the World's Business in *Seize the Day*," *Studies in American Jewish Literature* 17 (1998): 61.
11. Jonathan Franzen, *The Twenty-Seventh City* (New York: Farrar, Straus, and Giroux, 1988), 31.
12. Jane Smiley, *Good Faith* (New York: Alfred A. Knopf, 2003), 260.
13. Jane Smiley, *Ten Days in the Hills* (New York: Alfred A. Knopf, 2007), 22.
14. Saul Bellow, *Humboldt's Gift* (New York: Viking Press, 1975), 469.
15. Eichelberger, "Renouncing 'The World's Business,'" 63.
16. Jonathan Franzen, *Strong Motion* (New York: Farrar, Straus, and Giroux, 1992), 120.
17. Jane Smiley, *Duplicate Keys* (New York: Fawcett Columbine, 1984), 286.
18. Willa Cather, *The Song of the Lark* (New York: Signet, 1991), 191.
19. Jim Harrison, *The River Swimmer* (New York: Grove Press, 2013), 79.
20. Bernard G. Prusak, "When Words Fail Us: Reexamining the Conscience of Huckleberry Finn," *Journal of Aesthetic Education* 45, no. 4 (2011): 17.
21. Lionel Trilling. *The Liberal Imagination: Essays on Literature and Society* (New York: Charles Scribner's Sons, 1950), 112–113.
22. Sinclair Lewis, *Babbitt* (New York: New American Library, 1950), 46–47.
23. Sinclair Lewis, *Arrowsmith* (New York: New American Library, 1925), 430.
24. Sinclair Lewis, *Main Street* (New York: New American Library, 1948), 431.
25. Jane Smiley, *Moo* (New York: Fawcett Columbine, 1995), 355.
26. Jonathan Franzen, *Corrections* (New York: Farrar, Straus, and Giroux, 1988), 195.
27. Ty Hawkins, "Assessing the Promise of Jonathan Franzen's First Three Novels: A Rejection of 'Refuge,'" *College Literature* 37, no. 4 (2010): 86.
28. Jane Smiley, *The Greenlanders* (New York: Anchor, 1988), 581–82.
29. Neil Nakadate, *Understanding Jane Smiley* (Columbia: University of South Carolina Press, 1999), 126.
30. Sinclair Lewis, *It Can't Happen Here* (New York: New American Library, 1963), 85–86.
31. Tillie Olsen, *Yonnondio* (Lincoln: University of Nebraska Press, 2004), 1.
32. Jack Conroy, *The Disinherited* (Columbia: University Missouri Press, 1991), 206–07.
33. James Farrell, *Studs Lonigan* (New York: Library of America, 2004), 69.
34. Nelson Algren, *The Man with the Golden Arm* (New York: Seven Stories Press, 1976), 294.
35. Sherwood Anderson, *Perhaps Women* (Mamaroneck, NY: Paul P. Appel, 1970), 62–65.
36. Louise Erdrich, *The Plague of Doves* (New York: Harper Perennial, 2008), 78.
37. Bellow, *Humboldt's Gift*, 232.
38. Theodore Dreiser, *Sister Carrie* (New York: Dover, 2004), 339.
39. Toni Morrison, *Song of Solomon* (New York: Plume, 1987), 11.
40. Brenda Marshall, "The Gospel According to Pilate," *American Literature* 57, no. 3 (1985): 486.

Chapter Two

1. Hawthorne, *The Centenary Edition of the Works of Nathaniel Hawthorne*, 1:80.

2. George Montiero, "Innocence and Experience: The Adolescent Child in the Works of Mark Twain, Henry James, and Ernest Hemingway," *Estudos Anglo-Americanos* 1 (1977): 46.
3. Sherwood Anderson, *Winesburg, Ohio*, ed. Charles E. Modlin and Ray Lewis White (New York: W. W. Norton, 1996), 12.
4. Charles Baxter, *Gryphon: New and Selected Stories* (New York: Pantheon, 2011), 117–18.
5. Ernest Hemingway, *In Our Time* (New York: Charles Scribner's Sons, 1958), 16.
6. Ernest Hemingway, *The Old Man and the Sea* (New York: Scribner, 1980), 10.
7. Louise Erdrich, *The Plague of Doves*, 76–79.
8. Bellow, *Humboldt's Gift*, 423.
9. Louise Erdrich, *The Blue Jay's Dance* (New York: HarperCollins, 1995), 136.
10. Sherwood Anderson, *Letters to Bab*, ed. William A. Sutton (Urbana: University of Illinois Press, 1985), 80.
11. Tillie Olsen, *Yonnondio from the Thirties*, 50.
12. Charles Baxter, *First Light* (New York: Viking Press, 1987), 276.
13. Sherwood Anderson, *Windy McPherson's Son* (Chicago: University of Chicago Press, 1922), 11–16.
14. Sherwood Anderson, *Poor White* (New York: Viking Press, 1966), 5.
15. Walter Rideout, "Introduction" in Sherwood Anderson's *Poor White* (New York: Viking Press, 1966), xix.
16. Hill and Blair, *The Art of Huckleberry Finn*, 65–67.
17. Toni Morrison, "Introduction to *Adventures of Huckleberry Finn* in *The Mark Twain Anthology*, ed. Shelley Fishkin (New York: Library of America), 412.
18. Jim Harrison, *The Great Leader* (New York: Grove Press, 2011), 316.
19. Erdrich, *The Plague of Doves*, 161.
20. Louise Erdrich, *The Beet Queen* (New York: Harper Perennial, 1986), 337–38.
21. Jane Smiley, *A Thousand Acres* (New York: Fawcett Press, 1991), 305.
22. Sue Miller, *Lost in the Forest* (New York: Ballantine, 2006), 247.
23. Toni Morrison, *Sula* (New York: Vintage, 2004), 18.
24. Karen F. Stein, "Toni Morrison's *Sula*: A Black Woman's Epic," *Black American Literature Forum* 18, no. 4 (Winter 1984): 149.
25. Toni Morrison, *Love* (New York: Alfred A. Knopf, 2003), 199–200.
26. Louise Erdrich, *The Bingo Palace* (New York: Perennial, 2001), 209.
27. Louise Erdrich, *Love Medicine* (New York: Perennial, 2001), 39.
28. Jill Deans, "'File It Under 'L' for 'Love Child'": Adoptive Policies and Practices in the Erdrich Tetralogy" in *Imagining Adoption: Essays on Literature and Culture*, ed. Marianne Novy (Ann Arbor: University of Michigan Press, 2001), 233.
29. Thylias Moss, *Tale of a Sky-Blue Dress* (New York: Avon, 1998), 68.
30. Roni Natov, "Child Power in Louise Erdrich's Historical Fiction for Children," *International Research in Children's Literature* 2, no. 1 (2009): 137–38.
31. Thylias Moss, *I Want to Be* (New York: Picture Puffins, 1998), n. p.
32. Toni and Slade Morrison, *Little Cloud and Lady Wind* (New York: Simon & Schuster, 2010), n. p.
33. George P. Cunningham, "Afterword," in Langston Hughes, *The Sweet and Sour Animal Book* (New York: Oxford University Press, 1994), n. p.
34. Sherwood Anderson, *Short Stories*, ed. Maxwell Geismar (New York: Hill & Wang, 1962), 7.
35. Hemingway, *In Our Time*, 127–29.
36. Yvette Koepke and Christopher Nelson, "Genetic Crossing," *Studies in American Indian Literatures* 23, no. 3 (2011): 22.
37. Gerald Vizenor, *Father Meme* (Albuquerque: University New Mexico Press, 2008), 29.
38. James Farrell, *Reflections at Fifty* (New York: Vanguard, 1954), p. 166.
39. Carla Cappetti, *Writing Chicago: Modernism, Ethnography, and the Novel* (New York: Columbia University Press, 1993), 143.
40. Farrell, *Studs Lonigan*, 36.
41. Donald Pizer, *Twentieth-Century American Literary Naturalism: An Interpretation* (Carbondale: Crosscurrents/Modern Critiques, 1982), 23–24.
42. Daniel Shiffman, "Ethnic Competitors in *Studs Lonigan*," *Melus* 24 (Fall 1999), 76–77.
43. James Farrell, *A World I Never Made* (Urbana: University of Illinois Press, 2007), 7–8.
44. Jack Conroy, *The Disinherited* (Columbia: University of Missouri Press, 1991), 283.

45. Nelson Algren, *Never Come Morning* (New York: Seven Stories Press, 1987), 252.
46. Maxwell Geismar, "Nelson Algren: The Iron Sanctuary." *College English* 14 (March 1953): 313.
47. Tillie Olsen, *Tell Me a Riddle, Requa I, and Other Works* (Lincoln: University of Nebraska Press, 2013), 14.
48. Robert A. Perlongo and Nelson Algren, "Interview with Nelson Algren," *Chicago Review* 11, no. 3 (1957): 96.
49. Ernest Hemingway, *A Farewell to Arms* (New York: Charles Scribner's Sons, 1957), 185.
50. Jim Harrison, *Returning to Earth* (New York: Grove Press, 2007), 44.
51. Willa Cather, *One of Ours* (New York: Vintage, 1971), 243.
52. James Walsh, "Emblematical of War: Representations of Combat in Hemingway's Fiction," *Hemingway Review* 1 (Spring 1972): 50.
53. James Barloon, "Very Short Stories: The Miniaturization of War in Hemingway's *In Our Time*, *The Hemingway Review* 24 (Spring 2005), 13.
54. Ernest Hemingway, *The Nick Adams Stories* (New York: Scribner, 2003), 173.
55. Ibid., 228.
56. Alex Vernon, "War, Gender, and Ernest Hemingway," *The Hemingway Review* 22 (Fall 2002), http://www.questia.com/library/1G1-94775661/war-gender-and-ernest-hemingway.
57. Louise Erdrich, *The Master Butcher's Singing Club* (New York: Harper Perennial, 2005), 2.

Chapter Three

1. Hawthorne, *The Centenary Edition*, 1:263.
2. Toni Morrison, "Introduction to *The Adventures of Huckleberry Finn* in *The Mark Twain Anthology*," 409.
3. Dreiser, *Sister Carrie*, 350–53.
4. Algren, *Never Come Morning*, 213.
5. Jane Smiley, *The All-True Travels and Adventures of Lidie Newton* (New York: Fawcett Books, 1998), 450–52.
6. Willa Cather, *O Pioneers!* (New York: Dover, 1993), 28.
7. Judy Jones Tisdale, "Working Women on the Frontier: Capitalism and Community in Three Willa Cather Novels," in *The Image of the Frontier in Literature, the Media and Society*, ed. Will Wright and Steven Kaplan (Pueblo, CO: the Society for Inter-Disciplinary Study of Social Imagery, 1997), 183.
8. Clarence Major, *Such Was the Season* (San Francisco: Mercury House, 1987), 8.
9. Franzen, *Strong Motion*, 163.
10. Anderson, *Perhaps Women*, 132.
11. Precious McKenzie Stearns, "Sherwood Anderson: Between the Virgin and the Dynamo," in *Forces of Nature: Natural(-izing) Gender and Gender(izing) Nature in the Discourses of Western Culture*, ed. Bernadette H. Hyner and Precious McKenzie Stearns (Newcastle upon Tyne, England: Cambridge Scholars, 2009), 71.
12. Louise Erdrich, *Four Souls* (New York: Harper Perennial, 2005), 3.
13. Erdrich, *The Blue Jay's Dance*, 35.
14. Lisa Halliday, "Louise Erdrich, the Art of Fiction No. 208," *The Paris Review* http://www.theparisreview.org/interviews/6055/the-art-of-fiction-no-208-louise-erdrich.
15. Jane Smiley, "Can Mothers Think?" in *The True Subject: Writers on Life and Craft*, ed. Kurt Brown (St. Paul: Graywolf Press, 1993), 15.
16. Tillie Olsen, *Tell Me a Riddle, Requa I, and Other Works*, 14.
17. Rita Dove, *Fifth Sunday* (Lexington: University of Kentucky Press, 1985), 6.
18. Meridel Le Sueur, *The Girl* (Albuquerque: West End Press, 2006), 179–80.
19. Ann Pancake, "Story Time: Working-Class Women's Interpretations in Literary Temporal Conventions," *Narrative* 6 (October 1998): 300.
20. Melody Graulich, "Violence Against Women in the Literature of the Western Family," *Frontiers: A Journal of Woman Studies* 7, no. 3 (1984): 18.
21. Paula Rabinowitz, "Maternity as History: Gender and the Transformation of Genre in Meridel Le Sueur's *The Girl*," *Contemporary Literature*, 29 (Winter 1988): 545.
22. Erin V. Obermueller, "Reading the Body in Meridel Le Sueur's *The Girl*," *Legacy* 22, no. 1 (2005): 59.
23. Laura Coltelli, "Meridel Le Sueur: Connecting Class, Gender, Genre" in Marina Camboni, ed., *Networking Women: Subjects, Places, Links Europe-America towards a Re-Writing of Cultural History, 1890–1939* (Rome: Edizioni di storia e letteratura, 2004), 452.
24 Douglas Wixson, "The Question of

Meridel Le Sueur's Lost Patrimony," *Midamerica* 25 (1998): 106.
25. Sherwood Anderson, *Winesburg, Ohio*, Charles E. Modlin and Ray Lewis White, eds. (New York: W. W. Norton, 1996), 33.
26. Willa Cather, *Lucy Gayheart* (New York: Vintage, 1995), 86.
27. Willa Cather, *My Mortal Enemy* (New York: Vintage, 1990), 72–78.
28. Will Cather, *A Lost Lady* (New York: Vintage, 1972), 170.
29. Smiley, *The Greenlanders*, 108.
30. Jane Smiley, *Private Life* (New York: Alfred A. Knopf, 2010), 233.
31. Jane Smiley, *At Paradise Gate* (New York: Simon & Schuster, 1998), 203.
32. Tillie Olsen, *Tell Me a Riddle, Requa I and Other Works*, 89.
33. James R. Giles, *Confronting the Horror: The Novels of Nelson Algren* (Kent: Kent State University Press, 1989), 51.
34. Toni Morrison, *Paradise* (New York: Alfred A. Knopf, 1998), 177.
35. Sherwood Anderson, *Beyond Desire* (New York: Liveright, 1970), 208.
36. Franzen, *The Corrections*, 566.
37. Charles Baxter, *Shadow Play* (New York: W.W. Norton, 1993), 191.
38. Toni Morrison, *Home* (New York: Vintage, 2013), 103.
39. Louise Erdrich, the *Last Report on the Miracles at Little No Horse* (New York: Harper Perennial, 2009), 299.
40. Dana Kinnison, "Images of Possibility: Gender Identity in Will Cather's *My Antonia*," in *Women in Literature: Reading Through the Lens of Gender*, ed. Jerilyn Fisher and Silen S. Silber (Westport, CT: Greenwood Press, 2003), 206.
41. Charles Ruas, "Toni Morrison," in *Conversations with Toni Morrison*, ed. Danille Taylor-Guthrie (Jackson: University Press of Mississippi, 1994), 107.
42. Farrell, *Studs Lonigan*, 35.
43. Mark D. Noe, "Macho is all in the Mind: Studs Lonigan's Search for Paradise," *Aethlon* 11 (Fall 1993): 88.
44. Fitzgerald, *The Beautiful and Damned*, 90.
45. Baxter, *Gryphon: New and Selected Stories*, 239.
46. Anderson, *Winesburg, Ohio*, 29.
47. Louise Erdrich, *Tracks* (New York: Perennial, 1989), 167.
48. Erdrich, *Four Souls*, 156–161.
49. Saul Bellow, *Herzog* (New York: Fawcett Crest, 1965), 12.
50. Nancy Bunge, *Master Class* (Iowa City: University of Iowa Press, 2005), 149–150.
51. James I. McClintock, "*Dalva*: Jim Harrison's 'Twin Sister,'" *Journal of Men's Studies* 6 (April 30, 1998): 319.
52. Jim Harrison, *Returning to Earth* (New York: Grove Press, 2007), 47.
53. Michael Hardin, "The Trickster of History: *The Heirs of Columbus* and the Dehistorization of Narrative," *MELUS* 23, no. 4 (1988): 39.
54. Ernest Hemingway, *The Sun Also Rises* (New York: Charles Scribner's Sons, 1954), 247.
55. Ernest Hemingway, *Death in the Afternoon* (New York: G.P. Collier & Son, 1932), 213.
56. Hemingway, *The Green Hills of Africa*, 72–73.
57. Ernest Hemingway, *For Whom the Bell Tolls* (New York: Charles Scribner's Sons, 1940), 305.
58. Robert D. Crozier, S.J., "The Mask of Death, the Face of Life: Hemingway's Feminique," *The Hemingway Review* 4 (Fall 1984), 12.
59. Marc Hewson, "A Matter of Love of Death: Hemingway's Developing Psychosexuality in *For Whom the Bell Tolls*," in *Hemingway: Eight Decades of Criticism*, ed. Linda Wagner-Martin (East Lansing: Michigan State University Press, 2009), 372.

Chapter Four

1. Herman Melville, *Moby Dick* (New York: W.W. Norton, 1969), 155.
2. Shelley Fisher Fishkin, ed. *The Mark Twain Anthology* (New York: Library of America, 2010), 252.
3. Ibid., 259.
4. Toni Morrison, *Playing in the Dark: Whiteness and the Literary Imagination* (Cambridge: Harvard University Press, 1992), 56–57.
5. Shelley Fisher Fishkin, ed. *The Mark Twain Anthology*, 419.
6. Jane Smiley, "Say It Ain't So, Huck: Second Thoughts on Mark Twain's 'Masterpiece,'" in Mark Twain *The Adventures of Huckleberry Finn: A Case Study in Critical Controversy*, ed. Gerald Graff and James Phelan (Boston: Bedford/St. Martin's, 2004), 460.

7. Sanford Pinsker, "Huckleberry Finn and the Problem of Freedom," *The Virginia Quarterly Review* 77 (Autumn 2001): http://www.vqronline.org/articles/2001/autumn/pinsker-huckleberry-finn/.

8. Jane Smiley, "A Conversation with Jane Smiley in *The All-True Travels and Adventures of Lidie Newton* (New York: Fawcett Books, 1998), n. p.

9. Jim O'Loughlin, "Off the Raft: Adventures of Huckleberry Finn and Jane Smiley's *The All-True Travels and Adventures of Lidie Newton*, Papers on Language and Literature 43 (Spring 2007): 221.

10. Smiley, *The All-True Travels and Adventures of Lidie Newton*, 450–51.

11. Seymour Chwast, "Selling Huck Finn Down the River: A Response to Jane Smiley" in Mark Twain *Adventures of Huckleberry Finn: A Case Study in Critical Controversy*, ed. Gerald Graff and James Phelan (Boston: Bedford/St. Martin's), 469.

12. Vachel Lindsay, *Collected Poems* (New York: Macmillan, 1925), 183–84.

13. Langston Hughes, *The Ways of White Folks* (New York: Vintage, 1962), 19.

14. Robert Hayden, *Collected Prose*, ed. Frederick Glaysher (Ann Arbor: University of Michigan Press, 1984), 45.

15. Sherwood Anderson, *Dark Laughter* (New York: Liveright, 1970), 80.

16. Sherwood Anderson, *Letters of Sherwood Anderson*, ed. Howard Mumford Jones and Walter Rideout (Boston: Little, Brown, 1953), 142.

17. Saul Bellow, *Henderson the Rain King* (New York: Viking Press, 1959), 169.

18. Choko Ikeda, "Experiencing Africa in Joseph Conrad's *Heart of Darkness* and Saul Bellow's *Henderson the Rain King*," *Saul Bellow Journal* 18 (2002): 52.

19. Langston Hughes, "The Negro Artist and the Racial Mountain," in *Collected Works of Langston Hughes*, ed. Christopher De Santis (Columbia: University of Missouri Press, 2002), 9:45.

20. Morrison, *Playing in the Dark*, 45.

21. Ibid., 85–86.

22. Angela M. Salas, "Willa Cather's *Sapphira and the Slave Girl*: Extending the Boundaries of the Body," *College Literature* 24, no. 2 (1997): 97.

23. William Dean Howells, *An Imperative Duty* (New York: Harper & Brothers, 1892), 93–94.

24. Sinclair Lewis, *Kingsblood Royal* (New York: The Modern Library, 2001), 164.

25. Clarence Major, *The Dark & Feeling: Black American Writers and Their Work* (New York: Third Press, 1975), 147.

26. Olsen, *Tell Me a Riddle, Requa I, and Other Works*, 47.

27. Rose Kamel, "Literary Foremothers and Writers' Silences: Tillie Olsen's Autobiographical Fiction," *MELUS*, 12 (Autumn 1985): 63.

28. Joanne S. Frye, "Placing Children at the Fulcrum of Social Change: Antiracist Mothering in Tillie Olsen's 'O Yes.'" *Tulsa Studies in Women's Literature* 18 (Spring 1999): 23.

29. Algren, *Never Come Morning*, x.

30. Richard Wright, *Native Son* (New York: HarperPerennial, 1993), 446.

31. Ian Peddie "Poles Apart? Ethnicity, Race, Class, and Nelson Algren," *Modern Fiction Studies* 47, no. 1 (Spring 2001): 127.

32. James G. Kennedy, "The Content and Form of *Native Son*," *College English* 34 (November 1972): 273.

33. Benjamin Appel, "People of Crime," *Saturday Review of Literature* 25 (April 18, 1942): 7.

34. "Bigger Thomas Represents the Social Plight of the Lower Classes" in *Readings on Native Son*, ed. Hayley R. Mitchell (San Diego: Greenhaven, 2000): 118.

35. Toni Morrison, *A Mercy* (New York: Alfred A. Knopf, 2008), 160.

36. Justine Tally, "Contextualizing Toni Morrison's Ninth Novel: Why *Mercy*? Why Now?" in *Toni Morrison's* A Mercy, eds. Justine Tally and Shirley A. Stave (Newcastle upon Tyne: Cambridge Scholars, 2011), 77.

37. Geneva Cobb Moore, "A Demonic Parody: Toni Morrison's *A Mercy*," *Southern Literary Journal* 44, no. 1 (2011): 17.

38. Cathy Covell Waegner, "Ruthless Epic Footsteps: Shoes, Migrants, and the Settlement of the Americas in Toni Morrison's *A Mercy*," in *Post-National Enquiries: Essays on Ethnic and Racial Border Crossings*, ed. Jopi Nyman (Newcastle upon Tyne: Cambridge Scholars, 2009), 91.

39. Susan Strehle, "'I Am a Thing Apart': Toni Morrison, *A Mercy*, and American Exceptionalism," *Critique: Studies in Contemporary Fiction* 54, no. 2 (2013): 122.

40. Ira Wells, "'What I Killed For, I Am'" Domestic Terror in Richard Wright's America," *American Quarterly* 62 (December 2010): 893.

41. Lale Demiturk, "Mastering the Master's Tongue: Bigger as Oppressor in Richard Wright's *Native Son*," *The Mississippi Quarterly* 50 (Spring 1997): 276.
42. Chester Himes, *If He Hollers Let Him Go* (Cambridge, MA: Da Capo Press, 1986), 3.
43. Robert Bone, *The Negro Novel in America* (New Haven: Yale, 1965), 173–76.
44. Chester Himes, *The Lonely Crusade* (New York: Thunder's Mouth Press, 1997), 3.
45. Robert Skinner, "The Black Man in the Literature of Labor: The Early Novels of Chester Himes" in *The Critical Response to Chester Himes*, ed. Charles L.P. Silet (Westport, CT: Greenwood, 1999), 199.
46. Gwendolyn Brooks, *Maud Martha* (Chicago: Third World Press, 1993), 142.
47. Harry B. Shaw, "Maud Martha" in *On Gwendolyn Brooks: Reliant Contemplation*, ed. Stephen Wright (Ann Arbor: University of Michigan Press, 1996), 134.
48. Patricia H. Lattin and Vernon E. Lattin, "Dual Vision in Gwendolyn Brooks's *Maud Martha*" in *On Gwendolyn Brooks: Reliant Contemplation*, ed. Stephen Wright, 142.
49. Hughes, *The Ways of White Folks*, 122–23.
50. Ibid., 149.
51. Ralph Reckley, "On Looking into Morrison's *Tar Baby*" in *Amid Visions and Revisions: Poetry and Criticism on Literature and the Arts*, ed. Burney S. Hollis (Baltimore: Morgan State University Press, 1975), 133.
52. Toni Morrison, *Tar Baby* (New York: New American Library), 112.
53. Judylyn S. Ryan, "Contested Visions/Double-Vision in *Tar Baby*," *Modern Fiction Studies* 39, no. 3 (1993): 617.
54. Lothar Bredella, "Decolonizing the Mind: Toni Morrison's *The Bluest Eye* and *Tar Baby*," in *Intercultural Encounters*, ed. Heinz Antor and Kevin L Cope (Heidelberg: Carl Winter Universitätsverlag, 1999), 383.
55. Malin Walther Pereira, "Periodizing Toni Morrison's Work from *The Bluest Eye* to *Jazz*: The Importance of *Tar Baby*," *MELUS* 22, no. 3 (1997): 74.
56. Rita Dove, *Through the Ivory Gate* (New York: Pantheon, 1992), 203.
57. Margaret A. Reid, "The Poetry of Langston Hughes: 'Langston Hughes: Rhetoric and Protest,'" in *Civil Disobedience*, ed. Harold Bloom (New York: Bloom's Literary Criticism, 2010), 153.

58. Clarence Major, *Dirty Bird Blues* (San Francisco: Mercury House, 1996), 3.
59. Craig Werner, "Bigger's Blues: *Native Son* and the Articulation of Afro-American Modernism in *New Essays on Native Son*, ed. Kenneth Kinnamon (Cambridge: Cambridge University Press, 1990), 151.
60. William Ferris, "Richard Wright and the Blues," *The Mississippi Quarterly* 61 (Fall 2008): 550.
61. Jean Wyatt, "Failed Messages, Maternal Loss, and Narrative Form in Toni Morrison's *A Mercy*, *Modern Fiction Studies* 58 (Spring 2012): 146.
62. Langston Hughes, *Not Without Laughter* (Mineola, NY: Dover, 2008), 144.
63. Joan Stone, "Circles of Liberation and Constriction: Dance in *Not Without Laughter*" in *The Montage of a Dream: The Art and Life of Langston Hughes*, ed. John Edgar Tidwell and Cheryl R. Ragar (Columbia: University of Missouri Press, 2007), 283.
64. Hughes, *The Ways of White Folks*, 206.
65. Toni Morrison, *The Bluest Eye* (New York: Plume, 1970), 17.
66. Hughes, *The Ways of White Folks*, 9.
67. Toni Morrison, *Home* (New York: Alfred A. Knopf, 2012), 83.
68. Morrison, *What Moves at the Margin*, 25.
69. Morrison, *Song of Solomon*, 188.
70. Morrison, *What Moves at the Margin*, 21.
71. Claudia Tate, "Toni Morrison," in *Conversations with Toni Morrison*, ed. Danielle K. Taylor-Guthrie (Jackson: University Press of Mississippi, 1994), 161.
72. D. H. Melhem, "Maud Martha, Bronzeville Boys and Girls" in *Gwendolyn Brooks' Maud Martha: A Critical Collection*, ed. Jacqueline Bryant (Chicago: Third World Press, 2002), 30.
73. Dorothy Randall Tsuruta, "Regional and Regal: Chicago's *Extraordinary* Maud Martha" in *Gwendolyn Brooks' Maud Martha: A Critical Collection*, ed. Jacqueline Bryant (Chicago: Third World Press, 2002), 64.
74. Farah Jasmine Griffin, "On Women, Teaching and *Native Son*" in *Approaches to Teaching Wright's* Native Son, ed. James A. Miller (New York: Modern Language Association 1997), 80.
75. Masaya Takeuchi, "Bigger's Divided Self: Violence and Homosociality in *Native*

Son," *Studies in American Naturalism* 4, no. 1 (2009): 57.

76. Kimberly S. Drake, *Subjectivity in the American Protest Novel* (New York: Palgrave, 2011), 87–88.

77. Amanda Putnam, "Mothering Violence: Ferocious Female Resistance in Toni Morrison's *The Bluest Eye, Sula, Beloved*, and *A Mercy*," *Black Women, Gender and Families* 5 (Fall 2011), http://muse.jhu.edu.proxy2.cl.msu.edu/journals/black_women_gender_and_families/v005/5.2.putnam.html.

78. Butler E. Brewton, *Richard Wright's Women: The Thematic Treatment of Women in Uncle Tom's Cabin, Black Boy, and Native Son* (New York: Academica, 2010), 125.

79. Kathleen Ochshorn, "The Community of *Native Son*," *Mississippi Quarterly* 42 (Fall 1984): 392.

80. Toni Morrison, *Beloved* (New York: Alfred A. Knopf, 1987), 141.

81. Moss, *Tale of a Sky-Blue Dress*, 211.

82. Morrison, *What Moves at the Margin*, 59.

83. Alan Katz, "Transition Is Tugging at a Local Avant-Garde Author," in *Conversations with Clarence Major*, ed. Nancy Bunge (Jackson: University Press of Mississippi, 2002), 52.

84. Nancy Bunge, "'What You Know Gets Expanded,'" in *Conversations with Clarence Major*, ed. Nancy Bunge (Jackson: University Press of Mississippi, 2002), 115.

Chapter Five

1. Hill and Blair, *The Art of Huckleberry Finn*, 156.

2. Thoreau, *The Variorum Walden*, 260.

3. William Barillas, *The Midwestern Pastoral: Place and Landscape in Literature of the American Heartland* (Athens: Ohio University Press, 2006), 53.

4. Lawrence Buell, *The Environmental Imagination: Thoreau, Nature Writing, and the Formation of American Culture* (Cambridge: Harvard University Press, 1995), 25.

5. Aldo Leopold, *A Sand County Almanac* (New York: Ballantine Books, 1966), 3–5.

6. John Muir, *Nature Writings*, ed. William Cronon (New York: Library of America, 1997), 35–36.

7. Sherman Paul, "The Husbandry of the Wild," *Iowa Review* 17, no. 2 (1987): 17.

8. John Tallmadge, "John Muir, Emerson and the Book of Nature: The Explorer as Prophet," *Exploration: Journal of the MLA Special Session on the Literature of Exploration and Travel* 4, no. 2 (1977): 7.

9. Tim B. Rogers, "Revisioning Our Views of 'Nature' Through an Examination of Aldo Leopold's *A Sand County Almanac*," *Inter-Disciplinary Studies in Literature and the Environment*, 10, no. 2 (2003): 67.

10. Wright, *Native Son*, 241.

11. Himes, *If He Hollers Let Him Go*, 14.

12. Algren, *The Man with the Golden Arm*, 230.

13. Farrell, *Studs Lonigan*, 126–27.

14. Edgar M. Branch, "*Studs Lonigan*: Symbolism and Theme" *College English* 23, no. 3 (1961): 192–193.

15. Robert Butler, "Farrell's Ethnic Neighborhood and Wright's Urban Ghetto: Two Visions of Chicago's South Side" *MELUS* 18, no. 1, Irish-American Literature (1993): 110.

16. Cather, *O Pioneers!* 1.

17. Franzen, *The Corrections*, 537.

18. Erdrich, *Love Medicine*, 281.

19. Louise Erdrich, *The Painted Drum* (New York: Harper Perennial, 2006), 8.

20. Ibid., 77.

21. Hemingway, *The Old Man and the Sea*, 63.

22. Leo Gurko, "The Old Man and the Sea," *College English* 17 (1955): 15.

23. Anderson, *Short Stories*, 68.

24. Charles Baxter, *The Feast of Love* (New York: Vintage, 2001), 57.

25. Morrison, *Tar Baby*, 203–04.

26. Barbara Christian, "Community and Nature: The Novels of Toni Morrison," *Journal of Ethnic Studies* 7, no. 4 (1980): 78.

27. Jonathan Franzen, *Farther Away* (New York: Farrar, Straus, and Giroux, 2012), 13.

28. Cather, *O Pioneers!* 28.

29. Morrison, *Song of Solomon*, 278.

30. Willa Cather, *My Antonia* (New York: Barnes and Noble, 1994), 243.

31. Willa Cather, *Death Comes for the Archbishop* (London: Virago, 1981), 161.

32. Jim Harrison, *Off to the Side: A Memoir* (New York: Grove Press, 2002), 104.

33. Ibid., 114.

34. Jim Harrison *Returning to Earth* (New York: Grove Press, 2007), 176.

35. Baxter, *Gryphon: New and Selected Stories*, 229.

36. Anderson, *Short Stories*, 7.

37. Jane Smiley, *Horse Heaven* (New York: Ballantine Books, 2000), 196.

38. Lindsay, *Earth Man and Star Thrower*, 147.
39. Lewis, *Main Street*, 306.
40. Olsen, *Yonnondio*, 63.
41. Smiley, *A Thousand Acres*, 336.
42. Hemingway, *The Nick Adams Stories*, 33.
43. Lewis, *Main Street*, 147.
44. Lewis, *Kingsblood Royal*, 148.
45. Ibid., 148.
46. Cather, *Death Comes for the Archbishop*, 218.
47. Hemingway, *In Our Time*, 135.
48. Ibid., 139.
49. Luchen Li, "A Heart Enshrouded in the Landscape: An Impressionist Reading of 'Big Two-Hearted River,'" *MidAmerica: The Yearbook of the Society for the Study of Midwestern Literature* 31 (2004): 24.
50. Hemingway, *The Sun Also Rises*, 125.
51. Mark Spilka, "The Death of Love in *The Sun Also Rises*" in *Ernest Hemingway's* The Sun Also Rises, ed. Linda Wagner-Martin (Oxford: Oxford University Press, 2002), 39.
52. Erdrich, *The Blue Jay's Dance*, 79.
53. Baxter, *Feast of Love*, 174–75.
54. Erdrich, *Tracks*, 9.
55. Erdrich, *The Bingo Palace*, 133–34.
56. Bellow, *Henderson the Rain King*, 267.
57. Donald W. Markos, "Life Against Death in *Henderson the Rain King*," *Modern Fiction Studies* 17 (1971): 204.
58. Erdrich, *Painted Drum*, 25.
59. Erdrich, *The Blue Jay's Dance*, 183–84.
60. Saul Bellow, *The Dean's December* (Middlesex: Penguin Books, 1982), 59.
61. Erdrich, *The Blue Jay's Dance*, 182.
62. Ibid., 190–91.
63. Bellow, *Humboldt's Gift*, 356.
64. Erdrich, *Last Report on the Miracles at Little No Horse*, 348.
65. Louise Erdrich, *The Birchbark House* (New York: Scholastic, 1999), 239.
66. Erdrich, *The Last Report on the Miracles at Little No Horse*, 361.
67. Cather, *Death Comes for the Archbishop*, 82.
68. Carol Steinhagen, "Dangerous Crossings: Historical Dimensions of Landscape in Willa Cather's *My Antonia*, *The Professor's House*, and *Death Comes for the Archbishop*," *Interdisciplinary Studies in Literature and Environment* 6, no. 2 (1999): 79.
69. Vizenor, *The Heirs of Columbus*, 5.
70. Harrison, *Off to the Side*, 162.
71. Harrison, *The River Swimmer*, 196.
72. Willa Cather, *The Professor's House* (Lincoln: University of Nebraska Press, 2002), 241.

Chapter Six

1. Nathaniel Hawthorne, *Hawthorne as Editor*, ed. Arlin Turner (Baton Rouge: Louisiana State University Press, 1941), 210.
2. Thoreau, *The Variorum Walden*, 30.
3. Louise Erdrich, *The Antelope Wife* (New York: Harper Flamingo, 1998), 23.
4. Hill and Blair, *The Art of Huckleberry Finn*, 386.
5. Hawthorne, the Centennial Edition of the Works of Nathaniel Hawthorne, 11:7.
6. Dreiser, *Sister Carrie*, 78.
7. Cather, *Song of the Lark*, 398.
8. Bellow, *Humboldt's Gift*, 203.
9. Bellow, *Herzog*, 386–87.
10. Nathan A. Scott, "Sola Gratia: The Principle of Bellow's Fiction," in Nathan Scott, *Adversity and Grace: Studies in Recent American Literature* (Chicago: University of Chicago Press, 1968), 45.
11. Martin Corner, "Moving Outwards: Consciousness, Discourse and Attention in Saul Bellow's Fiction," *Studies in the Novel* 32 (2000): 283–84.
12. Anderson, *Windy McPherson's Son*, 187.
13. Sherwood Anderson, *Many Marriages* (New York: B. W. Huebsch, 1923), 12.
14. Lewis, *Arrowsmith*, 113.
15. Cather, *The Professor's House*, 265.
16. Stephen L. Tanner, "The Deeper Role of Gender Conflict in *The Professor's House*" in *Willa Cather: Family, Community and History*, ed. John J. Murphy (Provo: Brigham Young University Humanities Publication Center, 1990), 114.
17. Harrison, "The Land of Unlikeness" in *The River Swimmer*, 113.
18. Cather, *O Pioneers!*, 112.
19. Ibid., 122.
20. Warren Motley, "The Unfinished Self: Willa Cather's *O Pioneers!* and the Psychic Cost of a Woman's Success," *Women's Studies: An Interdisciplinary Journal* 12 (1986): 162.
21. Jonathan Franzen, *Freedom* (New York: Farrar, Straus and Giroux, 2010), 106–07.
22. Himes, *The Lonely Crusade*, 238.
23. Morrison, *Paradise*, 262.

24. Erdrich, *Four Souls*, 184.
25. Erdrich, *The Master Butcher's Singing Club*, 169.
26. Cather, *Death Comes for the Archbishop*, 219.
27. Willa Cather, *Willa Cather on Writing* (Lincoln: University of Nebraska Press, 1976), 4.
28. Cather, *Death Comes for the Archbishop*, 204.
29. Marilyn Arnold, "the Integrating Vision of Bishop Latour in Wills Cather's *Death Comes for the Archbishop*," *Literature and Belief* 8 (1988): 39.
30. Christina Murphy, "Mythopoetic Consciousness and the Structure of Willa Cather's *Death Comes for the Archbishop*," *North Dakota Quarterly* 55 (1987): 104.
31. Hemingway, *In Our Time*, 139.
32. Fredrik Brogger, "Whose Nature? Differing Perspectives in Hemingway's 'Big Two-Hearted River,'" in *Hemingway and the Natural World*, ed. Robert E. Fleming (Moscow: University of Idaho Press, 1999), 28.
33. Garland, *Crumbling Idols: Twelve Essays on Art, Dealing Chiefly with Literature, Painting and the Drama*, 45–46.
34. Anderson, *Winesburg, Ohio*, 135.
35. Morrison, *Song of Solomon*, 149–50.
36. Harrison, *Returning to Earth*, 47.
37. Charles Baxter, *The Soul Thief* (New York: Pantheon, 2008), 3.
38. Claude M. Simpson, Jr., "Theodore Dreiser, *Sister Carrie* in *The American Novel from James Fenimore Cooper to William Faulkner*, ed. Wallace Stegner (New York: Basic, 1965), 116.
39. Quoted in James R. Giles, *Confronting the Horror* (Kent, OH: Kent State University Press, 1989), 72.
40. Carla Cappetti, *Writing Chicago: Modernism, Ethnography, and the Novel* (New York: Columbia UP, 1993), 180.
41. Barbara Cantalupo, "Reclaiming the Inadvertent: Olsen's Visceral Voice in *Yonnondio:* from the Thirties," *Studies in Jewish Literature* 11 (Fall 1992): 137.
42. Heidi Slettendahl MacPherson, "Classifying Escape: Tilliem Olsen's *Yonnondio*," *Critique* 41 (Spring 2000): 270.
43. Stephanie Li, "Intimacy in the Radical Narratives of Toni Morrison" in *Reading America: New Perspectives on the American Novel*, ed. Elizabeth Boyle and Anne-Marie Evans (Newcastle upon Tyne, England: Cambridge Scholars, 2008), 126.
44. P. S. Polanah and Karl Precoda, "In the Vortex of Modernity: Writing Blackness, Blindness and Insight," *Journal of Modern Literature* 34 (Spring 2011): 46.
45. Stephen K. George, "The Ethical Dimensions of Richard Wright's *Native Son*" in *Ethics, Literature, Theory: An Introductory Reader*, ed. Stephen K. George (Lanham, MD: Rowman & Littlefield, 2005), 298.

Bibliography

Algren, Nelson. *Chicago City on the Make.* Chicago: University of Chicago Press, 2011.
_____. *The Man with the Golden Arm.* New York: Seven Stories Press, 1976.
_____. *Never Come Morning.* New York: Seven Stories Press, 1996.
Algren, Nelson, and Robert A. Perlongo. "Interview with Nelson Algren." *Chicago Review* 11, no. 3 (1957): 92–98.
Anderson, Sherwood. *Beyond Desire.* New York: Liveright, 1970.
_____. *Dark Laughter.* New York: Liveright, 1970.
_____. *Letters of Sherwood Anderson.* Edited by Howard Mumford Jones and Walter Rideout. Boston: Little, Brown, 1953.
_____. *Letters to Bab.* Edited by William A. Sutton. Urbana and Chicago: University of Illinois Press, 1985.
_____. *Many Marriages.* New York: B.W. Huebsch, 1923.
_____. *Perhaps Women.* Mamaroneck, NY: Paul P. Appel, 1958.
_____. *Poor White.* New York: Viking Press, 1966.
_____. *Short Stories.* Edited by Maxwell Geismar. New York: Hill & Wang, 1962.
_____. *Windy McPherson's Son.* Chicago: University of Chicago Press, 1922.
_____. *Winesburg, Ohio.* Edited by Charles E. Modlin and Ray Lewis White. New York: W.W. Norton, 1996.
Andrews, Tom, ed. *On William Stafford: The Worth of Local Things.* Ann Arbor: University of Michigan Press, 1993.
Antor, Heinz, and Kevin L. Cope, eds. *Intercultural Encounters.* Heidelberg: Carl Winter Universitätsverlag, 1999.
Appel, Benjamin. "People of Crime." *Saturday Review of Literature* 25 (April 18, 1942): 7.
Arnold, Marilyn. "The Integrating Vision of Bishop Latou in Willa Cather's *Death Comes for the Archbishop*." *Literature and Belief* 8 (1988): 39–57.
Barloon, James. "Very Short Stories: The Miniaturization of War in Hemingway's *In Our Time*." *The Hemingway Review* 24 (Spring 2005): 5–17.
Barillas, William. *The Midwestern Pastoral: Place and Landscape in Literature of the American Heartland.* Athens: Ohio University Press, 2006.
Baxter, Charles. *The Feast of Love.* New York: Vintage, 2001.
_____. *First Light.* New York: Viking Press, 1987.
_____. *Gryphon: New and Selected Stories.* New York: Pantheon, 2011.
_____. *Imaginary Paintings.* Latham, New York: Paris Review Editions, 1989.
_____. *Shadow Play.* New York: W. W. Norton, 1993.
_____. *The Soul Thief.* New York: Pantheon, 2008.
Bellow, Saul. *The Dean's December.* Middlesex, England: Penguin, 1982.

———. *Henderson the Rain King*. New York: Viking Press, 1959.
———. *Herzog*. Greenwich, CT: Fawcett Crest, 1965.
———. *Humboldt's Gift*. New York: Viking Press, 1975.
———. *Seize the Day*. New York: Viking Press, 1956.
Bloom, Harold, ed. *Civil Disobedience*. New York: Bloom's Literary Criticism, 2010.
Bly, Robert. *Iron John: A Book about Men*. Reading, MA: Addison-Wesley, 1990.
Bly, Robert, with Marion Woodman. *The Maiden King: The Reunion of Masculine and Feminine*. New York: Henry Holt, 1998.
Bone, Robert. *The Negro Novel in America*. New Haven: Yale, 1965.
Bouson, J. Brooks. *Quiet as It's Kept: Shame, Trauma, and Race in the Novels of Toni Morrison*. Albany: State University of New York Press, 2000.
Boyle, Elizabeth, and Anne-Marie Evans, eds. *Reading America: New Perspectives on the American Novel*. Newcastle upon Tyne, England: Cambridge Scholars, 2008.
Branch, Edgar M. "*Studs Lonigan*: Symbolism and Theme." *College English* 23, no. 3 (1961): 191–96.
Brewton, Butler E. *Richard Wright's Women: The Thematic Treatment of Women in* Uncle Tom's Cabin, Black Boy, and Native Son. New York: Academica, 2010.
Brooks, Gwendolyn. *Maud Martha*. Chicago: Third World Press, 1993.
———. *Selected Poems*. New York: Perennial Classics, 1999.
Brown, Kurt, ed. *The True Subject: Writers on Life and Craft*. St. Paul: Graywolf Press, 1993.
Bryant, Jacqueline, ed. *Gwendolyn Brooks' Maud Martha*. Chicago: Third World Press, 2002.
Buell, Lawrence. *The Dream of the Great American Novel*. Cambridge: Harvard University Press, 2014.
———. *The Environmental Imagination: Thoreau, Nature Writing, and the Formation of American Culture*. Cambridge: Harvard University Press, 1995.
Bunge, Nancy. *Finding the Words: Conversations with Writers Who Teach*. Athens: Swallow/Ohio, 1985.
———. *Master Class*. Iowa City: University of Iowa Press, 2005.
Butler, E. Brewton. *Richard Wright's Women: The Thematic Treatment of Women in* Uncle Tom's Cabin, Black Boy *and* Native Son. New York: Academia, 2010.
Butler, Robert. "Farrell's Ethnic Neighborhood and Wright's Urban Ghetto: Two Visions of Chicago's South Side." *MELUS* 18, no. 1, Irish-American Literature (1993): 103–11.
Caldwell, Stephen. *On Gwendolyn Brooks: Reliant Contemplation*. Ann Arbor: University of Michigan Press, 1996.
Callicott, J. Baird, ed. *A Sand County Almanac: Interpretive & Critical Essays*. Madison: University of Wisconsin Press, 1949.
Camboni, Marina, ed. *Networking Women: Subjects, Places, Links Europe-America Towards a Re-Writing of Cultural History, 1890–1939*. Rome: Edizioni di storia e letteratura, 2004.
Cantalupo, Barbara. "Reclaiming the Inadvertent: Olsen's Visceral Voice in *Yonnondio: From the Thirties*." *Studies in Jewish Literature* 11 (Fall 1992): 128–39.
Cappetti, Carla. *Writing Chicago: Modernism, Ethnography, and the Novel*. New York: Columbia University Press, 1993.
Cather, Willa. *Death Comes for the Archbishop*. London: Virago, 1981.
———. *A Lost Lady*. New York: Vintage, 1972.
———. *Lucy Gayheart*. New York: Vintage, 1995.
———. *My Antonia*. New York: Barnes and Noble, 1994.
———. *My Mortal Enemy*. New York: Vintage, 1990.
———. *O Pioneers!* New York: Dover, 1993.
———. *One of Ours*. New York: Vintage, 1971.
———. *The Professor's House*. Lincoln: University of Nebraska Press, 2002.
———. *The Song of the Lark*. New York: Signet, 1991.
———. *Willa Cather on Writing*. Lincoln: University of Nebraska Press, 1976.
Christian, Barbara. "Community and Nature: The Novels of Toni Morrison." *Journal of Ethnic Studies* 7 (1980): 65–78.
Clymer, Jeffory A. "Race and the Protocol of American Citizenship in William Dean Howells' *An Imperative Duty*." *American Literary Realism* 30 (1998): 31–52.
Conroy, Jack. *The Disinherited*. Columbia: University Missouri Press, 1991.
Cook, Emily Walker. "'But She Won't Set Foot/In His Turtle-Dove Nash': Gender Roles and Gender Symbolism in Rita Dove's *Thomas and Beulah*." *College English Association Journal* 38 (1995): 322–30.
Corner, Martin. "Moving Outwards: Con-

sciousness, Discourse, and Attention in Saul Bellow's Fiction." *Studies in the Novel* 32 (2000): 369–85.

Crozier, Robert D.S.J. "The Mask of Death, the Face of Life: Hemingway's Feminique." *The Hemingway Review* 4 (Fall 1984): 2–13.

Demiturk, Lale. "Mastering the Master's Tongue: Bigger as Oppressor in Richard Wright's *Native Son*." *The Mississippi Quarterly* 50 (Spring 1997): 267–76.

Dove, Rita. *Fifth Sunday*. Lexington: University of Kentucky Press, 1985.

———. *The Poet's World*. Washington, D.C.: The Library of Congress, 1995.

———. *Selected Poems*. New York: Vintage, 1993.

———. *Through the Ivory Gate*. New York: Pantheon, 1992.

Drake, Kimberly S. *Subjectivity in the American Protest Novel*. New York: Palgrave, 2011.

Dreiser, Theodore. *Sister Carrie*. New York: Dover, 2004.

Dylan, Bob. *Chronicles, Volume One*. New York: Simon & Schuster, 2004.

Eichelberger, Julia. "Renouncing 'The World's Business' in *Seize the Day*." *Studies in American Jewish Literature* 17 (1998): 61–81.

Emerson, Ralph Waldo. *Essays & Lectures*. New York: Library of America, 1983.

Epstein, Joseph. *The New York Times Book Review*, December 5, 1976, 92.

Erdrich, Louise. *The Antelope Wife*. New York: Harper Flamingo, 1998.

———. *The Beet Queen*. New York: Harper Perennial, 1986.

———. *The Bingo Palace*. New York: Perennial, 2001.

———. *The Birchbark House*. New York: Scholastic, 1999.

———. *The Blue Jay's Dance*. New York: HarperCollins, 1995.

———. *Four Souls*. New York: Harper Perennial, 2005.

———. *The Last Report on the Miracles at Little No Horse*. New York: Harper Perennial, 2009.

———. *Love Medicine*. New York: Perennial, 2001.

———. *The Master Butcher's Singing Club*. New York: Harper Perennial, 2005.

———. *The Painted Drum*. New York: Harper Perennial, 2006.

———. *The Plague of Doves*. New York: Harper Perennial, 2008.

———. *Tracks*. New York: Perennial, 2001.

Farrell, James. *The Fate of Writing in America*. New York: New Directions, 1946.

———. *Reflections at Fifty*. New York: Vanguard, 1954.

———. *Studs Lonigan*. New York: Library of America, 2004.

———. *A World I Never Made*. Urbana: University of Illinois Press, 2007.

Ferris, William. "Richard Wright and the Blues." *The Mississippi Quarterly* 61 (Fall 2008): 539–52.

Fisher, Jerilyn, and Silen S. Silber, eds. *Women in Literature: Reading Through the Lens of Gender*. Westport, CT: Greenwood Press, 2003.

Fishkin, Shelley Fisher, ed. *The Mark Twain Anthology*. New York: Library of America, 2010.

Fitzgerald, F. Scott. *The Beautiful and Damned*. New York: The Modern Library, 2002.

———. *The Great Gatsby*. New York: Scribner's, 1953.

———. *Tender Is the Night*. New York: Scribner, 1962.

Fleming, Robert E. *Hemingway and the Natural World*. Moscow: University of Idaho Press, 1999.

Franzen, Jonathan. *The Corrections*. New York: Farrar, Straus, and Giroux, 2001.

———. *Farther Away*. New York: Farrar, Straus, and Giroux, 2012.

———. *Freedom*. New York: Farrar, Straus, and Giroux, 2010.

———. *Strong Motion*. New York: Farrar, Straus, and Giroux, 1992.

———. *The Twentieth-Seventh City*. New York: Farrar, Straus, and Giroux, 1988.

Frye, Joanne S. "Placing Children at the Fulcrum of Social Change: Antiracist Mothering in Tillie Olsen's 'O Yes.'" *Tulsa Studies in Women's Literature* 18 (Spring 1999): 11–28.

Garland, Hamlin. *Crumbling Idols: Twelve Essays on Art, Dealing Chiefly with Literature, Painting and the Drama*. Chicago and Cambridge: Stone and Kimball, 1894.

Geismar, Maxwell. "Nelson Algren: The Iron Sanctuary." *College English* 14 (March 1953): 311–15.

George, Stephen K., ed. *Ethics, Literature, Theory: An Introductory Reader*. Lanham, MD: Rowman & Littlefield, 2005.

Giles, James R. *Confronting the Horror: The Novels of Nelson Algren*. Kent: Kent State University Press, 1989.

Graff, Gerald, and James Phelan, eds. *By Mark Twain—Adventures of Huckleberry Finn: a Case Study in Critical Controversy.* Boston: Bedford/St. Martin's, 2004.

Graulich, Melody. "Violence Against Women in the Literature of the Western Family." *Frontiers: A Journal of Woman Studies* 7, no. 3 (1984): 14–20.

Gurko, Leo. "The Old Man and the Sea." *College English* 17.1 (1955): 11–15.

Halliday, Lisa. "Louise Erdrich, the Art of Fiction No. 208," https://www.google.com/search?q=louise%20erdrich%20paris%20review&ie=utf-8&oe=utf-8&aq=t&rls=org.mozilla:en-us:official&client=firefox-a&source=hp&channel=np.

Hardin, Michael. "The Trickster of History: *The Heirs of Columbus* and the Dehistorization of Narrative." *MELUS* 23, no. 4 (1988): 25–45.

Harrison, Jim. *The Great Leader.* New York: Grove Press, 2011.

———. *Off to the Side: A Memoir.* New York: Grove Press, 2002.

———. *Returning to Earth.* New York: Grove Press, 2007.

———. *The River Swimmer.* New York: Grove Press, 2013.

Hawkins, Ty. "Assessing the Promise of Jonathan Franzen's First Three Novels: 'A Rejection of Refuge.'" *College English* 37 (2010): 61–87.

Hawthorne, Nathaniel. *The Centenary Edition of the Works of Nathaniel Hawthorne.* Columbus: Ohio State University Press, 1962.

Hayden, Robert. *Collected Poems.* Edited by Frederick Glaysher. New York: Liveright, 1985.

———. *Collected Prose.* Edited by Frederick Glaysher. Ann Arbor: University of Michigan Press, 1984.

Hemingway, Ernest. *Death in the Afternoon.* New York: G.P. Collier & Son, 1932.

———. *A Farewell to Arms.* New York: Charles Scribner's Sons, 1957.

———. *For Whom the Bell Tolls.* New York: Charles Scribner's Sons, 1940.

———. *Green Hills of Africa.* New York: Scribner's, 1963.

———. *In Our Time.* New York: Charles Scribner's Sons, 1958.

———. *Islands in the Stream.* New York: Scribner, 1997.

———. *The Nick Adams Stories.* New York: Scribner, 2003.

———. *The Old Man and the Sea.* New York: Scribner, 1980.

———. *The Sun Also Rises.* New York: Scribner, 1954.

Hill, Hamlin, and Walter Blair. *The Art of Huckleberry Finn.* San Francisco: Chandler, 1962.

Himes, Chester. *If He Hollers Let Him Go.* Cambridge, MA: Da Capo Press, 1986.

———. *The Lonely Crusade.* New York: Thunder's Mouth Press, 1997.

Hollis, Barney S., ed. *Amid Visions and Revisions: Poetry and Criticism on Literature and the Arts.* Baltimore: Morgan State University Press, 1975.

Howells, William Dean. *An Imperative Duty.* New York: Harper & Brothers, 1892.

Hughes, Langston. *Collected Works of Langston Hughes.* Edited by Christopher De Santis. Columbia: University of Missouri Press, 2002.

———. *The Collected Poems of Langston Hughes.* Edited by Arnold Rampersad. New York: Vintage, 1994.

———. "The Negro Artist and the Racial Mountain." http://www.english.illinois.edu/maps/poets/g_l/hughes/mountain.htm.

———. *Not Without Laughter.* Mineola, NY: Dover, 2008.

———. *The Sweet and Sour Animal Book.* New York: Oxford University Press, 1994.

———. *The Ways of White Folks.* New York: Vintage, 1962.

Ikeda, Choko. "Experiencing Africa in Joseph Conrad's *Heart of Darkness* and Saul Bellow's *Henderson the Rain King*." *Saul Bellow Journal* 18 (2002): 44–54.

Kamel, Rose. "Literary Foremothers and Writers' Silences: Tillie Olsen's Autobiographical Fiction." MELUS, 12 (Autumn 1985): 55–72.

Kennedy, James G. "The Content and Form of *Native Son.*" *College English* 34 (November 1972): 269–83.

Kilcup, Karen L., ed. *Soft Canons: American Woman Writers and Masculine Tradition.* Iowa City: University of Iowa Press, 1999.

Kinnamon, Kenneth, ed. *New Essays on* Native Son. Cambridge: Cambridge University Press, 1990.

Koepke, Yvette, and Christopher Nelson. "Genetic Crossing." *Studies in American Indian Literatures* 23, no. 3 (2011): 1–33, 140.

Leopold, Aldo. *A Sand County Almanac.* New York: Ballantine, 1966.

Le Sueur, Meridel. *The Girl*. Albuquerque: West End Press, 2006.
Levine, Philip. *The Bread of Time: Toward an Autobiography*. New York: Alfred A. Knopf, 1994.
_____. *Breath*. New York: Alfred A. Knopf, 2011.
_____. *New Selected Poems*. New York: Alfred A. Knopf, 2011.
_____. *News of the World*. New York: Alfred A. Knopf, 2011.
_____. *What Work Is*. New York: Alfred A. Knopf, 2011.
Lewis, Sinclair. *Arrowsmith*. New York: New American Library, 1925.
_____. *Babbitt*. New York: New American Library, 1950.
_____. *Elmer Gantry*. New York: New American Library, 1970.
_____. *It Can't Happen Here*. New York: New American Library, 1963.
_____. *Kingsblood Royal*. New York: The Modern Library, 2001.
_____. *Main Street*. New York: New American Library, 1948.
Li, Luchen. "A Heart Enshrouded in the Landscape: An Impressionist Reading of 'Big Two-Hearted River.'" *Midamerica: The Yearbook of the Society for the Study of Midwestern Literature*. 31 (2004): 17–24.
Lindsay, Vachel. *Collected Poems*. New York: Macmillan, 1925.
_____. *Earth Man & Star Thrower*. New York: The Eakins Press, 1968.
Lynn, Kenneth S. *Mark Twain and Southwestern Humor*. Boston: Little, Brown, 1959.
MacPherson, Heidi Slettendahl. "Class-ifying Escape: Tilliem Olsen's *Yonnondio*." *Critique* 41 (Spring 2000): 263–71.
Major, Clarence. *Configurations; New and Selected Poems 1958–1998*. Port Townsend, WA: Copper Canyon Press, 1998.
_____. *Conversations with Clarence Major*. Edited by Nancy Bunge. Jackson: University Press of Mississippi, 2002.
_____. *The Dark & Feeling: Black American Writers and Their Work*. New York: Third Press, 1975.
_____. *Dirty Bird Blues*. San Francisco: Mercury House, 1996.
_____. *Myself Painting*. Baton Rouge: Louisiana State University Press, 2008.
_____. *Such Was the Season*. San Francisco: Mercury House, 1987.
Markos, Donald W. "Life Against Death in *Henderson the Rain King*." *Modern Fiction Studies* 17 (1971): 193–205.
Marshall, Brenda. "The Gospel According to Pilate." *American Literature* 57 (1985): 486–89.
McClintock, James I. "*Dalva*: Jim Harrison's 'Twin Sister.'" *Journal of Men's Studies* 6 (April 30, 1998): 319.
Melville, Herman. *Moby Dick*. New York: W. W. Norton, 1969.
Miller, James A., ed. *Approaches to Teaching Wright's* Native Son. New York: Modern Language Association, 1997.
Miller Sue. *The Good Mother*. New York: Harper Perennial, 2002.
_____. *Lost in the Forest*. New York: Ballantine, 2006.
Mitchell, Hayley R., ed. *Readings on* Native Son. San Diego: Greenhaven, 2000.
Monteiro, George. "Innocence and Experience: The Adolescent Child in the Works of Mark Twain, Henry James, and Ernest Hemingway." *Estudos Anglo-Americanos* 1 (1977): 39–57.
Moore, Geneva Cobb. "A Demonic Parody: Toni Morrison's *A Mercy*." *Southern Literary Journal* 44, no. 1 (2011): 1–18, 163.
Morrison, Toni. *Beloved*. New York: Alfred A. Knopf, 1987.
_____. *The Bluest Eye*. New York: Plume, 1970.
_____. *Conversations with Toni Morrison*. Edited by Danille K. Taylor-Guthrie. Jackson: University Press of Mississippi, 1994.
_____. *Home*. New York: Alfred A. Knopf, 2012.
_____. *Love*. New York: Alfred A. Knopf, 2003.
_____. *A Mercy*. New York: Alfred A. Knopf, 2008.
_____. *Paradise*. New York: Alfred A. Knopf, 1998.
_____. *Playing in the Dark: Whiteness and the Literary Imagination*. Cambridge: Harvard University Press, 1992.
_____. *Song of Solomon*. New York: Plume, 1987.
_____. *Sula*. New York: Vintage, 2004.
_____. *Tar Baby*. New York: New American Library, 1981.
_____. *What Moves at the Margin*. Edited by Carolyn C. Denard. Jackson: University Press of Mississippi, 2008.
Morrison, Toni, and Slade Morrison. *Little Cloud and Lady Wind*. New York: Simon & Schuster, 2010.
Moss, Thylias. *I Want to Be*. New York: Picture Puffins, 1998.

———. *Tale of a Sky-Blue Dress.* New York: Avon, 1998.
Motley, Warren. "The Unfinished Self: Willa Cather's *O Pioneers!* and the Psychic Cost of a Woman's Success." *Women's Studies: An Interdisciplinary Journal* 12 (1986): 149–65.
Motley, Willard. *Knock on Any Door.* DeKalb: Northern Illinois University Press, 1989.
Muir, John. *Nature Writings.* Edited by William Cronon. New York: Library of America, 1997.
Murphy, Christina. "Mythopoeic Consciousness and the Structure of Willa Cather's *Death Comes for the Archbishop.*" *North Dakota Quarterly* 55 (1987): 99–105.
Murphy, John J., ed. *Willa Cather: Family, Community, and History.* Provo: Brigham Young University Humanities Publication Center, 1990.
Nakadate, Neil. *Understanding Jane Smiley.* Columbia, South Carolina: University of South Carolina Press, 1999.
Natov, Roni. "Child Power in Louise Erdrich's Historical Fiction for Children." *International Research in Children's Literature* 2 (2009): 135–38.
Nelson, Kay Holye, and Nancy Huse, eds. *The Critical Response to Tillie Olsen.* Westport, CT: Greenwood, 1994.
Nerad, Julie Cary. "Slippery Language and False Dilemmas: The Passing Novels of Child, Howells, and Harper." *American Literature* 75 (2003): 813–41.
Novy, Marianne, ed. *Imagining Adoption: Essays on Literature and Culture.* Ann Arbor: University of Michigan Press, 2001.
Nyman, Jopi, ed. *Post-National Enquiries: Essays on Ethnic and Racial Border Crossings.* Newcastle upon Tyne: Cambridge Scholars, 2009.
Noe, Mark D. "Macho is All in the Mind: Studs Lonigan's Search for Paradise." *Aethlon* 11 (Fall 1993): 87–94.
Obermueller, Erin V. "Reading the Body in Meridel Le Sueur's *The Girl.*" *Legacy* 22, no. 1 (2005): 47–62.
Ochshorn, Kathleen. "The Community of *Native Son.*" *Mississippi Quarterly* 42 (Fall 1984): 387–92.
O'Loughlin, Jim. "Off the Raft: Adventures of *Huckleberry Finn* and Jane Smiley's *The All-True Travels and Adventures of Lidie Newton.*" *Papers on Language and Literature* 43 (Spring 2007): 221.
Olsen, Tillie. *Tell me a Riddle, Requa I, and Other Works.* Lincoln: University of Nebraska Press, 2013.
———. *Yonnondio from the Thirties.* Lincoln: University of Nebraska Press, 2004.
Pancake, Ann. "Story Time: Working-Class Women's Interpretations in Literary Temporal Conventions." *Narrative* 6 (October 1998): 292–306.
Paul, Sherman. "The Husbandry of the Wild." *The Iowa Review* 17 (1987): 1–18.
Peddie, Ian. "'Poles Apart?' Ethnicity, race, class, and Nelson Algren." *Modern Fiction Studies* 47, no. 1 (Spring 2001): 118–44.
Pereira, Malin Walther. "Periodizing Toni Morrison's Work from *The Bluest Eye* to *Jazz*: The Importance of *Tar Baby.*" *MELUS* 22 (1997): 71–82.
Petrie, Paul R. "Racial Duties: Toward a Pragmatic Ethic of Race in W. D. Howells's *An Imperative Duty.*" *Nineteenth-Century American Literature* 63 (2008): 223–54.
Pinsker, Sanford. "*Huckleberry Finn* and the Problem of Freedom." *Virginia Quarterly Review* 77 (Autumn 2001): 612–649.
Pizer, Donald. *Twentieth-Century American Literary Naturalism: An Interpretation.* Carbondale: Crosscurrents/Modern Critiques, 1982.
Polanah, P. S., and Karl Precoda. "In the Vortex of Modernity: Writing Blackness, Blindness, and Insight." *Journal of Modern Literature* 34 (Spring 2011): 31–46, 208.
Primeau, Ronald, ed. *Midwestern Literature.* Ipswich, MA: Salem Press, 2013.
Prusak, Bernard G. "When Words Fail Us: Reexamining the Conscience of *Huckleberry Finn.*" *Journal of Aesthetic Education* 45 (2011): 1–22.
Putnam, Amanda. "Mothering Violence: Ferocious Female Resistance in Toni Morrison's *The Bluest Eye, Sula, Beloved,* and *A Mercy.*" *Black Women, Gender and Families* 5 (Fall 2011). http://muse.jhu.edu.proxy2.cl.msu.edu/journals/black_women_gender_and_families/v005/5.2.putnam.html
Rabinowitz, Paula. "Maternity as History: Gender and the Transformation of Genre in Meridel Le Sueur's *The Girl.*" *Contemporary Literature,* 29 (Winter 1988): 538–48.
Roethke, Theodore. *The Collected Poems of Theodore Roethke.* New York: Anchor, 1975.
———. *Straw for the Fire.* Edited by David Wagoner. Port Townsend, WA: Cooper Canyon Press, 2006.
Rogers, Tim B. "Revisioning Our Views of

'Nature' Through an Examination of Aldo Leopold's *A Sand County Almanac*." *Interdisciplinary Studies in Literature and the Environment* 10 (2003): 47–73.

Ryan, Judylyn S. "Contested Visions/Double-Vision in *Tar Baby*." *Modern Fiction Studies* 34 (1993): 597–621.

Salas, Angela M. "Willa Cather's *Sapphira and the Slave Girl*: Extending the Boundaries of the Body. *College Literature* 24 (1997): 97–108.

Sandburg, Carl. *The Complete Poems of Carl Sandburg*. New York: Harcourt, Brace, Jovanovich, 1970.

———. *Harvest Poems*. New York: Harcourt, Brace, 1960.

———. *The People, Yes*. New York: Harcourt, Brace, 1936.

———. *Poems of the Midwest*. Cleveland: The World Publishing Company, 1946.

———. *Smoke and Steel*. New York: Harcourt, Brace, and Howe, 1920.

Schirer, Thomas E., and Frederick Gilliard, eds. *Entering the 90's: The North American Experience: Proceedings from The Native American Studies Conference at Lake Superior University, October 7–28, 1989*. Sault Sainte Marie: Lake Superior University Press, 1991.

Scott, Nathan A. *Adversity and Grace*. Chicago: University of Chicago Press, 1968.

Shiffman, Daniel. "Ethnic Competitors in *Studs Lonigan*." *MELUS* 24 (Fall 1999): 67–79.

Silet, Charles L. P., ed. *The Critical Response to Chester Himes*. Westport, CT: Greenwood, 1999.

Smiley, Jane. *The All-True Travels and Adventures of Lidie Newton*. New York: Fawcett, 1998.

———. *At Paradise Gate*. New York: Simon & Schuster, 1998.

———. *Duplicate Keys*. New York: Fawcett Columbine, 1984.

———. *Good Faith*. New York: Alfred A. Knopf, 2003.

———. *The Greenlanders*. New York: Anchor, 1988.

———. *Horse Heaven*. New York: Ballantine, 2000.

———. *MOO*. New York: Fawcett Columbine, 1995.

———. *Private Life*. New York: Alfred A. Knopf, 2010.

———. *Ten Days in the Hills*. New York: Alfred A. Knopf, 2007.

———. *A Thousand Acres*. New York: Fawcett, 1991.

Spendal, R. J. "Wright's 'Lying in a Hammock at William Duffy's Farm in Pine Island, Minnesota.'" *Explicator* 34 (1976): 64.

Stafford, William. *Stories That Could Be True: New and Collected Poems*. New York: Harper & Row, 1977.

———. *The Way It Is: New and Selected Poems*. St. Paul: Graywolf Press, 1998.

Stafford, William, with Marvin Bell. *Segues: A Correspondence in Poetry*. Boston: David R. Godine, 1983.

Stearns, Precious McKenzie, and Bernadette H. Hyner, eds. *Forces of Nature: Natural(izing) Gender and Gender(-izing) Nature in the Discourses of Western Culture*. Newcastle upon Tyne, England: Cambridge Scholars, 2009.

Stegner, Wallace, ed. *The American Novel from James Fenimore Cooper to William Faulkner*. New York: Basic, 1965.

Stein, Karen F. "Toni Morrison's *Sula*: A Black Woman's Epic." *Black American Literature Forum* 18 (Winter 1984): 146–50.

Steinhagen, Carol. "Dangerous Crossings: Historical Dimensions of Landscape in Willa Cather's *My Antonia*, the *Professor's House*, and *Death Comes for the Archbishop*." *Inter-Disciplinary Studies in Literature and Environment* 6 (1999): 63–82.

Strehle, Susan. "'I Am a Thing Apart': Toni Morrison, *A Mercy*, and American Exceptionalism." *Critique: Studies in Contemporary Fiction* 54, no. 2 (2013): 109–23.

Sullivan, Rosemary. "A Still Center: A Reading of Theodore Roethke's 'North American Sequence.'" *Texas Studies in Language and Literature* 61 (1975): 765–83.

Takeuchi, Masaya. "Bigger's Divided Self: Violence and Homosociality in *Native Son*." *Studies in American Naturalism* 4, no. 1 (2009): 56–74.

Tallmadge, John. "John Muir, Emerson, and the Book of Nature: The Explorer as Prophet." *Exploration: Journal of the MLA Special Session on the Literature of Exploration and Travel* 4 (1977): 1–8.

Tally, Justine, and Shirley A. Stave, eds. *Toni Morrison's A Mercy*. Newcastle upon Tyne: Cambridge Scholars, 2011.

Thoreau, Henry David. *The Variorum Walden*. Edited by Walter Harding. New York: Twayne, 1962.

Tidwell, John Edgar, and Cheryl R. Ragar, eds.

Montage of a Dream: The Art and Life of Langston Hughes. Columbia: University of Missouri Press, 2007.

Trilling, Lionel. *The Liberal Imagination: Essays on Literature and Society*. New York: Charles Scriber's Sons, 1950.

Turner, Arlin, ed. *Hawthorne as Editor: Selections from his Writings in the* American Magazine. Baton Rouge: Louisiana State University Press, 1941.

Twain, Mark. "James Fenimore Cooper's Literary Offenses." *North American Review* 161, no. 464 (1895): 1–12.

Vernon, Alex. "War, Gender, and Ernest Hemingway." *The Hemingway Review* 22 (Fall 2002): 34–55.

Vizenor, Gerald. *Father Meme*. Albuquerque: University New Mexico Press, 2008.

_____. *The Heirs of Columbus*. Hanover: University Press of New England, 1991.

Wagner-Martin, Linda, ed. *Ernest Hemingway's* The Sun Also Rises. Oxford: Oxford University Press, 2002.

_____. *Hemingway: Eight Decades of Criticism*. East Lansing: Michigan State University Press, 2009.

Walsh, James. "Emblematical of War: Representation of Combat in Hemingway's Fiction." *Hemingway Review* 1 (Spring 1972): 45–57.

Weber, Ronald. *The Midwestern Ascendancy in American Writing*. Bloomington: Indiana University Press, 1992.

Wells, Ira. "'What I Killed for, I Am'" Domestic Terror in Richard Wright's America." *American Quarterly* 62 (December 2010): 873–95, 1015.

Wheatcroft, John. "Naughty Child: Poet on Top of Greenhouse." *North Dakota Quarterly* 66 (1999): 60–68.

Wilbur, Richard. *Responses: Prose Pieces, 1953–1976*. New York: Harcourt, Brace, Jovanovich, 1976.

Wixson, Douglas. "The Question of Meridel Le Sueur's Lost Patrimony." *Midamerica* 25 (1998): 98–108.

Wonham, Henry B. "Writing Realism, Policing Consciousness: Howells and the Black Body." *American Literature* 67 (1995): 701–24.

Wright, James. *Selected Poems*. New York: Farrar, Straus, and Giroux, 2005.

Wright, Richard. *Black Boy*. New York: HarperPerennial, 1993.

_____. *Native Son*. New York: HarperPerennial, 1993.

Wright, Stephen Caldwell. *On Gwendolyn Brooks: Reliant Contemplation*. Ann Arbor: University of Michigan Press, 1996.

Wright, Will, and Steven Kaplan, eds. *The Image of the Frontier in Literature, the Media, and Society*. Pueblo, CO: the Society for Interdisciplinary Study of Social Imagery, 1997.

Wyatt, Jean. "Failed Messages, Maternal Loss, and Narrative Form in Toni Morrison's *A Mercy*." *Modern Fiction Studies* 58 (Spring 2012): 128–51, 188.

Index

abuse see childhood
The Adventures of Augie March (Bellow) 156
Adventures of Huckleberry Finn (Twain): childhood in 49–50, 58–59, 76; compassion in 11, 31, 32, 41, 166–67; conformity in 19–22, 30–32; gender in 78, 103; as midwestern literature 4, 6; nature in 130–31, 134; optimism in 54; race in 7, 104–7; self-acceptance in 151; as southern literature 4, 6–7
African Americans 10, 13, 104–29; American dream and 13, 114, 115; nature and 135–36; *see also* race
Algren, Nelson 3
    literary themes: addiction 75; childhood 70–71; compassion 8–9, 173; conformity 43–45, 153; gender 79, 90–91; nature 136; war 75
    works: *The Man with the Golden Arm* 45, 75, 136, 153; *Never Come Morning* 3, 12, 43–45, 70–71, 79, 90–91, 113–14, 153, 173
All-Night Visitors (Major) 128
The All-True Adventures of Lidie Newton (Smiley) 79–80, 106
American dream 9, 26, 65; African Americans and 13, 114; alienation and 10, 14–15, 21–22, 25, 26, 114; children and 65; class and 41–48; competition and 9, 10, 21, 27, 38, 41, 49, 51, 82; conformity and 11
American literature: impact of *Huckleberry Finn* on 6; regional literature 5–6
The American Midwest: An Interpretive Encyclopedia (Sisson, Zacher, and Cayton) 3, 4, 6
Anderson, David 2, 4

Anderson, Sherwood 2, 9
    literary themes: authenticity 9, 14, 159; childhood 50–51, 54, 56–58, 65–66; class 45; compassion 159, 168; conformity 45; gender 78, 82–83, 85–87, 92, 97–98; industrial age 82–83; nature 139, 141; race 107, 111
    works: *Beyond Desire* 92; *Dark Laughter* 107, 111; "I Want to Know Why" 65–66, 141; *Kit Brandon* 78; "The Man Who Became a Woman" 139; *Many Marriages* 159; *Perhaps Women* 10, 12–13, 82–83; poetry 16; *Poor White* 57–58; *Tar* 68; *Windy McPherson's Son* 56–57, 159; *Winesburg, Ohio* 50–51, 85–87, 97–98, 168
androgyny see gender
The Antelope Wife (Erdrich) 151
Appel, Benjamin 114
Arnold, Marilyn 165
Arrowsmith (Lewis) 34, 143, 159
authenticity 2, 15, 17, 151–65
    authors' treatment: in Anderson 159; in Bellow 156–58; in Cather 154–56, 159–60, 161, 164–65; in Dreiser 153–54; in Erdrich 151, 163–64; in Farrell 153; in Fitzgerald 23–24; in Franzen 161–62; in Garland 15; in Harrison 158, 160–61; in Hemingway 165; in Himes 162; in Lewis 159; in Major 158–59; in Morrison 8, 160, 162–63; in poetry 17; in Twain 151
    issues: authenticity and Chicago 153–57, 158–59; authenticity and compassion 15, 165–67, 171–73; authenticity and renunciation 159–62, 171–73; Midwest as authentic 28–30

193

Babbitt (Lewis) 11, 32–34; optimism in 32, 34
Barillas, William 144; *The Midwestern Pastoral* 3, 131
Barloon, James 73
Baxter, Charles
    literary themes: childhood 51–52, 55–56, 66–67; compassion 172–73; gender 92–93; nature 139, 141, 145; relinquishing the American dream 9, 14
    works: *The Feast of Love* 139, 145; *First Light* 55–56; "Gryphon" 51–52; "Kiss Away" 141; poetry 16; *Saul and Patsy* 66–67; *Shadow Play* 92–93, 139; *The Soul Thief* 14, 171, 172–73
The Beautiful and Damned (Fitzgerald) 22, 28, 97
The Beet Queen (Erdrich) 59–60
Bellow, Saul 2, 7
    literary themes: alienation 28; American dream 25, 27; authenticity 2, 9, 14, 165–66; childhood 54; compassion 54, 156–58; conformity 25, 27–28, 35; gender 99–100; nature 138, 145–46, 146–47; race 107
    works: *The Adventures of Augie March* 156; *The Dean's December* 146; *Henderson the Rain King* 107, 138–39, 145–46; *Herzog* 14, 99–100, 156–58; *Humboldt's Gift* 27–28, 45–46, 54, 147, 157, 165–66; *Seize the Day* 25, 28, 35
Beloved (Morrison) 120, 121, 126–27
Beyond Desire (Anderson) 92
"The Big Two-Hearted River" (Hemingway) 74–75, 124, 144, 165, 169
The Bingo Palace (Erdrich) 62, 145
Birchbark series (Erdrich) 65, 147–48
"The Birthmark" (Hawthorne) 77
Black Boy (Wright) 3, 9
"The Blue I'm Playing" (Hughes) 119
The Blue Jay's Dance (Erdrich) 83–84, 146
The Bluest Eye (Morrison) 120, 122–23, 170
Bly, Robert 16
Bone, Robert 116–17
Bouson, J. Brooks 100
The Boy Who Ran to the Woods (Harrison) 65
Branch, Edgar M. 137
Bredella, Lothar 120
Brewton, Butler 126
Brogger, Fredrik 165
Brooks, Gwendolyn 16; gender 12, 16; *Maud Martha* 118–19, 125; as poet 16; race 14–15, 29–30, 87, 118–19
Buell, Lawrence 136; *The Dream of the Great American Novel* 5; *The Environmental Imagination* 131–32
Burnham, Daniel 137
Butler, Robert 137

Cantalupo, Barbara 173
Cappetti, Carla 68, 173
Cather, Willa
    literary themes: authenticity 154–56, 159–60, 161, 164–65; childhood 71–72, 159–69; compassion 168, 169–70; gender 80–81, 87–88, 95–96; nature 138, 140–41, 142, 143–44, 145, 148, 150; race 108; relinquishing the American dream 14–15; war 71–72
    works: *Death Comes for the Archbishop* 14–15, 140–41, 142, 143–44, 145, 148, 164–65, 169–70; *A Lost Lady* 88; *Lucy Gayheart* 87, 155–56; *Mortal Enemy* 88; *My Antonia* 81, 138, 140; *O Pioneers!* 14, 80–81, 95–96, 138, 140, 161, 168; *One of Ours* 12, 71–72; *The Professor's House* 150, 159–60; *Sapphira and the Slave Girl* 108; *Song of the Lark* 29–30, 81, 154–55
Catholicism 71
Cayton, Andrew 3, 6
"The Celestial Railroad" (Hawthorne) 152
Chicago, Illinois 2, 15, 18, 137–38, 153–59
childhood 10, 11–12, 49–76
    authors' treatment: in Algren 70–71; in Anderson 50–51, 54, 56–58, 65–66; in Baxter 51–52, 55–56, 66–67; in Bellow 54; in Cather 71–72; in Conroy 70; in Erdrich 50, 53–54, 59–60, 62–63, 65, 75; in Farrell 68–70, 71; in Franzen 50, 58; in Harrison 59, 65, 71; in Hawthorne 49; in Hemingway 52–53, 66, 71, 72–75; in Hughes 65; in Miller 60; in Morrison 61–62; in Moss 63–64, 65; in Olsen 54–55, 71; in poetry 16; in Smiley 60, 64–65, 67; in Twain 20, 49–50, 58–59; in Vizenor 67, 149
    issues: abuse 12, 58–64, 67, 121–23; adult corruption 49–50, 65–67, 122–24; authenticity 64–66; compassion 50–56, 64; impact of childhood on adulthood 55–58; race 122–24; society's damage of children 67–71, 76, 149; war 12, 71–76, 123–24
Christian, Barbara 140
Chwast, Seymour 106
Clark, Harry Hayden 1
class, social 10; in Algren 9, 41, 43–45; in Anderson 45; common people 15; conformity 21, 32–34, 41–48; in Conroy 41–43; in Dreiser 46; labor unions 18, 41, 114; lower class midwesterners 11, 46, 47; middle-class midwesterners 11, 32–34, 47; in Morrison 46–48; music and 16, 43; in Olsen 41–42; in poetry 16; upper-class midwesterners 11, 22–24, 27–28, 46
Clymer, Jeffory 110
Coltelli, Laura 85
Come by Here (Major) 128–29

compassion 8–11, 14–15, 167–74
  authors' treatment: in Algren 153, 173; in Anderson 50–51, 168; in Baxter 171–73; in Bellow 54, 165–66; in Cather 168, 169–70; in Dreiser 167, 173; in Emerson 151; in Erdrich 53, 171; in Fitzgerald 168–69; in Harrison 171–72; in Hawthorne 151–52; in Hemingway 52–53, 169; in Himes 166; in Morrison 160, 170–71, 174; in Olsen 173–74; in Thoreau 151–52; in Twain 166–67; in Wright 174
  issues: childhood 50–55; failure and 162–63; women 77, 80, 81, 85, 92, 93, 99, 102, 103
competition *see* American dream
conformity 19–48
  authors' treatment: in Algren 43–45; in Bellow 25, 27–28, 35; in Conroy 41–43; in Dreiser 46; in Fitzgerald 22–24, 28; in Franzen 37–39; in Harrison 30; in Lewis 24, 32–35, 40–41; in Morrison 46–48; in Olsen 41–42; in Smiley 11, 26–27, 29, 35–37, 40; in Twain 19–22, 30–32, 41
  issues: versus authenticity 28–30, 35–37; destroying cultures 39–41; social class 41–48; success 11
Conroy, Jack 18
  literary themes: childhood 70; class 114
  works: *The Disinherited* 11, 41–43, 70, 114
"Cora Unashamed" (Hughes) 123
Corner, Martin 183
The Corrections (Franzen) 37–39, 50, 92
Crozier, Robert 102
Crumbling Idols: Twelve Essays on Art, Dealing Chiefly with Literature, Painting and the Drama (Garland) 15–16
Cunningham, George P. 65

Dalva (Harrison) 100
Dark Laughter (Anderson) 107, 111
The Dean's December (Bellow) 146
Death Comes for the Archbishop (Cather) 14–15, 140–45, 148, 164–65, 169–70
Death in the Afternoon (Hemingway) 101–2
Demiturk, Lale 115
Detroit, Michigan 18
Dewey, John 18
The Dictionary of Midwestern Literature (Society for the Study of Midwestern Literature) 3, 4, 6
Dirty Bird Blues (Major) 121, 158–59
The Disinherited (Conroy) 11, 41–43, 70, 114
"Divinity School Address" (Emerson) 19–20
domination 13, 15, 22, 77, 85–91
Dove, Rita 16, 17; *Fifth Sunday* 84; gender 84; music 17, 120; *Through the Ivy Gate* 120

Drake, Kimberly S. 126
The Dream of the Great American Novel (Buell) 5
Dreiser, Theodore 2
  background: midwestern ties 3
  literary themes: authenticity 153–54; class 46; compassion 153–54, 167, 173; gender 10, 78–79
  works: *Jennie Gerhardt* 9; *Sister Carrie* 9, 46, 78–79, 153–54, 167
Dunbar, Paul Lawrence 10
Duplicate Keys (Smiley) 29
Dylan, Bob 17–18

"Earth's Holocaust" (Hawthorne) 20
education 42
Eichelberger, Julia 25, 28
Eliot, T. S. 2; "The Love Song of J. Alfred Prufrock" 1
Ellison, Ralph 104–5
Elmer Gantry (Lewis) 24
Emergency Exit (Major) 128
Emerson, Ralph Waldo 104; contrasted with Muir 133; "Divinity School Address" 19–20; ideology of 10–11, 19–20, 133, 139, 151
The Environmental Imagination (Buell) 131–32
Erdrich, Louise 9
  literary themes: authenticity 151, 163–64; childhood 12, 50, 53–54, 59–60, 62–63, 75; compassion 53, 171; gender 83, 94–95, 98–99; nature 14, 138, 144–45, 146–47, 147–48; relinquishing the American dream 14; war 75
  works: *The Antelope Wife* 151; *The Beet Queen* 59–60; *The Bingo Palace* 62, 145; Birchbark series 65, 147; *The Blue Jay's Dance* 83, 146; *Four Souls* 14, 83, 98–99, 163, 171; *The Last Report on the Miracles at Little No Horse* 94–95, 147, 148; *Love Medicine* 62–63, 75, 138; *The Master Butchers Singing Club* 75, 164; *The Painted Drum* 138, 146; *The Plague of the Doves* 45, 53–54, 59; *The Round House* 12, 50; *Tracks* 98, 145
"Ethan Brand" (Hawthorne) 20, 49, 152
evil, concepts of: Hawthorne 11, 20, 21, 49; Melville 11, 21; social 26, 29, 37, 43; Twain 11, 21, 22, 32

Fabi, M. Giulia 110
A Farewell to Arms (Hemingway) 71, 101
Farrell, James 3
  literary themes: authenticity 153; childhood 68–70, 71; gender 96; nature 136–37; political stance 9
  works: *Reflections at Fifty* 68; *Studs Loni-*

gan 12, 68–70, 96, 136–37, 153; *A World I Never Made* 69–70, 137, 153
Father Meme (Vizenor) 67
The Feast of Love (Baxter) 139, 145
Ferris, William 121
Fifth Sunday (Dove) 84
First Light (Baxter) 55–56
Fitzgerald, F. Scott 17
    literary themes: compassion 168–69; conformity 11, 22–24, 28; women 97
    works: *The Beautiful and Damned* 22, 28, 97; *The Great Gatsby* 22–23, 97, 168–69; *Tender Is the Night* 23–24, 28; *This Side of Paradise* 22
For Whom the Bell Tolls (Hemingway) 102–3
Four Souls (Erdrich) 14, 83, 98–99, 163, 171
Franzen Jonathan
    literary themes: authenticity 161–62; childhood 50, 58; conformity 37–39; gender 81–82, 92; nature 139, 140, 143
    works: *The Corrections* 37–39, 50, 92; *Freedom* 58, 143, 161–62; *Strong Motion* 28–29, 81–82, 139; *Twenty-Seventh City* 25–26, 29, 50
Freedom (Franzen) 58, 143, 161–62
Frye, Joann 113

The Garden of Eden (Hemingway) 101
Garland, Hamlin 15–16, 138, 167
Geismar, Maxwell 71
gender 10, 12, 13, 77–103
    authors' treatment: in Algren 79, 90–91; in Anderson 78, 82–83, 85–87, 92, 97–98; in Baxter 92–93; in Bellow 99–100; in Cather 80–81, 87–88, 95–96; in Dove 84; in Dreiser 78–79; in Erdrich 83, 94–95, 98–99; in Farrell 96; in Fitzgerald 97; in Franzen 81–82, 92; in Harrison 100–101; in Hawthorne 77–78; in Hemingway 101–3; in Le Sueur 84–85; in Lewis 78, 79; in Major 81, 128–29; in Miller 84; in Morrison 91–92, 93–94, 96; in Olsen 84; in Smiley 79–80, 88–90; in Twain 78; in Vizenor 10
    issues: androgyny 13, 16, 95–103; assertion 92–95; compassion 77, 79–82, 85, 92, 93, 99, 102, 103; domination 88–91; female self-sufficiency 78; industrial age 82–83; marriage 88–90; maternity 83–85; race 124–29
George, Stephen 174
George Washington University 1
The Girl (Le Sueur) 11, 84–85
Good Faith (Smiley) 11, 26–27, 29
The Good Mother (Miller) 84
Good Will (Smiley) 67
Graulich, Melody 85

The Great Gatsby (Fitzgerald) 22–23, 97, 168–69
The Great Leader (Harrison) 59
The Green Hills of Africa (Hemingway) 102
Greenlanders (Smiley) 40, 88–89
Griffin, Farah 126
"Gryphon" (Baxter) 51–52
Gurko, Leo 139

Hardin, Michael 101
Harrison, Jim 17
    literary themes: authenticity 158, 160–61; childhood 59, 65, 71; compassion 171–72; conformity 30; gender 100–101; nature 141, 143, 149–50; war 71
    works: *The Boy Who Ran to the Woods* 65; *Dalva* 100; *The Great Leader* 59; "The Land of Unlikeness" 30, 160–61; poetry 16, 17; *Returning to Earth* 14–15, 71, 100–101, 141, 143, 149–50, 158, 171–72; "The River Swimmer" 150, 158; *Sundog* 100; *True North* 141
Hartley, Marianne 54
Hawkins, Ty 39
Hawthorne, Nathaniel
    literary themes: evil 11, 20, 49; gender 77–78; intellectual growth 151; treatment of children 12, 49
    works: "The Birthmark" 77; "The Celestial Railroad" 152; "Earth's Holocaust" 20; "Ethan Brand" 20, 49, 152; "Rappaccini's Daughter" 77; *The Scarlet Letter* 12, 20, 49, 77–78; "The Snow Image" 152
Hayden, Robert 16, 107
Haymarket Bombing 18
Heirs of Columbus (Vizenor) 14, 67, 148–49
Hemingway, Ernest 2, 6, 7
    literary themes: authenticity 165; childhood 52–53, 66, 71, 72–75; compassion 52–53, 169; gender 101–3; nature 139, 143, 144; war 71, 72–75
    works: "The Big Two-Hearted River" 74–75, 124, 144, 165, 169; *Death in the Afternoon* 101–2; *A Farewell to Arms* 71, 101; *For Whom the Bell Tolls* 102–3; *The Garden of Eden* 101; *The Green Hills of Africa* 102; *In Our Time* 12, 52, 66, 72–75, 101, 124, 169; "Indian Camp" 52; "My Old Man" 66; "Now I Lay Me" 74; *The Old Man and the Sea* 52–53, 139; "Soldier's Home" 74, 169; *The Sun Also Rises* 101, 144; "Ten Indians" 143; "A Way You'll Never Be" 74
Henderson the Rain King (Bellow) 107, 138, 145–46
Herzog (Bellow) 14, 99–100, 156–158
Hewson, Marc 102–3

Himes, Chester 3, 18
    literary themes: authenticity 162; compassion 166; gender 125–26; nature 136, 142; race 116–17
    works: *If He Hollers Let Him Go* 116–17, 127, 136, 142; *Lonely Crusade* 117, 125, 127, 162, 166
Holt, Debra 110
Home (Morrison) 93–94, 123–25
Horse Heaven (Smiley) 141–42
"How Bigger Was Born" (Wright) 3, 113
Howells, William Dean 10; *An Imperative Duty* 108–11; race 108–11
Huckleberry Finn see *Adventures of Huckleberry Finn* (Twain)
Hughes, Langston 17, 107
    literary themes: childhood 65, 121–22; music 120–21; race 107–8, 119, 121–22, 123
    works: "The Blues I'm Playing" 119; "Cora Unashamed" 123; "The Negro Artist and the Racial Mountain" 108; *Not Without Laughter* 121–22; "One Christmas Eve" 122; poetry 16; "Poor Little Black Fellow" 119; "Rejuvenation through Joy" 107–8; *Sweet and Sour Animal Book* 65
Humboldt's Gift (Bellow) 27–28, 45–46, 54, 147, 157, 165–66

"I Stand Here Ironing" (Olsen) 71, 84
I Want to Be (Moss) 65
"I Want to Know Why" (Anderson) 65–66, 141
If He Hollers Let Him Go (Himes) 116–17, 127, 136, 142
Ikeda, Choko 107
An Imperative Duty (Howells) 108–11
In Our Time (Hemingway) 12, 52, 66, 72–75, 101, 124, 169
"Indian Camp" (Hemingway) 52
individualism 25, 133, 166; and industrial age 82–83
International Workers of the World 18
It Can't Happen Here (Lewis) 40–41

James, Henry: pairing with Twain 5
"James Fenimore Cooper's Literary Offenses" (Twain) 20
Jazz (Morrison) 120, 125
Jennie Gerhardt (Dreiser) 9

Kamel, Rose 113
Katz, Alan 128
Kennedy, James G. 114
Kingsblood Royal (Lewis) 111–12, 143
Kinnison, Dana 96
"Kiss Away" (Baxter) 141
Kit Brandon (Anderson) 78

Knock on Any Door (Motley) 113, 127
Koepke, Yvette 67
Kosiba, Sara 8

"The Land of Unlikeness" (Harrison) 30, 160–61
The Last Report on the Miracles at Little No Horse (Erdrich) 94–95, 147, 148
Lattin, Patricia H. 118–19
Lattin, Wernon E. 118–19
Leopold, Aldo 14, 17, 132–35; contrasted with Thoreau 133; *A Sand County Almanac* 132–35
Le Sueur, Meridel 10; gender 84–85; *The Girl* 11, 84–85
Levine, Philip 16, 17
Lewis, Ida 125
Lewis, Sinclair 2, 3, 7, 10, 17
    literary themes: authenticity 159; conformity 11, 24, 32–35, 40–41; gender 10, 78, 79; nature 142, 143; race 111–12
    works: *Arrowsmith* 34, 143, 159; *Babbitt* 11, 32–34; *Elmer Gantry* 24; *It Can't Happen Here* 40–41; *Kingsblood Royal* 111–12, 143; *Main Street* 34–35, 78, 79, 142, 143
Li, Luchen 172
Li, Stephanie 174
Lindsay, Vachel 142; "The Congo" 107
literary criticism 173, 174; class criticism 10; gender criticism 10, 78, 85, 125; New Criticism 10; race criticism 10, 13, 104–8
Little Cloud and Lady Wind (Morrison) 64–65
Liveright, Horace 107
Lonely Crusade (Himes) 117, 125–26, 127, 162, 166
Lost in the Forest (Miller) 60
A Lost Lady (Cather) 88
Love (Morrison) 62
Love Medicine (Erdrich) 62–63, 75, 138
Lucy Gayheart (Cather) 87, 155–56
Lynn, Kenneth 6–7

MacPherson, Heidi 173–74
Main Street (Lewis) 34–35, 78, 79, 142, 143
Major, Clarence 16
    literary themes: authenticity 158–59; gender 81, 128–29; race 121
    works: *All-Night Visitors* 128; *Come by Here* 128–29; *Dirty Bird Blues* 121, 158–59; *Emergency Exit* 128; *One Flesh* 129; *Such Was the Season* 81
Malcolm X 18
"The Man Who Became a Woman" (Anderson) 139
The Man with the Golden Arm (Algren) 45, 75, 136, 153

Many Marriages (Anderson) 159
Markos, Donald 146
Marshall, Brenda 47
The Master Butchers Singing Club (Erdrich) 75, 164
Matthiessen, F. O. 6
Maud Martha (Brooks) 118–19, 125
McClintock, James 100
McKenie Stearns, Precious 82–83
Melville, Herman 11, 20; *Moby Dick* 104
A Mercy (Morrison) 114–15, 121
Michigan State University 2
The Midwestern Ascendency in American Writing (Weber) 3–4, 6
midwestern literature: difficulties in defining 7–8; fundamental assumptions of 10–11; intellectual humility 134; Midwest as place of authenticity 28–30, 39; social goals 8–9 (*see also* American dream); tolerance and 132
Midwestern Literature (Primeau) 3
The Midwestern Pastoral: Place and Landscape in Literature of the American Heartland (Barillas) 3
Milhem, D. H. 125
Miller, Sue
    literary themes: childhood 60; gender 84
    works: *The Good Mother* 84; *Lost in the Forest* 60
Montiero, George 50
MOO (Smiley) 35–37
Moore, Geneva Cobb 115
Moore, Michael 18
Morrison, Slade 64–65
Morrison, Toni 7, 9, 58
    criticism: on Cather 108; on Hemingway 108; on politics and literature 8; on Twain 58–59, 78, 105
    literary themes: childhood 61–62, 64–65; class 46–48; compassion 160, 170–71, 174; conformity 46–48; gender 91–92, 93–94, 96, 125, 126–27; nature 139–40; race 108, 111, 114–15, 119–20, 121, 122–23, 123–25; relinquishing the American dream 14; war 123–24
    works: *Beloved* 120, 121, 126–27; *The Bluest Eye* 120, 122–23, 170; *Home* 93–94, 123–25; *Jazz* 120, 125; *Little Cloud and Lady Wind* 64–65; *Love* 62; *A Mercy* 114–15, 121; *Paradise* 91–92, 162–63; *Playing in the Dark* 105; *Song of Solomon* 14, 46–48, 96, 120, 125, 140, 160, 170–71; *Sula* 61, 120; *Tar Baby* 111, 119–20, 139–40
Mortal Enemy (Cather) 88
Moss, Thylias 16–17
    literary themes: childhood 63–64, 65; gender 127

    works: *I Want to Be* 65; *Tale of a Sky Blue Dress* 63–64, 127
Motley, Warren 161
Motley, Willard 3, 161
    literary themes: gender 113, 127; race 113
    works: *Knock on Any Door* 113, 127
Muir, John 14, 17, 132–35; contrasted with Emerson 133
Murphy, Christina 165
music 17, 42, 43, 45–46, 112, 120; blues 120–21; dance 122; jazz 108, 121
My Antonia (Cather) 81, 138, 140
"My Old Man" (Hemingway) 66

Nakadate, Neil 40
Native Americans 145–50
Native Son (Wright) 2, 3, 113–14, 115–16, 126, 135, 174
Natov, Roni 65
nature 10, 13–14, 17, 130–50
    authors' treatment of: in Algren 136; in Anderson 139, 141; in Baxter 139, 141, 145; in Bellow 138, 145–46, 147; in Cather 138, 140–41, 142, 143–44, 145, 148, 150; in Erdrich 14, 138, 144–45, 146–48; in Farrell 136–37; in Franzen 139, 140, 143; in Garland 138; in Harrison 141, 143, 149–50; in Hemingway 124, 139, 143, 144; in Himes 142; in Leopold 132–35; in Lewis 142, 143; in Lindsay 142; in Morrison 139–40; in Muir 132–35; in Olsen 132–35; in Smiley 141–42, 142–43; in Thoreau 130–31, 133, 134–35; in Twain 130–31, 134; in Vizenor 14, 148–49; in Wright 135
    issues: connection 14, 134, 144; death 147; disempowered groups 132; dogs 135, 141; domestication 135, 140–43; dreams 147; horses 141–42; inhabiting nature 145–50; intellectual humility 134; love 140; nature for nature's sake 131–32; pastoral 130–31; race 135–36; regional attitudes 131–32; restoration 143–45; solitude 14, 130; transcendence 7, 13, 14, 17, 131, 134, 144; wilderness 135, 140
"The Negro Artist and the Racial Mountain" (Hughes) 108
Nerad, Julie Carey 110
Never Come Morning (Algren) 3, 12, 43–45, 70–71, 79, 90–91, 113–14, 153, 173; introduction to 3, 113–14
New Criticism 10
New York City 28, 29
Nobel Prize 7
Noe, Marcia 7
Noe, Mark 96
Not Without Laughter (Hughes) 121–22
"Now I Lay Me" (Hemingway) 74

O Pioneers! (Cather) 14, 80–81, 95–96, 138, 140, 161, 168
"O Yes" (Olsen) 112–13
Obermueller, Erin V. 85
Ochshorn, Kathleen 126
The Old Man and the Sea (Hemingway) 52–53, 139
O'Loughlin, Jim 106
Olsen, Tillie
  literary themes: childhood 54–55, 71; class 41–42; compassion 9, 173–74; conformity 41–42; gender 84; nature 142; race 112–13
  works: "I Stand Here Ironing" 71, 84; "O Yes" 112–13; *Yonnondio* 41–42, 54–55, 142, 173–74
"One Christmas Eve" (Hughes) 122
One Flesh (Major) 129
One of Ours (Cather) 12, 71–72
optimism 32, 34; in childhood 54; music 17, 42–43, 45–46, 120–21

The Painted Drum (Erdrich) 138, 146
Pancake, Ann 85
Paradise (Morrison) 91–92, 162–63
Paradise Gate (Smiley) 89–90
passivity *see* conformity
Paul, Sherman 133
Peddie, Ian 114
Pereira, Malin Walther 120
Perhaps Women (Anderson) 10, 12–13, 82–83
Perlongo, Robert A. 71
Petrie, Paul 110
Pinsker, Sanford 105
Pizer, Donald 69
The Plague of the Doves (Erdrich) 45, 53–54, 59
Playing in the Dark (Morrison) 105
poetry 16–17; authenticity and 17; compassion and 17; music and 17; nature and 17
Poetry Magazine 2
Polanah, P. S. 174
"Poor Little Black Fellow" (Hughes) 119
Poor White (Anderson) 57–58
Pound, Ezra 2
Precoda, Karl 174
Primeau, Ronald 3
Private Life (Smiley) 89, 90
The Professor's House (Cather) 150, 159–60
Prusak, Bernard G. 31
Pullman Strike 18
Putnam, Amanda 126

Rabinowitz, Paula 85
race 10, 13, 104–29
  authors' treatment: in Algren 113–14; in Anderson 107, 111; in Bellow 107; in Brooks 14–15, 29–30, 87, 118–19; in Cather 108; in Himes 116–17; in Howells 108–11; in Hughes 107–8, 119, 121–22; in Lewis 111–12; in Lindsay 107; in Major 112; in Morrison 108, 111, 114–15, 119–20, 121, 122–23, 123–25; in Motley 113; in Olsen 112–13; in Twain 104–7; in Wright 113–14, 115–16, 174
  issues: blacks adopted by whites 119–20; children 122–23; gender 124–29; music 108, 120–22; nature 135–36; primitivism 107; war 123–24
"Rappaccini's Daughter" (Hawthorne) 77
Reckley, Ralph 119
Reflections at Fifty (Farrell) 68
Reid, Margaret A. 120
"Rejuvenation through Joy" (Hughes) 107–8
Returning to Earth (Harrison) 14–15, 71, 100–101, 141, 143, 149–50, 158, 171–72
Reynolds, Michael 75
"The River Swimmer" (Harrison) 150, 158
Rodgers, Tim B. 133
Roethke, Theodore 2, 16, 17
Roger and Me (Moore) 18
The Round House (Erdrich) 12, 50
Ryan, Judylyn S. 120

Salas, Angela M. 108
Sandburg, Carl 16, 17; music 120
Sapphira and the Slave Girl (Cather) 108
Saul and Patsy (Baxter) 66–67
Saunders, James 114
The Scarlet Letter (Hawthorne) 12, 20, 49, 77–78
Scott, Nathan A. 157
Seize the Day (Bellow) 25, 28, 35
Shadow Play (Baxter) 92–93, 139
Shaw, Harry B. 118
Shiffman, Daniel 69
Simpson, Claude 173
Sisson, Richard 3, 6
Sister Carrie (Dreiser) 9, 46, 78–79, 153–54, 167
Smiley, Jane
  literary criticism: Twain 105–6
  literary themes: childhood 60, 64–65, 67; conformity 11, 26–27, 29, 35–37, 40; gender issues 79–80, 88–90; horses 141–42; nature 141–42, 142–43
  works: *The All-True Adventures of Lidie Newton* 79–80, 106; *Duplicate Keys* 29; *Good Faith* 11, 26–27, 29; *Good Will* 67; *Greenlanders* 40, 88–89; *Horse Heaven* 141–42; *MOO* 35–37; *Paradise Gate* 89–90; *Private Life* 89, 90; *Ten Days in the Hills* 11, 27, 29; *A Thousand Acres* 60, 142–43
"The Snow Image" (Hawthorne) 152

social status 1–2, 21, 125; *see also* American dream; conformity
Society for the Study of Midwestern Literature 3, 4
"Soldier's Home" (Hemingway) 74, 169
Song of Solomon (Morrison) 14, 46–48, 96, 120, 125, 140, 160, 170–71
Song of the Lark (Cather) 29–30, 81, 154–55
The Soul Thief (Baxter) 14, 171, 172–73
speech, authentic 15, 20
Spilka, Mark 144
Stafford, William 16, 17
Stegner, Wallace 5–6
Stein, Karen F. 61
Steinhagen, Carol 148
Stone, Joan 122
Strong Motion (Franzen) 28–29, 81–82, 139
Studs Lonigan (Farrell) 12, 68–70, 96, 136–37, 153
Such Was the Season (Major) 81
Sula (Morrison) 61, 120
The Sun Also Rises (Hemingway) 101, 144
Sundog (Harrison) 100
Sweet and Sour Animal Book (Hughes) 65

Takeuchi, Masaya 126
Tale of a Sky Blue Dress (Moss) 63–64, 127
Tallmadge, John 133
Tally, Justine 114
Tanner, Stephen L. 160
Tar (Anderson) 68
Tar Baby (Morrison) 111, 119–20, 139–40
Tate, Claudia 125
Ten Days in the Hills (Smiley) 11, 27, 29
"Ten Indians" (Hemingway) 143
Tender Is the Night (Fitzgerald) 23–24, 28
Terkel, Studs 18
This Side of Paradise (Fitzgerald) 22
Thoreau, Henry David 10–11, 19–20, 104, 130–31, 133, 134–35, 139; contrasted with Leopold 133; ideology of 10–11, 130–31, 133, 139, 151, 152; *Walden* 19–20
A Thousand Acres (Smiley) 60, 142–43
Through the Ivy Gate (Dove) 120
Tisdale, Judy Jones 81
Tracks (Erdrich) 98, 145
Trilling, Lionel 31
True North (Harrison) 141
Tsurata, Dorothy Randall 125
Turow, Scott 9
Twain, Mark 9
   literary themes: authenticity 151; childhood 49–50, 58–59, 76; common people 10, 20, 30–32; compassion 166–67; conformity 19–22, 30–32, 41; evil 11, 21, 22, 32; gender 10, 78, 103; nature 130–31, 134; pairing with James 5; race 104–7
   works: *Adventures of Huckleberry Finn* 4, 6, 7, 11, 19–22, 49–50, 58–59, 76, 78, 103, 130–31, 151, 166–67 (see also *Adventures of Huckleberry Finn*); "James Fenimore Cooper's Literary Offenses" 20
Twenty-Seventh City (Franzen) 25–26, 29, 50

University of Chicago laboratory school 18
University of Wisconsin at Madison 1

Vernon, Alex 75
Vizenor, Gerald
   literary themes: childhood 67, 149; gender 101; nature 14, 148–49
   works: *Father Meme* 67; *Heirs of Columbus* 14, 67, 148–49; poetry 16

Waegner, Cathy 115
Walden (Thoreau) 19–20
war 12, 43, 71–76, 123–24
"A Way You'll Never Be" (Hemingway) 74
Weber, Ronald 3–4, 6
Werner, Craig 121
Windy McPherson's Son (Anderson) 56–57, 159
Winesburg, Ohio (Anderson) 50–51, 85–87, 97–98, 168
Wisconsin 18
Wixson, Douglas 85
women *see* gender
Wonham, Henry B. 110
A World I Never Made (Farrell) 69–70, 137, 153
Wright, James 17
Wright, Richard
   background: impact of reading 9; midwestern ties 3
   literary themes: compassion 174; gender 126; nature 135; race 113–14, 115–16, 174
   works: *Black Boy* 3, 9; "How Bigger Was Born" 3, 113; introduction to Algren's *Never Come Morning* 3, 113–14; *Native Son* 2, 3, 113–14, 115–16, 126, 135, 174
Wyatt, Jean 121

Yonnondio (Olsen) 41–42, 54–55, 142, 173–74

Zacher, Christian 3, 6

www.ingramcontent.com/pod-product-compliance
Ingram Content Group UK Ltd.
Pitfield, Milton Keynes, MK11 3LW, UK
UKHW042007140426
5217IPUK00015B/1033